Blog It Out, Bitch

Nina Perez

For all of my Myspace peeps. Consider this your handy-dandy guide to our time together at BIOB on Myspace. May you never again have to venture there. I'm serious. That place will give your computer AIDS.

Introduction

In the summer of 2005 I found myself laid off from a decent-paying job and completely clueless as to what I'd do next. I was married to a great man, Donny, and we were raising a beautiful little girl, Kali, in the house of our dreams. I may not have known what I was going to do, but I knew I was tired of working in a job in service of others, helping them achieve their goals while ignoring my own. I was 31-years-old and hadn't taken any real steps to make things happen for *me*.

I decided to go back to school, and without giving it much more thought than, "I should go back to school," I enrolled in an Associate's program for Journalism. Then I got the bright idea that I would teach myself one new thing a year. It could be something I'd always wanted to learn or had an interest in, or something completely foreign and terrifying. That first year, it was cake decorating. And for awhile I thought I'd actually try to make an income selling fondant-covered sugary treats, but it became clear pretty quickly that in order to do it for a living, you have to have a passion for it. Beyond making a birthday cake here or there for my daughter or husband, I wasn't feeling baking as a career choice.

My passion was, and has always been, writing. So, at the end of 2005 I decided to start blogging. I'd found myself on a site called MySpace. It was like a really cheesy internet disco – all funky colors and scantily-clad women.

If websites had an aroma, MySpace would smell like Drakkar Noir. But it had a place where I could write about anything that popped into my head, and amazingly enough, people wanted to read it. I would tell my best friend, Sophie, about the crazy things that happened to me at school or the witty things Kali – then, six-years-old - had said, and she'd say, "Don't tell me. Blog it out, bitch," altering the famous "Hug it out, bitch," line from the popular HBO show, *Entourage*.

Blog It Out, Bitch became the name of my blog. At first, the only people commenting were the seven friends I had on MySpace, who also happened to be my relatives. Slowly, other people began reading, commenting, and staying. I consistently ranked in the top blogs on the site and within minutes of posting a blog it wasn't uncommon to receive a dozen comments and three times the views. Being the first to comment, "First, bitches!" on one of my blogs became a rite of passage and, to this day, when I see it on other sites around the web, I am confident that somewhat annoying trend started on my blog.

One of the things I'm most proud of when I look back at those early years of blogging is that it wasn't just a place for me to talk about me – even though there was definitely *a lot* of that. I posted commentary on pop culture and current events and regularly "pimped out" other bloggers to help them build an audience. It got to the point where I never bothered to check the top rankings and only became aware of my standing on them when others brought it to my attention. Logging into MySpace, I'd head directly to my blog to interact with the readers and friends I'd made all over the world.

After about two years, I started my own website with the same name (www.blogitoutb.com) and started to focus more on storytelling and talking about the things that most interested me: motherhood, marriage, writing, books, and watching massive amounts of movies and television.

It's been six years and I've moved, written a book, graduated, and had another baby – a little boy named Jack, whose gestation and birth were chronicled in the spin-off blogs, *Blog It Out, Baby*.

The greatest things to come out of my time writing these blogs are the wonderful, supportive friends I've made. They are not minions. They are more than readers. So, for them I have compiled some of the best blogs I've written over the past six years. They remain in chronological order, though some of the dates may have been changed by a day or two.

I'm a different person than I was when I first started blogging, and that's a good thing, but in many ways I'm the same… and that's a good thing, too. I'm grateful that I have these reminders of conversations and moments I might have otherwise forgotten. I appreciate that I have reminders of the lessons I've learned in being a wife and mother. And I cherish the people that bothered to read them the first time.

Nina

Wife. Mother. Blogger. Bitch.

White Boy Crazy

July 9, 2005

One day my husband will kill me while I sleep. He will take his pillow and calmly place it over my face and press down until I am no longer breathing. I know this to be true because I am lazy, I am bossy, and I am bitchy. I would rather watch TV than do housework. Most of all, I know this because he is white. And that is just how white boys roll.

Being a black woman married to a white man has increased my chances of death by homicide about 74% according to the recent findings of a study I just made up. White men have a history of flipping the fuck out more fabulously than any other race of man. That's not to say that Black, Hispanic, Eskimo, etc., men are not capable of committing horrible crimes. Of course they are. We all know it. But when white men snap they just take it to a whole 'nother level.

I'm sure many of you reading this may be related to, or married to, a white man. Hell, you might even *be* a white man. And you're thinking, "This isn't true. Nina, this is a racist generalization."

Here me out: I believe that all white men have this special dormant gene I've dubbed, "The White Boy Crazy Gene," or WBCG for short, which remains inactive until it is triggered. When the switch is flipped, a white man will commit the most heinous, scratch-your-head, that-motherfucker-is-crazy crimes you could never have imagined. The most common trigger seems to be pregnancy.

My husband, Donny, and I have a six-year-old daughter and over the course of our marriage we've discussed the possibility of having other

1

children, but something always comes up that causes us to push the blessed event back a few months.

Sometimes, it's been lack of money and other times my desire to finish school. I've even argued that we should wait until I lose the baby weight I'm still carrying from my first pregnancy 'cause who wants to add fat to fat? The truth is: I'm scared. I don't want to be six months pregnant and find my black ass crammed into a drum, weighted down by chains and cinder block, under Lake Linear. That would suck.

Donny is probably the last guy you would expect to snap and go W.B.C., and that is *exactly* why he's a likely candidate! It's always the most handsome, mild-mannered, even-tempered ones that snap. Just look at Scott Peterson! Then you see their neighbors and co-workers on the news talking about, "He was always so nice. We're in shock."

Bullshit. *Somebody* had to see that shit coming, and you can just consider this your fair warning so you're not one of the completely snowed people on the news, or worse, the one crammed in the drum.

I'm so prepared for the day when Donny finally snaps I've even given my family and friends ways to save themselves, and the police, a whole lot of trouble trying to find out what happened to me. For instance, you ever notice that when men go W.B.C. and kill their wives they always give the same story as to when they last saw their wives alive?

"She went for a run in the park. She went for a walk. She went for a hike."

My black ass does *none* of that. If Donny ever tried that sorry line everyone knows to head straight for the nearest cop and say, "He did it. You may want to check the backyard." Now, if he said something like, "The last time I saw her she was sitting on the couch watching TiVo," then he just may be telling the truth.

Separation Anxiety
August 19th, 2005

Yesterday, due to car trouble, I couldn't pick Kali up from school and I had to make arrangements for her to ride the school bus home for the first time. The stop is directly across the cul-de-sac from our house so it wasn't that bad. It's just that I had visions of those hidden camera news reports where you see kids beating the shit out of each other on school buses and the drivers sitting there like everything's cool. I had worked myself into such a tizzy that by the time the bus pulled up to the curb, and I waited for her to come off, I was giving every kid looking out the window the stink eye.

Donny wasn't able to figure out what was wrong with the car last night, so Kali had to take the bus again today to go to school. By this time, I'd worked myself into a downright mental breakdown. It was like I was sending her off to war instead of the elementary school five minutes away.

As the bus pulled off and I headed for home, I turned around expecting to see her little sad face in the back window. Instead, I was greeted with exhaust fumes and not a glimpse of my baby as she had promptly taken a seat in the front - not thinking about anything except that she *finally* gets to take the bus like a big girl.

Idle Threats, They Work

September 22, 2005

I cringe every time I catch myself sounding like my mother. Not that there's anything wrong with my mother – except she kills pets, but more on that later – it's just that mothers of my generation like to fancy ourselves more contemporary and understanding than our own mothers who, most likely, grew up in that era of "spare the rod, spoil the child." You know, a time when it was not only okay for parents to spank their kids without fear of reprisal, but it wasn't uncommon for other relatives and neighbors to take it upon themselves to discipline the nearest kid getting out of hand.

We choose not to spank to discipline. Sparing a rod leading to a spoiled child doesn't fly with me. Prisons, detention centers, and "special" classes for kids who don't know how to act are filled with people whose parents disciplined by spanking. On the other hand, there are plenty of people who didn't get spanked, who grew up to be well-adjusted, productive members of society. I refuse to believe the only way to get a child to behave is to incorporate hitting them.

But I will threaten like there's no tomorrow.

"Kali, I'm gonna count to three and then you're gonna get it."

I never make it to two. I guess she figured, "I don't know what this spanking business is all about, but I'm not tryna find out."

Actually, she has had one spanking, but she doesn't remember it. When she was a toddler, we let my little sister babysit while we went out to see a movie. When we returned, we found Kali had drawn all over the walls of her room. My little sister's defense? "She said you let her!" Since we'd been trying to break Kali of the habit and this latest offense was massive (it took up a whole wall), I spanked her by way of three quick swats on her diaper. I felt so awful, and she looked so betrayed, that I cried harder than she did… for two days.

Note: Her wall art included lots of smiley faces with all the facial features in the correct places and her name spelled properly. She was three and I was proud. She may be hard-headed, but by God, my child was also a genius!

Here we are, three years later, and I'm still dealing with the same stubbornness. Only now, she's old enough to understand threats and when I deliver them, I sound exactly like my mother. Our latest battle is bedtime. I try to put Kali to bed between seven-thirty and eight. It's frustrating to tuck her into bed, only to find her out of bed an hour and a half later asking for water or another bedtime story – mainly because I know this means she's going to be a grumpy mess when it's time to get up for school the next morning.

The other night she came downstairs at 9:45, and sensing I was about to lose it, she cut me off as soon as I opened my mouth.

"Mommy, there are three things wrong with me: My stomach hurts, my ears itch, and my forehead is hot."

And sounding every bit like my mother I said, "There's about to be four things wrong with you if you don't get back in that bed."

This kid doesn't realize how good she has it. I don't make her turn off the T.V. at night and she has a night light. My mother wasn't so accommodating. Bedtime meant no T.V., lights out, and she didn't want to see hide nor hair of you once she said good night.

Every morning I wake Kali up with snuggles and kisses and tickles and love, and most mornings I get grumbling, crying, and stiff-armed for my troubles. A far cry from how my Mama used to wake us up. She'd come in the room, flipping the lights on, clapping loudly and yelling, "Come on, get up! Rise and shine." A drill sergeant had more finesse. I guess she thought this was invigorating – inspiring, even. It would be like, five-thirty in the morning, before the sun was even up. I remember the one morning I was brave enough to ask, "Why do we have to rise if it ain't even shining?" A thrown slipper was her reply.

This morning, Kali gave me the roughest time yet. I got in the bed with her and started kissing, cuddling, and cooing, "Get up, Stinkerbell." She immediately started grumbling and clutched the blanket in a vice-like grip. I finally managed to remove the blanket and tried to get her dressed. I attempted to put her right leg in her jeans. No luck. So I threatened a spanking. Right leg goes in.

When it came time to try for the left leg, she got creative on me. She stretched her left leg as far away from her body as it would go and held it in place by the ankle with her left hand. Just imagine when a cheerleader kicks her leg up and holds it at her side. That was my child, yet flat on her back. All the while I'm coaxing and laughing because I cannot believe she is giving me such a hard time. She had that leg *locked*. I couldn't bend it to save my life.

"Kali, come on. We're going to miss the school bus."

"I don't want to go to school."

"Why? Because you're tired?"

She nodded.

"Then maybe you should go to bed when I tell you to."

"I don't want to go to school."

"You have to."

"Why?"

Another way I differ from the way my Mom raised me is that I don't believe in "because I said so," as an answer. Making children aware of the consequences behind the things we deny them the opportunity of doing isn't a bad thing. But, "because an education is important," wasn't going to fly with a cranky, sleep-deprived, hard-headed six-year-old who wants nothing more than to stay in bed, warm and toasty, instead of going to school on a cold, rainy day. So, I went for the jugular and ventured to a place that even my mother dared not go.

"Because if I don't send you to school, I'll go to jail. Is that what you want? You want Mommy to go to jail?"

Left leg went in.

Hey, I never said I wouldn't exaggerate the consequences.

Boy Wizard, Girl Geek

September 30, 2005

It's three o'clock on a hot, July, Friday afternoon when I enter my neighborhood Borders, excited that I'm about register for an early copy of the new *Harry Potter* book. There's a big purple and gold sign outside, announcing that the book will be on sale at midnight, but that the "festivities" start at 9pm.

There's a sign-up table near the entrance and there's already a rather large man and a slightly less large boy signing up. Apparently, the large man called ahead months ago and his name is on a list. He is handed a ticket and told that at 11:45pm ticket holders one through twenty-five will be allowed to get in line and purchase the first twenty-five books at midnight. After that, they will call ticket numbers randomly, twenty-five at a time, and allow those ticket holders to purchase books - no more than three copies per customer. Just when I think it's my turn, the large man asks if the less large boy can register now for his own copy. He can. Before they walk away, the large man says to the sign-up guy, "I like your name tag."

As he moves away, I can finally see the Borders employee forced to deal with all the anxious Potter fans. He's pale, a little heavy, and his mouth droops on one side. His name tag reads, *Professor Flitwick*. Cute.

I tell him I want to sign up, give him my last name, which he notes on a list and then hands me a ticket. It is done with all the fanfare of opening night on Broadway. I'm extremely embarrassed and quickly stuff my ticket in my faux Prada bag, but not before glancing at my ticket number.

1893.

Were these things handed out consecutively? I heard this particular store was only getting fifteen hundred books. Thank God the numbers are being called randomly, but what if my number isn't called? I don't have much time to ponder as I quickly head to the magazine section, still embarrassed for even being there. I wonder if there are any new logic puzzle books in.

As I peruse, I notice large man and slightly less large boy sitting down next to the comics, each reading one. *Figures,* I think as I smirk in their direction. *Good luck ever getting laid, you two.*

This grown ass man has reserved a copy of a *Harry Potter* book months ago, he recognizes the name of a character on the employee's name tag, not for its lameness, but because he has memorized all things Potter. Now he's sitting in a corner, in all his geek glory, reading comics.

What a loser. What could be lamer than that? I put back a Math & Logic puzzle book because it has too many math puzzles and not enough logic puzzles. It hasn't yet occurred to me that the answer to my question could be: shopping for logic puzzle books.

I'm about to leave when I decide to ask Flitwick if this ticket guarantees me a copy of the book later that night, but when I get to the table, there's a short Filipino woman trying to sign up. He's explaining about the ticket and the lottery and the festivities at 9pm in the tent outside, but she's just not getting it. Between her thick accent and his speech impediment, it's like watching two paraplegics compete in a potato sack race - not much is getting accomplished.

"So, I can get book tomorrow?

"Yes, at midnight. The festivities begin at nine p.m. We'll have prizes and treats and games."

Sadly, I find myself thinking what I would be missing on T.V. at 9 o'clock if I brought my ass back to Borders. "Then why sign say Saturday?" she asks.

"Well, the festivities are Friday, but you can get the book at midnight."

"Then why sign say Saturday?" she repeats.

I want to yell, "Bitch, cause midnight *is* Saturday! Now come on before someone I know sees me standing here!" But I don't. The useless exchange goes on for another minute or so, and I'm starting to think it's not so bad to wait and get the book next week when he's finally done dealing with the lady and confirms for me that holding a ticket doesn't guarantee a book. Lovely.

I high-tail it to my car. I'm disgusted by the whole process. *Damn nerds. Stupid geeks.* I'm halfway home before it hits me: *I am a damn nerd, a stupid geek.* Am I not just as excited to get my mitts on this book? Do I not know all the inconsistencies between the *X-men* comics and the movies? Did I not get just a tad giddy when handed my purple and gold ticket? What made me better than the overweight guys and the clock-challenged Filipino woman? I realized that the answer is absolutely nothing.

Now, if you'll excuse me, I must go take a nap. I have someplace to be at midnight…er…nine.

Please Don't Let 2006 Suck

January 2, 2006

Entering the real world again is going to suck. I register for classes in two days and they start five days after that. With Kali being home on Christmas break, I've gotten used to getting up pretty much when I want to and going to bed whenever. I'd forgotten what it feels like to have to be somewhere by a specific time. I'm slowly remembering that it sucks.

And worst yet, I'm pretty sure I'll need to work part-time while I go to school. Which, you guessed it, sucks. It's not so much that I don't want to go back to work. Well, it is so much that. But it's also that I know anything part-time is going to, yeah, suck.

In a perfect world, I'd be able to put my child on the bus and go about my day of school and/or work and be home by the time the school bus returns. But, I know the world ain't perfect. I'll most likely *not* find a job that will allow me to do that and not want to shoot myself in the process.

Most part-time jobs will require weekend shifts and possibly holidays. Most part-time jobs will require me to do a whole bunch of shit I don't wanna do. I should probably make a list. It will cut down on me applying to – and interviewing for – a bunch of crap jobs.

So here is my list of things I refuse to say and/or do for money. No matter how much I love my house and want to pay the mortgage.

I do not want a job where I am obligated to say the following:

"Would you like to hear our specials?"

"Yes, tonight is dollar draft night."

"Do you have a penny?"

"Have a nice day."

"Welcome to...."

"Can I start you off with something to drink?"

I do not want a job where someone can be heard saying:

"And coming to the main stage..."

"Let me see some I.D."

"Would you like to dance?"

(Or worse yet, a job where there is music playing so loudly you can't hear anything and come home smelling of cigarette smoke.)

I will not take a job where I am required to:

Sweep, fold clothing, count out any kind of cash register, greet people when they walk in, watch people to make sure they're not stealing, sell people stuff, be nice when I don't want to, touch food, wear a name tag, and work on the weekends.

Yeah. This is going to suck.

Really?

January 5, 2006

I love my daughter more than anything in this world. I'm absolutely convinced that I love my child more than any parent loves a child. Even more than you love yours. What I have found over the years though, is that the older they get, the less fascinated you become with what they have to say.

When they're babies and toddlers and just learning to talk, you hang on to every coo, every giggle, and every new word they utter. But between the ages of five and eight, when they're just getting into the swing of this talking thing and learning to string together thoughts and ideas to form stories, you start to realize that a lot of what they say just doesn't make sense. Your child is talking just to talk, and any good parent would learn to navigate through these conversations without hurting their child's feelings.

Never underestimate the beauty of a perfectly timed, "Mmm hmm," people. Unfortunately, because I love my child so much - remember, much more than you love yours - I can't lie to Kali for very long and one day I had to come clean.

"Mommy, I just saw my first ladybug in the house!"

"Really?" I asked, totally transfixed on online banking and not really paying attention.

"Yeah. Hey, that's the same thing Daddy just said when I told him."

"That's because it's the standard response when parents aren't really listening to their children, honey."

"Oh."

This revelation has since prompted my child to ask, "Mommy, are you listening? I mean, *really* listening?" before beginning any story. And it has forced me to get into the habit of stopping whatever I'm doing and listen to my child. *Really* listen.

Death by Gordita

January 8, 2006

Approximately one week before my period is due several changes occur in my house. Not all of them bad. My breasts grow from a 36C to a D cup easily. Most of you are probably thinking that's a good thing. Sometimes it is. It certainly looks nice, but it doesn't feel so nice. If I sit still and close my eyes, I can almost feel them growing. Think David Banner turning into The Hulk, but sexier. They get sore, feel really heavy, and make sleeping on my stomach impossible and uncomfortable. Once my period comes they shrink back to their normal size. I guess they figure they won't be seeing any action for the next five days so, what's the point?

Of course my husband notices, realizes what it means, and takes every opportunity to have as much sex as he can with me in the next seven days.

I also get cravings for fast food and chocolate. Not just any chocolate. Usually Ben and Jerry's, *Everything But The…* or Entenmann's Chocolate Cake. Last night I craved Taco Bell which brings me to how I almost died.

So, Donny says he's running to the supermarket for snacks before we sit down for a season two *Roswell* marathon and he asks if I want anything.

"Taco Bell, please."

"They don't sell Taco Bell at Publix."

"Your point is?"

He just sighs and leaves. Now before you think he just does what I tell him to, please remember that my boobs at this point are each the size of a small child's head. He's not going to argue with me for the next seven days if he wants to play with these puppies. He returns a few minutes later with two steak Gordita Supremes and to push aside any doubt that I'd be putting out that night, a pint of the aforementioned Ben and Jerry's. I was in premenstrual heaven. We pop in the DVD, I grab a Sprite, and my Taco Bell, and it's on!

For those unfamiliar with the glorious Gordita, here's the definition straight from their website: Warm, pillowy flatbread filled with seasoned ground beef, creamy pepper jack sauce, crisp, shredded lettuce, a blend of three cheeses – cheddar, pepper jack and mozzarella, and fiesta salsa.

In other words: a tortilla-wrapped orgasm.

Usually, I'll brush off most of the excess lettuce and tomato and get right down to the good stuff: cheese, steak, and sour cream. But I was a pig being led by my menses-fueled greed. I bit into it trying to get as much in my mouth as possible.

I don't know if it was the way I was holding it or how fast I bit into it, but two things happened at once. All the cold food at the top (tomato and lettuce) landed on my tongue. All of the warm stuff (steak, cheese, and sour cream) shot like a rocket to the back of my throat.

Surprised, I inhaled. And then I started to choke. On reflex, I spit out as much as I could which amounted to most of the tomato and lettuce. Actually, I didn't so much spit it out as I had to let it just fall out my mouth and onto the floor. My husband is just looking at me, mid-sip of his soda, like this is normal. Like I'm some fucking retard with a helmet who suddenly spits out her food all the time. (Note to self: check that husband hasn't suddenly increased life insurance policy on my dumb ass.)

The food is going down the wrong pipe, not sure which pipe, but I know it's not the food pipe. My chest is burning as I imagine carne asada steak infiltrating my heart. Donny decides to get up off his ass, finally, and administer the ghetto Heimlich: slapping me on the back.

"What's wrong with you?"

I'm thinking, "Motherfucker, I'm choking. What does it look like?" But, of course I can't say that because I have cheese and steak and snot coming out of my nose. This wasn't a satisfying response for my husband because he asks, "Can you hear me?" as he continues to beat the shit out of my back. Like choking caused my ear drums to rupture.

This continues for a few seconds more and I've lost all control of my bodily functions. I'm hacking and spewing food and I think I even farted. By the time it's all over, the room is a mess and I feel like my nostrils are on fire.

This, of course, didn't stop me from eating the other Gordita a short while later (Don't judge me!) or my husband from having sex with the woman he nearly killed with his rescue efforts.

Stinky Hands

January 21, 2006

So I'm sitting at the computer in the study and Kali is on the floor behind me watching cartoons. After a while, I realize the whole room smells like lilac. I don't pay too much attention because one of her stocking stuffers this past Christmas was some lilac lotion. But then, after another few minutes, the smell becomes overwhelming. It's like a fucking lilac explosion. Without turning around I ask, "Kali, what are you doing?"

"Putting lotion on my armpits."

"Ok, well, that's enough."

"Wait, I have to put some on my hands because today in school, Makayla said my hands stink."

This gets my attention. My head whips around. "What? Why would she say that?"

Kali shrugs. "I don't know."

"Come here."

She walks over to me and I start hugging her, wanting to kick little Makayla's ass. "Did you smell your hands after she said that?" I ask and Kali nods.

"And did they stink?" She nods again.

"Why were your hands stinking? Were you digging in your butt or something?"

The question was purely rhetorical, intended to make her laugh, not feel so bad about her odorous digits, and forget about what a bitchbag Makayla was. Kali does laugh, but also answers, completely unaware of what a rhetorical question is.

"No! I would never dig in my butt… at school."

"I would appreciate it if you never dug in your butt at all."

"My teacher says, 'Never say never.'"

Down With Deer

January 23rd, 2006

I'm afraid of deer. Everyone knows this. I am not embarrassed. Deer are gross. They are evil, stupid, little creatures who don't have the good sense to not run in the middle of the road. Unfortunately, there are a lot of deer where I live. It seems with the insurgence of strip malls and subdivisions in my neck of the woods, these little fuckers have been left uprooted. Sucks for them, even worse for me.

New York wildlife, I'm used to: roaches, mice, rats, pigeons, cats, and dogs. For the purpose of this blog, however, we will limit this discussion to things that primarily roam the streets. That leaves us with rats, pigeons, cats, and dogs. It must be the New York mentality because a rat, pigeon, cat or dog crossing the road in New York will most definitely get its ass out the way should you suddenly slam on your brakes and honk your horn. They ain't stupid. They may shoot you a, "Damn bitch, calm down" look and take their sweet time, but they *will* move. I'm convinced that any dead animal on the side, or middle, of the street in New York was the victim of intentional homicide. Hey, it's New York. That's how we roll.

Now in the south, and I am referring to the cities I've lived in, an animal's stupidity will get *you* killed and the most dangerous of these dimwitted animals are deer. I've lived in Atlanta for almost three years now and I can tell you every place I've ever seen a deer, dead or alive. I log that shit in my mental rolodex. When I approach that area again, I immediately slow down and do "the shake." Both are involuntary. "The shake" is this very quick, very violent shudder that overcomes me whenever I encounter a particularly gross animal, which are *most* animals. I cannot help it.

I remember when it started. Over ten years ago, when I was living in Durham, I heard two stories that stuck with me. They were probably deer urban legends, but I didn't care. They seemed *completely* plausible.

The first involved a lady who had just picked her kids up from school, a boy and a girl, and as usual they were arguing over who got to sit in the front seat. Instead of picking one, the frustrated mother instructed them both to sit in the back. A short while later she hit a deer, which landed smack dab in her passenger seat where one of her kids would have been sitting. The second story: A woman is driving home, on I-40, and hits a deer. It goes through her windshield, kicking violently. It kicks her in the chest a few times and she dies instantly.

After I heard those stories, I was on deer alert whenever I drove at night and in rural areas. Then one day, I was driving to Raleigh, down a busy four-lane street, in the middle of the day, and a deer ran across the road right in front of me. I nearly pissed myself. The brazen little fuckers traveled during the day! No one had told me this. I have been on the red threat level ever since.

I realize my fear may be a bit irrational and has led to some irrational actions. Such as: I used to drive down one convenient road to get to work every morning. I would leave my house at the ungodly hour of 5am. I was later informed that this is the time of day that deer are traveling from their resting place to their eating place or vice versa. Either way, the fuckers are out in full force. So, one morning I'm driving down this road and it's still dark out. A deer runs across the road, in front of my car, very quickly. I have never, ever seen a deer run the way this one did. He had his body really low to the ground and was *booking*. It looked like the pictures of the greyhound on the side of the buses. (I swear to God, I just did "the shake" recalling the image. Thanks, guys.)

After that morning, I started going the long way around, even if it meant that I had to leave the house ten minutes earlier. It was inconvenient, but I'd never seen a deer going the long way and out of sight, out of mind. That worked well for a few months until one early morning, I'm again on my way to work, when I see something up ahead on the side of the road. As I get closer, I realize it is *five* deer. And they weren't just standing there. The mofos were frolicking and shit.

One of them looked like he was timing his sprint in front of my car, bobbing on the side of the road like his ass was about to jump double-dutch. But instead of jumping in between two spinning cords of telephone wire, he was going to jump in front of my car and kill me. I was too scared to even speed up, in fact, I went ridiculously slow. As I passed, I'm not even looking in front of me, but instead turning my whole head to keep an eye on the deer. They, in turn, followed me with their heads as I drove by. Like, "What the fuck is her problem?" Needless to say, I shook violently the whole way to work. The other motorists probably thought I was having a seizure.

The most irrational moment had to have been when we still lived in North Carolina. When our house in Atlanta was being built, Donny, Kali and I would visit once a month to check on the status. On one particular trip, we left in the evening - something I never liked to do - and I was driving. We had just gotten onto I-40 when I saw at least six deer on the side of the road.

"Oh my God, oh my God!"

"Nina, calm down."

"Oh my God." By this time I'm shaking like a junkie. I reach over and lock the car doors. As if they would suddenly develop opposable thumbs and try to jack my ride.

"You are retarded."

"Where's Kali?" I kind of squeal, as if they had developed opposable thumbs and wanted to kidnap my child.

Kali responds in a calm voice, like she's talking to a fairly stupid child. "I'm still right here. In the car."

Yes, I felt like an ass. But I still don't like 'em.

My Mama on MySpace

February 20, 2006

My mother and I have always had somewhat of a weird co-existence. She had me when she was fifteen, and then eleven days later, she turned sixteen. I have vague memories of her playing handball wearing little short-shorts, tennis shoes, and long socks. She had an afro to rival Foxy Brown. I thought she was the most beautiful woman in the world. I suppose every little girl thinks of her mother that way. My parents' teenage romance ended shortly after I was born. I often wondered what it would have been like to have had another sibling that came from both my mother and father together. Instead, I have siblings from their relationships that developed after they split.

As I got older, I realized that my mother was a regular person. She had flaws, she made mistakes, and for many years I struggled with that. When I was a teenager our relationship was very strained. My mother had always been a spanker, and as my brother, sisters, and I got older, our spankings got bigger. Belts were replaced with shoes. Open hands became closed fists. I once took a ketchup bottle to the knee because I said something smart from across the room while my mother was in the kitchen. She couldn't reach me in time so she lobbed the bottle instead and this was before the days of plastic, squeezable ketchup bottles.

Our relationship didn't improve until I moved out at eighteen. Not living under the same roof worked wonders for us. We actually became more like friends. Around that same time she separated from my stepfather and joined the New York City Police Department. I would hang out with my mother and her police officer friends in Manhattan bars. I'd handed down the role of babysitter to my sister who, at the time, was fourteen. She was now left home alone to watch our two younger siblings.

It was now her turn to deal with the anger and resentment, and the longing for a normal family. You would think I'd have reached out to her, try to ease the burden for her, but I was too busy appreciating the fact that it was no longer me. I was reveling in my new role as "friend" as opposed to eldest child. Drinking, dancing, swearing, and smoking cigarettes in front of my mother replaced fighting and arguing. She had come full circle and was once again, "the coolest Mom ever."

My friends always marvel at the dynamics of our relationship and cannot believe the things I'm allowed to say around her. I think it has something to do with the fact that the older we get, the smaller our age difference seems to be. 31-year-olds have friends that are 46-year-olds and it's no big deal.

As close as we've become, there are still things I'm not comfortable sharing with her and my blogs are one of them. When you write a blog entitled *Fellatio Connoisseur,* you kinda wanna keep your Mom away from it. That's why I damn near birthed a small farm animal when I found out she'd been reading my blogs on MySpace.

"Girl, I have something funny for your blog!"

"You have a what for my who? I don't want you reading my blogs."

"Too late, I read your shit every day."

Silence.

"You there?"

"Yeah, I just threw up in my mouth a little."

"Here's my email and password… Can you log into my page and hook it up for me? It asked who I wanted to meet and I put Denzel, Jamie Foxx, Orlando Jones, and the black guy who played the president on *24*."

"Dennis Haysbert?"

"Yeah, him. I only have one friend. Some white boy named Tom. Who the fuck is Tom?"

"He's the founder of MySpace."

"Oh. And then someone sent me a message that said, 'This is MySpace, ho! Wanna get a hassle free credit card?' I was like, 'Oh no this bitch didn't!'"

"It's spam, Ma. Just delete it. Don't respond to it."

"I did. Anyway, I know all those people commenting on your stuff are wondering what kind of mother you have. Everything is 'motherfucker this', 'coochie that', and 'bitches and whores.'"

I held my breath. If I heard the word "fellatio", I was hanging up the damn phone.

"Ma, please don't leave comments embarrassing me."

"I'm not gonna say anything! I just know they wonder what kind of mother you came from talking like that."

"They ain't thinking 'bout you, and look who's talking!"

"I don't cuss like that anymore. I'm a Christian now."

"Mmm hmm."

"Okay, well, only when people piss me the fuck off. Anyway, you should write your sister, she thinks you're mad at her."

"I'm not mad anymore. I just don't want Dina reading my blogs either. It's full of adult content. I can't be myself if I'm worried about what you guys are thinking."

"Girl, please. She's a young lady now, she probably knows more than you."

"She's still a virgin."

"So, that doesn't mean she doesn't know stuff. She just hasn't put it to use yet."

Throw up in mouth part two.

Dashing Dreams, One Little Girl at a Time

May 5, 2006

For a full week, Kali's fourth loose tooth hung on for dear life before conceding defeat and making room for its replacement, which had already begun to push its way through her gums. She would move the outgoing tooth around with her tongue, trying to pry it from its home in her top gums, but it wasn't having it. I would get frustrated just looking at it. Like when you're tempted to pull an errant string on a sweater though you know it's not a good idea and might possibly cause the whole thing to unravel. Kali must have seen the look in my eye and recognized it for what it was. "Don't touch it, Mommy!" she'd warn.

Needless to say we were both excited the day she came home from school with the tooth rolling around in a little Ziploc bag. I because I no longer had to look at the tooth hanging from a bit of skin no wider than dental floss, and Kali because she knew she was due for some cold hard cash.

At around midnight, I was on the computer engaged in some titillating online conversation with another blogger, and by conversation I mean gossip, when it suddenly hit me that I didn't have any cash to leave under Kali's pillow.

I check every purse I own, but all that produces is long forgotten makeup and old breath mints. Sucking on a breath mint, I search through jean pockets and Donny's wallet. No cash. We are a check card/check household; rarely do we have cash. So, now I'm stressing. It's late and I really don't feel like going to an ATM machine, and even then, I'd have to go find change since she gets five bucks per tooth. I head to Kali's room to check under her pillow. Maybe Donny already took care of it? Tippy-toeing into her room, I quietly check under her pillow and there is the tooth still in the baggie, mocking me. "Whatcha gonna do now, you no cash having bitch?"

By now I'm kicking myself for introducing her to this silly myth and all others like it. For many years, Kali thought Santa Claus was some guy who worked in the mall. Then she began school and some big mouth kid told her tales of Old Saint Nick swooping down the chimney and taking credit for all the gifts we, her parents, busted our asses to buy. She was a little put off at the idea of a strange man coming into our home in the middle of the night, but if he dropped off *Strawberry Shortcake* DVDs and a *Dora the Explorer* talking van, she was willing to deal with it.

When she lost her first tooth, I explained The Tooth Fairy. She didn't seem to like that concept either. She basically said, "Wait a minute. Some strange chick is going to come into my house, into my bedroom, lift my head off of my pillow and leave money?" Adults are pretty fucked up, huh? We tell our children we will protect them from strangers... unless strangers come bearing cash and prizes. Then we will leave out milk and cookies and even our teeth for the bastards.

I turned to leave Kali's room wondering how evil it would be to wake Donny and make him drive to Wal-Mart, or if I should just go myself, when I spot them: Kali's collection of piggy banks! Don't judge me! You know, desperate times and all that. I knew she had *at least* fifteen dollars in one of those suckers from the previous lost teeth. Not to mention all the times my Dad slips her a five here and there. All of the piggy banks were the kind you had to break open to reach the goods... except for one; a big, black, lady piggy bank, brought back from the cruise my parents took to the Bahamas. We call her Bahama Mama.

I grabbed her fat ass and removed the little rubber plug from her butt. Change went everywhere. I looked at Kali. She was still sleeping. Nice! I dug around the bowels of the piggy bank as much as the small opening would allow. I came up with *two freaking dollars*! I contemplated leaving two in singles and three in quarters. I considered calling the whole thing off and writing my child either a check or I.O.U.

Fuck it; I decided to go with the two bucks. It was better than nothing. Hell, in my day we were lucky to get a dollar. She'd be happy with...

"What are you doing, Mommy?"

Busted. I slowly turn my head and look into my baby's sleepy eyes. And for once, words fail me. I have no suitable excuse. I have been caught with my hand in the proverbial cookie jar... or in this case, my hand in a fat black woman's ass. My creative juices began to simmer and produced...

"Nothing. Go back to sleep."

Miraculously, she did. I gathered up the change from the floor, pocketed the two bucks in my robe's pocket, and went back downstairs to finish my conversation. I decided it would be safer to wait until she'd once again fallen into a deep slumber before I carried out the final act of my covert mission.

I know what you're thinking. I am a horrible mother for re-gifting my child's old tooth fairy loot. Don't worry. Karma paid me back in spades the very next morning.

Karma and My Boobies

May 6, 2006

It sort of felt like some dirty drug deal when I switched out the Ziploc bag for the two bucks, while my child innocently slept. Proving she is truly her mother's child, also under her pillow were her pink DVD and TV remote controls. I moved them aside when I left the money.

The next morning, when I tried to wake her up as I always did - with kisses - I sensed resistance. I used the best weapon I had. "Kali, don't you want to see what the tooth fairy left you?" Her eyes popped open and her head shot from the pillow with lightening speed.

As I turned my back to rummage through her dresser for socks I heard, "She only left me one dollar!?" Not even thinking, I whipped around and protested, "It should be two!" Quickly realizing my mistake, I recovered, "Uh, I mean... that's weird... you sure it's not more?"

Kali unfolded the money, seemed to feel slightly better that she got two bucks instead of one, but I could still see her wondering why the tooth fairy started slacking. "Look, Mommy, she straightened my remotes."

Gee, isn't the tooth fairy nice?

Twenty five minutes later I'm preparing to stand at the front door and watch Kali travel the short walk across the street and up the block to the bus stop. A Mexican family lives in the house directly across from ours in the cul-de-sac. Their house is the same model as ours complete with this big gallery window on the second floor. That window is awesome. From our position at the back of the subdivision, one could spy on the whole neighborhood if they were so inclined. Not that I would.

Anyway, the Mexican mom watches her daughter walk to the bus stop from that window. I mention all this to point out that I'm a better mother than she is. At least if some shit went down, I could sprint across the street in my PJs. She has to go through the halls, down the stairs, through the foyer, and out the front door. What was she thinking?

That morning, in an effort to cut down on the amount of time I'd be standing in the doorway, freezing in my robe, Kali and I waited an extra five minutes before heading to the door. All I had on was that robe: no panties, no bra, no nothing under it. No sooner had we gotten to the front door, we could hear the bus approaching. Crap! Kali still had to put on her coat and backpack.

At the exact moment I unlocked our front door, across the street the little Mexican girl and one of her teenage brothers were leaving their house. The brother has a male friend waiting for him at the curb. And then a few things happened at once...

I was trying to help Kali into her coat, I was also casting quick glances up the block to see if it was indeed the school bus I heard, and I was doing all of this while trying to keep my robe closed. As Kali walked out the door, I realized her hood was stuck inside her coat. I called out, "Wait!"

This gets the attention of my teenage neighbor who looks over, I instinctively reach for Kali's hood with both hands, letting go of the robe. Here are your choices for what happened next:

a. my boobs fell out

b. my boobies fell out

c. my titties fell out

d. all of the above.

I quickly tried to close the robe. (I lost the belt to it ages ago.) One glance across the street told me my efforts were futile. My neighbor began slapping the shit out of his friend's arm, in attempt to get him to look at the free titty show across the street. I was so mortified!

Kali, thankfully, missed it all and was now hauling ass across the street. And the worst part of it all was that the bus wasn't even coming! That's what I get for stealing from my child the night before.

In related news, I am now bombarded with offers from all the neighborhood boys to mow my lawn... for free.

The Hunt for April

May 17, 2006

When Kali was less than a year old, my sister Christine gave her a stuffed bear named April. Now, over seven years later, Kali and April are inseparable. She sleeps with April, and on occasion she has taken April to school though April stays in her backpack the whole time so that the other kids won't think that Kali's a baby. Her words, not mine. I guess she just likes knowing that April is close.

One night, after midnight, Donny is dead to the world in bed next to me. I'm surrounded by textbooks, a notebook, pencils, a pencil sharpener, and a graphing calculator. Sexy.

Kali knocks, and then peaks her head in our room. Seeing the "what the hell are you doing up" look all over my face, she cuts me off...

"I can't find April, and I can't sleep without her."

"Where did you have her last?

"In the red room."

Our study is painted Ralph Lauren's Hunting Coat Red and we refer to it as the red room.

"Go look in the red room then."

"I'm scared."

The red room is on the first floor and all the lights were out downstairs. I didn't feel like moving 'cause I'm literally covered in books and I have a flow going.

"Kali, just turn on the lights as you go."

She comes back a few moments later.

"I can't find her."

Sighing, I get out of bed, take her by the hand, and we head downstairs together in search of April.

We search the red room. No April. We pass through the kitchen on our way to the family room to search. I turn around and notice Kali bent over studying the kitchen floor.

"Where did they go?"

"Where did who go?" I ask.

"The ants."

We had an insurgence of ants the other day and Kali had a grand old time slapping them with her flip flops till Donny sprayed, and then mopped, the floor.

"Daddy sprayed."

"But where are the dead bodies?"

"Daddy cleaned them up."

"Oh, I thought maybe we had zombie ants. That would be cool."

"Girl, come on."

We searched the family room. I'm on all fours looking under the couch when...

"Mommy, can I ask you something? And don't laugh!"

"What?"

"Are you a playful parent?"

"A what? Yes, I'm a playful parent. Don't you think so? Look at me!"

"Yes, you're very playful."

I get up, dust my hands off. No April.

"I'm also a parent of infinite patience."

"What does that mean?"

"That means most parents would have sent your butt to bed without April ten minutes ago."

"Oh."

Through the kitchen we go again, this time Kali goes to the back door and peers into the backyard.

"Where are the possums?"

"Girl, get away from that door and come on. I'm tired." We head into the formal dining room. For the first time I notice that Kali's hair is styled in manner I'd never seen before.

"What happened to your hair?"

"Daddy did it. I asked him to."

"It's going to be a tangled mess in the morning and I don't want to hear your mouth when I try to brush it."

We finally find April on Kali's piano in the formal living room - looking like a little, filthy, tan lounge singer. Kali kisses her and squeals in delight.

"Kali, she's dirty. Don't put your mouth on her."

"You kiss my boo-boos when I'm dirty."

"That's different. You came from my vagina."

"You're the best Mom I ever had!"

"I'm the only Mom you've ever had."

Attack of the Opossums

June 8, 2006

I like New York City critters better than Georgia critters. Simply because I'm used to them: roaches, rats, pigeons, squirrels, and the occasional stray dog or cat. Not here in the southern suburbs though. Here, I can't drive a mile without seeing deer, cows, horses, raccoons, foxes, and the nastiest of them all; opossum. Those things freak me out. They're so gross and sneaky looking. I once Googled "opossum poison" with the hopes of littering my backyard with it, but my Dad told me that might be illegal.

Several nights in a row I'd noticed the little bastards creeping around my backyard and couldn't figure out why they considered our house the Do Drop Inn of the neighborhood. One particular night I came downstairs for a drink and noticed one sniffing around outside.

First, I shat myself. Then I screamed for Donny. Why do all husbands do this? How come they will hear their wives screaming bloody murder and still call back, "What?!"

"Come here!"

Donny appears at the top of the staircase. "What?"

"Come here! I want to show you something!"

He starts making his way down the stairs.

"What?" He calls out again.

"Am I where you are? Is that here? Hurry up before you miss it."

So of course he gets to the backdoor in just enough time to see the fat little fucker scurry into the woods behind the house.

"He just wants the garbage." Donny says reasonably.

"What garbage?"

And I finally crane my neck to get a good look, and I'll be damned if there weren't like ten bags of garbage piled up against the back of our house.

What the shit?

"I forgot to pay the garbage bill."

Now, I too had forgotten to pay the garbage bill a few months ago and nearly had a social heart attack when pick-up day came and the garbage men told us to kiss their asses. No, seriously. They didn't take my trash, instead left a note that read, *Kiss my ass*. My main fear was that come Wednesday night all the neighbors would see that our trash hadn't been taken.

"I don't want them to think we didn't pay our bill." I explained to Donny in a panicked voice after he questioned why I was suggesting he gather our trash and dump it somewhere else; like behind a supermarket or restaurant with their trash.

"Well, we *didn't* pay our bill."

"Yeah, but I don't want them to *know* that!"

Now the situation was completely reversed, but I couldn't say anything because he didn't make me feel like an ass when I did it. Instead, I seethed and went back to Googling, "husband poison."

I Got Served

July 2, 2006

You're aware of my garbage problem right? I noticed lots of opossums in our backyard, husband revealed that there are mounds of garbage piled up behind the house due to nonpayment of garbage bill, husband decided to keep this from me because it is his turn to handle the bills and he didn't want me to know he'd dropped the ball. We switch off the responsibility of handling the bills every few months. It keeps each of us from wanting to shoot ourselves in the temple if we share the financial burden that comes with being homeowners.

Donny assured me that he'd handled the garbage situation. He said that an online payment had been sent the next day after his confession. It has been three weeks now, and still no picking up of garbage. My backyard was beginning to resemble *Sanford & Son.* To add insult to injury, last Wednesday (pick-up day) they took the garbage out of the can, sat it on top of the mounds of bags on the curb that couldn't fit in said can, and *took our can away.*

Donny called them last week to find out what the deal was. Turns out they never received our payment, and even worse, they say that the address we sent it to via our bank's online bill pay is incorrect. They claim they didn't move, but that we had the wrong address all along. I called bullshit on that because it's the same way we've always paid the bill for the three years we'd been in our house. And guess how much money caused this whole drama? $40! They were boycotting our garbage for forty measly bucks! Donny pays the money over the phone, stops payment on the check that is floating around God knows where, and the lady assures him we will have our can back on Monday and our trash picked up on Wednesday.

Monday comes, no can. They dropped it off Tuesday. There was so much trash sitting on our curb in anticipation of pick-up day, it was downright embarrassing. I'm sitting at the computer, working on my morning blog when I hear the garbage truck come and go. I run to the front door, peek out the sidelights, and there is the trash at the curb, overflowing with trash. Grrrr.

I grab the phone, and call the number on the side of the can. Before the lady can get the words, "How can I help you" out of her mouth, I'm cussing her out. I'm being sarcastic and I'm using foul language and big words. I do that on purpose when I'm being outraged with customer service. I use really big words to make them feel even smaller than they already must for having a shitty job like taking sanitation complaints.

I tell her that I spend more than forty dollars on lipstick, that they can take their forty dollars and shove it up their asses, that there's no way in hell we've been sending the money to the wrong address for three years, and that somebody better come and get this damn trash before possums invade my house and bite my baby, then I'll have to come to her shit hole of an office and slit her throat. By the end of it, I'm pretty sure I was foaming at the mouth.

She places me on hold to contact the driver, and after she does I can see the truck pause at the cul-de-sac down the street from ours. "That's right, bitches. Come get my trash!" Customer service girl with a freshly ripped asshole comes back on the line.

CSGWFRA: "Ma'am?"

N: "Yes?"

CSGWFRA: "That wasn't the garbage pick-up. That was the recycling pick-up. The garbage truck hasn't come by yet, but when they do, they will definitely pick up your trash."

N: "Oh."

I felt like the biggest twat in the history of twats. I mumbled some final lame ass, "Well, they better." And hung up.

Field Day

July 14, 2006

Last night, around midnight, after not being able to sleep, I decided to watch *Cold Case Files*. It's a true crime show where they show how cold, unsolved crimes were solved after many years. I love it, but it spooks me out.

As the show finished I heard a noise downstairs. I nudged Donny. Nothing. I nudged him again. Nothing. Finally, I slapped his arm, and asked one of two stupid questions usually asked in this situation. The first being, "Are you sleeping?" I mean, he was just softly snoring two seconds before. I *knew* he was sleeping. I went with stupid question number two.

"Did you hear that?"

"No."

And that's it. He made no move to get out of bed, to investigate, or to check that our child was still snug as a bug in bed. Nothing makes a person think, "Why the hell did I marry your ass again?" more than watching your husband roll over and spoon his pillow when a rapist could be in the house.

I checked all of downstairs, came back upstairs, and he had the nerve to ask, "Everything ok?"

"Yeah, glad to know you had my back, dickass."

"I had your back."

"Yeah, I coulda been raped and murdered two times over. Get off of me. Don't try to cuddle me now."

This morning he redeemed himself. Kali wouldn't get up for school. She cried that she didn't want to go. It was Field Day, but she didn't care. As a matter of fact, I suspect that may be the reason she didn't want to go. Donny and I were sitting on her bed trying to talk her into getting up.

I'm a wimp. I was thisclose to letting her stay home, but Donny put his foot down and explained to Kali that she had to go and she'd be sad if she missed Field Day. He encouraged her to try her best, and told her that she just may surprise herself with how well she did and how much fun she had.

I remember hating Field Day as a kid. I was always tall, lanky, and skinny. Any kind of organized sports activity scared me. My days as a cheerleader came to crashing halt after I slipped on another girl's pom-poms during a basketball game, and busted my ass in front of the whole school. Field Day was like asking me to come to school naked and do jumping jacks. I felt Kali's pain, however; I didn't want her to be one of *those* kids afraid to *try*. Donny reminded me of that. He helped motivate her into going.

As I evaluate my life and marriage and try to figure out what is working, and what needs improvement, I maintain a list of pros and cons. In Donny's pro column I have, "Great father." On the con side: "Totally okay with me getting raped and murdered."

Cucumber Melon Ass

August 2, 2006

So, yesterday was Donny's second day of vacation, and the first day we actually *did* anything. We went out to the movies, did a little shopping, and had dinner. After the movie, I was cranky. They saw *Over the Hedge*, and I saw *Miami Vice*. I leave the theatre and Donny's sitting in the lobby watching Kali play a video game.

"How was it?" he asked.

"I hate you."

See, I thought I was actually *doing* something by seeing *Miami Vice*. I was trying to prove a point. Donny hates the idea of us seeing movies we both want to see alone. If I even *suggest* that I might go see a movie alone, his lower lip quivers and his eyes water. This time, I refused to give in. I put my foot down. I had a big old rant.

"I don't want to see some chick flick. I hate chick flicks! I wanna see *Miami Vice*! You can go see it alone another time or rent it. Why we gotta do everything together? Damn. I can't go see what I want, when I want, by myself? Is this not America? Are you my master now? Massah, can I's go see *Miami Vice*, suh? Give us free!"

Fast forward to the end of the movie and I'm crying and Donny has a smug look on his face.

"*Over the Hedge* was good."

"Fuck you and *Over*... Oh hey, Kali. How was your movie?"

"It was sooo good! It was awesome. It was the funniest movie I've ever seen. It was the *best* movie I've ever seen. How was your movie, Mommy?"

"It was...the exact opposite of your movie."

We head to Wal-Mart. I need a wax kit, we want to pick up Kali's school supply list, and I want the *Smallville* season three box set. As we're walking through the parking lot, I realize that it's hot as fucking balls outside. Kali and Donny are in shorts. My dumb ass is in jeans. Call that my jackass move-of-the-day number two. That's what my Dad calls it when someone does something stupid. "Then he went and made the jackass move...."

So, we're walking across the parking lot and my jeans are literally clinging to me and they feel heavy and wet. I'm wearing this shirt that kinda hangs off my shoulders and I'm trudging across the parking lot, boobs practically hanging out, my hair pinned up, squinting behind a pair of sunglasses, and feeling like a big, fat, sweating cow.

"You are so sexy."

"Donny, are you delirious from the heat? I look a hot ass mess."

"No, you look sexy as hell."

"Ah, that's sweet. Grab a shopping cart."

We shop for a bit. I stock up on some *Nair* for my legs, a *Nair* stick for my upper lip, a *Sally Henson* eyebrow wax kit, and lots of *Oil of Olay* face products. Then hunger hits me so suddenly that my whole body goes weak. My hands start shaking and I'm overcome with waves of heat. We pass the candy aisle and I start tossing shit in my cart. First, two big Symphony bars.

"How can you eat that? They're just blocks of sugar." Donny stares at the candy.

"Leave me alone."

A bag of mini Snickers go in next. Then, a bag of Reese's Peanut Butter Cups. And the biggest bag of Skittles ever. We head over to electronics to get *Smallville*, and while Donny looks, I can't take it anymore. I reach in the cart and rip open one of the Symphony bars.

"Ooooh, can I have some?" Kali asks.

I toss her a few squares to keep her quiet. I hate when people eat in the supermarket, but fuck it, I'm starving. These are extenuating circumstances. I really thought I would faint. As we walk through the aisles I catch Donny shooting me looks every so often.

"What?"

"You. You're moaning."

"I am?"

"Yes. Is it *that* good?"

"Hey, don't judge me. I'm hungry." We get everything we need and go to check out. I barely let go of the huge chocolate bar long enough for the woman to scan it. As we're exiting, the alarm goes off. Normally, I'd be mortified, but as the lady with the scanner gun goes over our receipt, and she and Donny try to figure out what caused the alarm to sound, all I care about is my chocolate. I'm standing there, as people pass us by looking at us as if we're thieves, licking my fingers and stuffing my face.

In the car, Donny asks, "Where do you want to go eat?"

I'm sprawled out in the passenger seat, chocolate on my face. "I don't care...I want hot wings... and vegetables... with sweet tea. And maybe some beef."

Donny snickers. "You want..."

"If the words hot beef injection leave your mouth, I will punch you in it."

We decide on Buffalo's because I know I'll like their wings since we've had them many times.

"Or we can try that new place," Donny says. "They have a sign up for all you can eat wings."

"No, what if I don't like them? I'm too hungry to take a chance on a new place."

"Yeah, that's true. We need to get you what you want or the world will end."

"What the hell is that supposed to mean?"

Donny laughs. "Oh, you know what I mean."

Kali chimes in from the backseat. "He doesn't mean *literally.*" Apparently, this is my child's new word. Literally. Kali's decided she's had enough of this conversation. "Daddy, guess what? Thursday, Mommy and I are going to the aquarium." I told Kali the week before that, "When Daddy's on vacation, we're going to the aquarium."

"I know. I'm going too." Donny smiles at her in the rearview mirror.

"I thought you were going on vacation." Kali says.

"I am on vacation."

"When do you leave?"

"I'm not going anywhere. This is my vacation... spending time with you guys."

"Oh, I thought you were leaving on vacation and Mommy and I were going to the aquarium."

He laughs again. "Is it okay if I come too?"

"It's okay with me, ask Mommy."

The restaurant was uneventful. I ate a lot, and drank like ten glasses of sweet tea. Much later, Kali's in bed, I'm standing at the kitchen table in a little white nightie, and I'm elbow deep in that big ass bag of Skittles. Donny's playing some football game on the XBOX in the next room.

"You know what I just thought of? I grabbed this little sample bottle of cologne at Wal-Mart. I sat it in the cart. I think that's what was going off. Maybe Kali was sitting on it, but when I unpacked the bags, I didn't see it and it's not on the receipt. I think we just left it in the cart."

"Why the fuck are you buying cologne from Wal-Mart?" I ask through a mouth full of Skittles.

"It was a little sample bottle, like five bucks, and I wanted to try it out."

"So?"

"It was Perry Ellis."

"It's still Wal-Mart."

"Who cares?"

I shrug. "Hmmm. Well. I guess if that's how you were raised."

We head up to bed and I start using my new face stuff. I'm all scrubbed and exfoliated and moisturized, but my top lip looks fuzzy. I decide to try my new *Nair* stick.

Note: I've never used a Nair product in my life.

Sensing possible comedic relief, Donny joins me in the master bathroom. I apply the cream to my upper lip using the little, pink, tube applicator. I look like a milk ad, or porno, gone wrong.

"How long do you leave it on?" Donny asks.

"Five minutes."

Donny reads from the direction for *Nair* that goes on my legs. "This only takes three minutes."

"Well, let's test that while we wait for my lip."

So, we spread a towel on the bed and I lay there as he lathers my right leg in *Nair*.

After a few minutes I ask, "What's that smell?"

"The Nair... eating away the flesh on your face."

"That's not funny!"

"That's what it smells like!"

He's right. The shit on my lip smells like hair relaxer, and that doesn't make me feel good at all about it being on my face. The stuff on my leg doesn't smell any better even though it's supposed to be Cucumber Melon scented.

"Does that smell like cucumber melon to you?" I ask.

"It smells like cucumber melon ass."

"Go get me a wet washcloth so I can wipe this off my lips. It's been five minutes and it's burning." I wipe it off. "Did it work?"

Donny's cracking up. Apparently it worked straight across the top of my lip, under my nose, but the sides (corners of my mouth) still had whiskers. And because the top was freshly removed, the area is lighter and slightly red which only makes the corners look darker and hairier. I hobble to the bathroom mirror; my right leg covered in stinky *Nair* like it's a full cast.

"Fuck! Stop laughing. I have to do the corners again." My top lip looked like a reverse Hitler mustache. It's at that point that I realize my right leg is on fire. "Damn! It's been three minutes; help me wipe this off my leg." I stand in the tub and we both start wiping away at the *Nair* with wet rags. It worked in some areas better than others, but I still felt like the stuff was on me so I jumped in the shower. As soon as the water hit, I regretted it. It didn't really hurt, just very prickly. My skin was too sensitive to be touched after I'd just willingly smeared it with lye. I look down in the shower, and I'll be damned if my right leg wasn't lighter than my left. It's like it removed hair and skin.

I crawl into bed with Donny. One hairy leg, one smooth. We watch two episodes of *Rescue Me*, and pretend that our bedroom doesn't smell like cucumber melon ass.

I'm Joining a Gym... Now!

August 17, 2006

Um, yeah so... I just got back from my walk/run around the subdivision. My calves feel like they've been bitten by dogs. Let me tell you why it's so hard for me to get on the right track for diet and exercise. Life gets in the way!

First of all, after I put Kali on the bus and posted my morning blog I had planned on going for my walk/run then. I say walk/run because I really wasn't sure what I'd be in the mood to do once I got out there. It was really cool out this morning and somewhat cloudy so I thought that would be perfect. I have a thing with the sun. I don't like it. My family calls me a vampire because I never open the blinds and will rarely turn on a light unless absolutely necessary. I had Donny install a dimmer in the dining area of the kitchen because I felt like McDonald's fries sitting under a heat lamp every time we sat down for a meal.

ANYWAY, where was I? Oh yeah, my plan to go fairly early before it got much hotter was foiled when Donny called. "I'm coming home soon. We have to take the blue car to get an emissions test before Monday. I need you to go with me to drop the car off."

This summer we got away with having one car. Kali was out of school and Donny was home from work before my classes began. Now that she's back in school and my fall classes start on Monday, we need to get our other car (a blue Toyota something or other) registered as most of my classes are during the day while he's at work.

I contemplate going for my walk/run anyway, and then making his ass drive around the subdivision to find me, but I stay home and fart around MySpace. He finally shows and I follow him to the emissions place. We get there and guess what? They don't do emissions anymore. So, we head down the road to another place. By this time the sun is rearing its ugly head and I'm getting cranky. Visions of cardiac arrest dance in my head. I glance in the rearview mirror and notice that I have more grey hairs than ever before. Oh, joy. And I turn 32 tomorrow.

We finally make it back home. "What's wrong with you?" Oh, he was so sorry he asked that.

I don't feel like walking/running in this hot ass heat.

You ruined my day.

The house is a mess and I don't feel like cleaning, but I have to or else I'll wake up to a messy house on my birthday.

These Nikes feel too tight. I think my feet got fatter too. Can feet get fat? Mine did.

Tomorrow's my birthday and I don't have shit to do.

"Well, that's why I wanted to take care of the car stuff today so you can keep the Saturn and do something."

Do what? Call my girlfriends and go out? What girlfriends?! Go where?!

The stupid financial aid office won't answer the phone, and I want to know if my grant money is on my ID card so I can buy my books before Monday.

And finally, I had fruit and Crystal Lite for breakfast. I'm about to eat my own titties I'm so hungry.

Donny scurries back to work, wondering why he didn't marry that cute little blonde he was dating before me.

Off I go. Oh wait, I need a key. Donny has one set of keys with the Saturn, and the other set is with the Toyota at the auto place. I search the junk drawer for a spare key. When we closed on our house they gave us like, fifteen copies of the house key. Of course, I can't find one now that I finally need it. After much searching and cussing, I find one. *Now*, I'm ready to go.

By this time, it's high fucking noon. I start walking. I have my iPod in my left hand, and a bottled water and house key in my right hand. I turn around because I think I hear something behind me. *Wack!* I knock one earphone out of my ear and the iPod hits the ground. Fuck me!

I need one of those stupid armband thingies to hold the iPod. Maybe I should go to Wal-Mart first and get one before I do this? Hmmm, I don't have a car. I could walk to Wal-Mart. Inner self kicks in.

IS: "Bitch, you ain't walkin' to no Wal-Mart."

She's right. I re-adjust and continue walking. I suppose I should pump my arms and blow out breaths like those power walkers do, but they look stupid. These are my neighbors. I have to live with these people. They will not see me looking like a retarded mall walker. I do realize, though, that I need to do more than just stroll. It seems kinda pointless unless I put some pep in my step. Some motion in my ocean. You know, move my ass. I opt for the only other "walk" I know.

Pretty soon I look like I'm auditioning for *America's Next Top Model: The Geriatric Edition.* I don't care. It's better than looking like a power walker.

As I listen to my music and strut my stuff, I realize that this would be a good time to reflect. I try to reflect, but I'm not sure what I should be reflecting on. I decide clearing my mind might be better. I clear my thoughts, but that, and the sun, just makes me sleepy.

I decide to play a little game where I envision the music videos to the songs that play on my iPod. I'm halfway through Guns n' Roses' *You Could*

Be Mine and contemplating watching *Terminator 2* later, when I realize I have a wedgie.

IS: "You should have worn panties."

Bitch.

So, now I'm strutting like a supermodel, sweating like a pig, and picking a wedgie as I walk by a house with a black couple unloading groceries from their car in their driveway. Their mouths are moving, but I can't make out their greeting over Pearl Jam's *Glorified G.* I just give a half wave with my water bottle/key hand, and pick my pants out of my ass with my iPod hand. They look a bit disgusted, but I don't care. They should have their black asses at work anyway. It's the middle of the fucking day.

I'm four long blocks away from my cul-de-sac when my left calf starts to burn. Holy. Mother. Of. God. But I can't stop now. Four blocks ain't shit. In my heyday, I'd walk from 23rd St. to 42nd in Manhattan without breaking a sweat. I sadly realize this isn't my heyday, and I'm pretty sure my eyeballs are sweating. I drink some water and soldier on.

I walk another two blocks before turning back. This is why I love the gym. It's air conditioned, and if I get tired of the treadmill I can always hop on the bike or elliptical. Your only options walking the subdivision are: you can either continue, turn around and walk back, or sit on the curb and cry like a bitch. I was seriously contemplating option three.

The walk back to the house was only slightly less torturous because I was able to tell myself I was headed home where there was central air waiting. Three blocks from my house, my hips start to hurt.

IS: "Stop switching them so hard. Nobody's looking. You don't have to be cute all the time, you know."

Eat me.

The last block was the worst. It was uphill and my calves felt like little pins were being poked into them. I couldn't get the key in the front door fast enough. As soon as my eyes adjusted from leaving the sun, I was hit with a headache. I don't care what our budget looks like. I'm rejoining Gold's Gym. This walking out in the elements is for the birds.

I need a shower. And a cheeseburger.

He Works Hard For the Money

August 25, 2006

You know what I've noticed? No matter how forward thinking and modern your man is, if he's the bread winner he will take on certain caveman type characteristics. Donny is a sweetie pie, but lately I've noticed a change in him. And I don't just mean his constant threats of backhanding me. Everyone knows that he works while I go to school full time. I've found that no matter what the situation, Donny's answer for everything has now become, "Because I work." Or some variation of that. For instance...

"Why are you so tired?"

"Because I work."

Or...

"I don't feel good."

"What's wrong?"

"I've been working."

Or...

"What do you want for dinner?"

"Work."

The other day he came in and kissed me hello.

"Ew, you stink."

"'Cause I been working!"

I'd finally had enough. "Alright, I get it. Damn! You work and I don't! Must you remind me every three hours?! I know you work!"

My favorite part of all of this is how he thinks this means that I'm automatically going to be a housewife. Um, no. Don't get me wrong. I clean and cook. But I don't do it like it's my *job*.

Donny leaves the room to get something to drink...

"Can you bring me something to drink too?"

"Sure."

"And maybe a slice of pizza. But only put it in the microwave for like forty-five seconds. And don't forget a napkin."

"You're bossy."

"Are you new?"

Outsourced

September 14, 2006

In this day and age, we are all familiar with how much of a pain in the ass it is to cancel an account. Some of us had to learn the hard way the correct way to do this. In the beginning, when asked, "May I ask why you wish to cancel your account/subscription?" I would try to be nice and general.

"Oh, I just don't need it anymore." Or, "I never really use it."

What I realize now is that the customer service person has a book of rebuttals propped up in front of him just waiting for me. His finger travels down the page of rebuttals until he gets to "I never really use it." It slides to the right.... "Well, ma'am, perhaps you were not aware of all the fine features our product offers. Did you know that besides providing you with hours of entertainment, it can also mow your lawn, clip your toenails, braid your hair, and help you save on car insurance?"

"Really? One little magazine can do all that?"

"That's right. Perhaps you would like to get the next month free, and try out these new features."

My stupid ass says, "Okay."

Over the years, I've learned to be ready for them. "Ma'am, may I ask why you're canceling your account?"

"Because I want to, that's why! As a free, black woman, it is my right to cancel. I woke up this morning and decided to cancel and that's just what I'ma do. Cancel. What you questioning me for? Can't a black woman cancel some shit if she wants to? Bet if I was white you wouldn't be questioning me like this. What? You think I don't know myself? A black woman can't know what she wants? Fuck you. Cancel. That. Shit. Now!"

"Your confirmation number is…."

See? Leave no room for argument.

Perfect example: I finally called to cancel my Napster subscription yesterday. Now that I have an iPod with iTunes, I don't need it.

"Ma'am, may I ask why you want to cancel your Napster subscription?"

My exact words: "Cause it sucks! It was a big old rip off. I pay $10 a month and 99 cents per song. When I bought my MP3 player and tried to download the songs to it, I kept getting licensing errors and was told I need to buy the songs again. Screw that. Then when I tried to get some sort of help, it took me two days to find the customer service number. Who are you? The CIA? Why the difficulty? Just cancel it. I got an iPod now and it's so much nicer. Yup, I missed Prison Break last week and got the episode for $2 on my iTunes. Napster sucks."

Done and done. He hurried up and got my ass off the phone.

Just now I called Real Player to cancel my Super Pass. I get it every summer for the *Big Brother* live feeds and cancel as soon as the show is done. Every fucking summer they ask me why I want to cancel and I tell them. They still try to get me to stick around. When I called today I was prepared for a fight, but got so much more.

Some Indian lady answered the phone. There was a ton of noise in the background. It was really loud and I almost hung up thinking I had the wrong number.

"Can I have your email address please to look up your account?"

Now my last name is hyphenated. Perez-married last name. I always have to spell them both. My email address is the letter "n" followed by my married name. Let's just say it's Cuashka.

"N as in Nancy- C as in Cat – U as in Unicorn – A as in Apple – S as in Sam…"

You get the picture. She's typing for a moment. I think I hear a goat in the background.

"Let me confirm that email address for you. That's M as in Mary, F as in Frank, A as in Apple."

I cut her off. "No, no, no, there's no F anywhere in there. Where'd you get an F?"

"I'm sorry. Can you repeat that?"

"It's N as in Nancy, C as in Cat, A as in…"

I do it all over again.

"Thank you. Please hold while I pull up your account."

I hear her typing and breathing. In the background the goat sounds restless. "Ok, Ma'am can I have your credit card number on the account?"

"Can I just give you the last four digits?"

"No, I need the whole number."

"I don't want to give you the whole number."

"Well, I need to prove you are who you say you are."

"Well, I don't know who *you* are and I'm not giving out the number. Now what?"

"One moment."

The goat brays. Or whinnies. Or whatever the fuck it is goats do.

"Ok, can you give me your first and last name?"

"Nina. N as in Nancy, I as in Igloo, N as in Nancy, A as in Apple."

"Ok."

Then I say my last name and proceed to spell it.

"P as in Paul…" When I'm done she repeats it back to me… "Did you say E as in Paul?"

Silence.

I blink.

"Yes, that's exactly what I said. That silent *e* in Paul."

Jesus fucking Christ.

Projectile Tampons

November 2, 2006

Donny and I were watching this show on VH1 where they did a countdown of the top one hundred songs of the 80's. That song by David Bowie and Queen, you know, the one Vanilla Ice sampled, made the list. My young husband says, "I didn't know they did this song."

"You thought Vanilla Ice came up with that?!" So then I ask, "Don't you remember that interview with Vanilla Ice where he's defending himself?" And I tell Donny how Vanilla Ice said, "Their beat goes like this... dun dun dun dun dun dun dun. And my beat goes like this... dun dun dun dun dun dun dun *tsk* dun dun dun dun. See, that little *tsk* is the difference"

And Donny is looking at me like I'm on crack, like I'm making it up. And at that exact moment what comes on but the *actual* interview? And I had it right! Down to the very last "dun." Donny starts laughing, I start laughing, and I'm laughing so hard I say, "Stop! I think my tampon is going to come out!"

That only makes Donny laugh harder. He says, "I saw a tampon commercial yesterday where tampon have grips. And I thought, do tampons really need grips? Do they come out?"

And we continued to laugh like children while I clenched my vagina.

The Morphine Statue

December 28, 2006

Kali is The Big Dipper, and my best friend's daughter, who is three years old, is The Little Dipper. So named are they because they have the uncanny ability to find themselves within earshot every time we are on the phone having inappropriate conversations. Next thing I know, I'm answering questions like this:

"Mommy, what's Chlamydia?"

"A seasoning, honey. Go play." I gotta get that child a bell or something.

My best friend, Sophie, has a female stalker - a poor soul who can't take a hint and continues to call her and invite her places even though Sophie repeatedly declines, and most times, won't even answer the phone. We talk about this girl at least every two weeks, and were totally unaware that the Little Dipper had been paying attention to these conversations until one day she informed Sophie that "Mommy doesn't like Miss Cathy." So, now we're just waiting for the day when Sophie and Little Dipper run into Miss Cathy at the Shop N' Save and she repeats it. Cause that's how kids roll.

My favorite Little Dipper moment was a few months ago as Sophie and I were on the phone one weekday around 4pm.

Sophie: "Oooh, I can't watch Oprah today."

Nina: "Why? What's it about?"

Sophie: "It's about a D-A-D that killed his five-year-old twins."

There's a shocked gasp from Little Dipper in the background.

Nina: "I think you spelled the wrong word, jackass."

My biggest fear is that one day Kali will repeat something in school that will cause them to call child services. For instance, Christmas Eve day was the first day I met my new nephew and as I was "eating his little ass up" (kissing him all over) I said, "Ooh, just wait till tomorrow when the rest of the family sees you." Then I looked at my sister and said, "We're going to be passing him around like a joint."

"What's a joint?" See? Big Dipper, dippin' in grown folks' conversation.

Yesterday, Sophie had her second child, a beautiful baby boy. She was hopped up on morphine most of the day and our conversation last night was hysterical. She sounded like a crack head. Her speech was slurred, she kept repeating herself. I kept waiting for her to ask to borrow money.

Tonight, we're on the phone talking about it as Kali is drawing at the coffee table.

Nina: "So, you still getting morphine?"

Sophie: "Nah, I've been downgraded to Percocet."

Kali interrupts to show me her drawing and how she can't wait to show it to her teacher.

Nina: "That's nice, honey."

Kali: "Thanks! I call it, *The Morphine Statue.*"

Big Dipper strikes again.

Picking up Tips

January 3rd, 2007

Last night I made Donny go out and rent *Snakes on a Plane* and *The Covenant*. Morbid curiosity made it so that he didn't mind the first one, but...

"What the hell is *The Covenant*?"

"Remember? That movie that Chrissa wanted to see and was crying about because she couldn't find it in any theatre, and then it turned out it wasn't out for a few weeks so I mocked her privately in IM instead of blogging about it?"

"Oh, yeah. You don't want to see that!"

"How you gonna tell me what I want to see? I said I want to, didn't I?"

"Fine. Who's in it, Nina?"

"White boys and vampires. Two of my favorite things. Now go get it."

We watched *SOAP* last night. Not bad. I actually liked it. If you don't go into it expecting Oscar material, you won't be disappointed.

After the movie, we watched *Dateline*. Chris Hansen, who we love in this house due to his *To Catch a Predator* series, was doing a story on a man accused of killing his wife in Michigan. Donny was particularly interested as he's from Michigan and I was interested because I didn't want his ass picking up tips.

The story was the usual: The couple started out great, married out of college, two kids, nice home, then the husband becomes addicted to everything from porn, to pills, to gambling. The wife wants a divorce and then looky here; she turns up face down in the river with a bloody head. And the husband is left with this dumb ass, "I don't know nuffin' 'bout nuffin'" look on his face.

I turned to Donny in bed and said, "What is it with you white men? I mean, really? Why you always gotta kill your wives?"

He just smiled, flashing deep dimples. I stuck my finger in one dimple and told him, "Don't go smiling at me! I'm not playing. Don't even think about killing me cause your ass gonna get caught! See (pointing to the screen), they always get caught!"

"At least I'll get to meet Chris Hansen."

I slept with one eye open the whole night.

A Whale's Tail

January 4th, 2007

Yesterday morning, around 10am, I found myself sitting at the kitchen table with Kali, waiting for her hot chocolate to cool down enough so that she could sip it without burning off a taste bud or twelve, and then I planned on taking her to school. You may be wondering what she was doing home at ten in the morning on a Wednesday, but the better question would be, "Why did she stay home the day before when all the other kids in our county returned to school?"

Simple: Her mother, that would be me, assumed that she returned to school next week. Why? Because that's when her mother, again me, is returning to school and in true Nina form, she believed that everything (in the world, universe, galaxy) revolved around *her* - her being Nina, not Kali. By extension everything in her (Nina's, not Kali's) world revolved around Kali. With the exception, obviously, of her education as this story so blatantly proves.

When asked lovingly - and with all the patience one musters for a mildly retarded child - by Donny, where she obtained the information that Kali returned to school on January 9th, and not the 2nd, I replied, "From myself." Donny sighed. The same sigh exhaled when said mildly retarded child poops and then plays in it.

I was already in a pretty lousy mood considering that the weekend before, Donny and I had *a moment*.

I can count on one hand the number of times we've actually fought, and most of those took place last year. I can count on the other hand the number of times I've actually seen him mad...because of me...that I know of. I'm sure there are dozens of times that I inspired some unseen, festering beneath the surface, "white boy crazy" rage.

Those of you who are married know exactly what *a moment* is. In fact, you don't have to be married to experience this. Just live with someone. This can be a significant other or roommate. Inevitably, you will experience a moment with this person. A moment is when, for no apparent reason, the two of you decide you want absolutely nothing to do with one another.

Ours started on New Year's Eve night. We went to my Dad's house and around 1am I decided I wanted to go home. Donny was fine with this but informed me that should we go, I would have to drive as he had too much to drink. I commented that was odd since I'd only seen him have one beer - a honey lager if memory serves.

Anyway, the drive home was really quiet, the trip to bed even quieter, and the next morning (yesterday) was downright icy. I woke up at eleven and went downstairs to find coffee brewing and Donny outside dumping garbage.

Oh, okay, it's going to be one of *those* moments. You know, where you each try to outdo the other in an effort to make each look like a lazy bastard. Not much work required on Donny's part, I should add. I grab a cup of coffee and head upstairs. As I hit the second floor I can hear the washer and dryer going. *Oh, he's gooood.*

I get in bed with my coffee and book, and wait to hear the washer stop so I can switch out the laundry. Unfortunately, I got so engrossed in my book that I missed it and moments later Donny comes in the room carrying clean clothes.

"What are you doing?"

"Laundry."

"I was going to do that. You don't have to."

He takes one look me, still in PJs, gripping a coffee mug in one hand, novel in the other, with the comforter up to my chin, looking every bit the opposite of someone ready for housework.

"Don't worry about it," he says dryly.

Bastard.

He takes a basket of clean clothes downstairs to fold. This is normal during a moment. We have a big house, and during a moment, we try to stay on opposite ends of it. In fact, if I were truly playing by the rules, my ass would be huddled in the master bedroom's closet with my book as that's about as far away from the family room as one could get without actually leaving the house.

Since there wasn't much housework to be done yesterday, we used the only tool available to us to prove "I'm the better spouse." Kali. Anything that poor child needed yesterday, Donny and I damn near broke our necks to be the one to get it.

"Can someone pour me some soda?"

That would usually be met with, "Go ask your mother/father." Not yesterday. We were practically tackling each other to get to the Cherry Coke first. Unfortunately for Kali, she never caught on to what was happening or she'd have been asking for a lot more, and getting it, more's the pity.

Anyway, at one point in the afternoon I was back in bed, watching *The Unit* without Donny, which is another moment tactic. You watch a show you would normally watch together off the TiVo, leaving the other to wonder if you're actually going to be bitch enough to delete it when you're done. (I wasn't.)

Donny comes into the bedroom, sits on the edge of the bed, and starts to put on a pair of socks.

"I'm going to the store. Do you need anything?"

Now, don't go *awwwwing* and taking his side. He had an ulterior motive and you're about to read about it.

"No. What are you going to the store for?"

"Ingredients."

"For what?"

"Dinner."

Son of a bitch.

A few hours pass, Donny's making his world famous chili and watching college football, I'm still upstairs, and Kali's in the study on the first floor playing an *I Spy* computer game we got her for Christmas. She comes upstairs and asks, "Can you come downstairs and help me find something in my game?"

She had me at "can you." Moments later I'm at the computer trying desperately to find a whale's tail in an underwater scene. I tried everything I could think of. I squinted, I turned my head left, right, upside down, I sat close the screen (which only gave me a headache) and I sat far from the screen, I even found Waldo, *but I could not find the damn whale's tail.*

"I'll go ask Daddy."

"No!" I said a little too quickly and loudly.

I was determined to find the whale's tail all alone without any help from his attitude having, laundry folding, chili making ass. At some point I was so into finding the tail, I didn't notice that Kali had left the room and returned with Donny. Traitor.

So, now we're both sitting at the computer trying to find the whale's tail. The tension is thick. I was sweating and I'm pretty sure Donny was drooling. We were determined to be the parent to find the whale's tail first.

Wanna know the kicker? *I could not, for the life of me, remember what a whale's tail looked like! And I refused to ask!* Was it rounded, spiked, curled, or forked? I tried to conjure up images of Shamu and Willy. Nothing.

Finally, from Donny, "Oh. There it is."

He clicks at a place on the screen, near the top, amongst the blue sky and clouds, and I'll be damned if a part of the blue sky wasn't actually a tiny whale. As he clicked, the whale shook his little whale tail, mocking me no doubt, and disappeared behind a cloud.

Son of a bitch.

Hookers Fascinate Me

January 6th, 2007

Hookers amaze me. They really do. First of all, I know there are different kinds of hookers. There are the high-priced call girls, the streetwalker who hits the stroll to feed addictions and/or children, the pseudo strippers giving hand jobs for an extra fiver (Well, hopefully more than that), and massage ladies who deliver happy endings.

If you want to get all deep with it, some say married women and women in relationships are hookers as well. That's if you just go by the definition of "trading sexual favors for goods or services" and omit the "with strange men" part. Although, some ladies may argue that their men are pretty strange, but that's for another blog.

Did I engage in a little prostitution last year when, while on my lunch break, some girlfriends and I hit up Macy's and I spent $275 on a purse, two pairs of shoes, and some MAC cosmetics, stashed the stuff in the trunk of the car until I could make love to my husband before showing him my purchases? Po-TAY-toes, Po-TA-toes.

Anyway, for all intents and purposes of this blog we will be discussing the traditional prostitute: sex for money with strangers. In particular, I'm talking about the high-priced call girls like the two arrested here in Atlanta on Wednesday.

The head hooker, madam, H.H.I.C., whatever you want to call her, is a former Playboy Playmate (and I think porn star) who ran the business from her very nice home in the Sugarloaf Country Club subdivision. Now, this is very near where I live and I can tell you that these houses are fabulous. Michael Vick (Atlanta Falcons QB) lives in there - just to give you an idea of the kind of money and houses we're talking about.

So, the first news reports were that two women were arrested for operating a prostitution ring out of a house. There was no shot of the house, just their two mug shots. No matter how hot you look before the picture is taken, everyone looks busted in their mug shots. It's just physics.

By Thursday it was all over the news, all the sordid details of their business: the location of the house complete with an aerial shot of the sprawling estate, the fact that the madam was a former Playmate ("North America's Most Published Centerfold and one of Penthouse Magazine's Most Published Pets"), and the website listing their fees.

Ready for the fees?

The smallest package was $500. The largest was $15,000. They would entertain at the house sometimes, but most times the clients would be entertained in high-end hotels all around Atlanta, and sometimes the clients would pay to fly the girls to different cities.

Wanna know what you get for $500?

Oral sex.

For one hour.

Now, oral is great, but an hour is a really long time. And five hundred dollars?! What the *hell* are these girls putting in these blowjobs? Crack? Diamonds?

The women were released on bail yesterday, and now there's talk of their customer and financial records seeing the light of day. Now, I'm going to go out there and ready myself for ridicule when I say this: I don't know why this is illegal. I think they should be left alone. They're consenting adults and these men can obviously afford it. Who are they hurting? And that's not rhetorical. I really want to know. Maybe you guys know something I don't. Maybe I'm not thinking about this deep enough.

Now, could I do this personally? No. Strange penis makes me queasy and I have this pesky little habit of loving the men I sleep with or falling in love with the men I sleep with -whichever comes first. But, for these women, I think it is fine. Let 'em do what they want to do.

They interviewed some of the hoity-toity residents of the subdivision, and they were all shocked, amazed, and had no idea what was going on in the house. Although, it was reported that some of what started this investigation was complaints from neighbors of heavy traffic to the house and loud parties. You would think hookers would be a bit more discreet ... unless some of the neighbors were getting their freak on, too!

That's right. It's been reported that the client list of this house o' hookers includes some of the rich and respected residents of Atlanta, including those in the subdivision. For some reason Donny is downright giddy with the idea that Michael Vick might be on the list.

Note: Of course, we'd later come to find out that Michael Vick had other worries.

More arrests were promised in the coming weeks. More girls and clients. I'm willing to bet that we will see plenty of girls doing the perp walk in front of news cameras in the weeks to come, and every time they have a court date you can be sure news cameras will be there, but I seriously doubt we'll see any of their clients taking the walk of shame... and that's a shame.

iPod Resuscitation

January 8th, 2007

I have issues with charging things. Just ask my friends. My cell phone has been uncharged since December 13th or thereabouts. My house phones are never on their chargers so when I'm in the middle of a very good conversation they start beeping. It's to the point now where they won't even do that. Mid-sentence a voice interrupts my conversation, "Time's up, bitch!"

Last night, I had a panic attack. I went to connect my iPod to the computer after many, many, many days of inactivity. I opened up iTunes and noticed it wasn't acknowledging my iPod. I pick it up, look at the screen and it's black. No, wait. There's the little apple symbol. What's that doing there? Wait. It's gone again. As so for a few minutes I'm watching this apple flicker off and on. I'm crying and calling for Donny.

"Dooooonny! My iPod's broken!"

Actually, I might have said it the ghetto way, "broke," which I realize now means my iPod was low on funds, but he seemed to understand what I meant.

"Don't tell me that."

So, he starts doing what all husbands do to fix a situation: every fucking thing I already tried before he got there!

"I tried that already," I sob.

"Well, let *me* try it."

Men.

Finally, I notice that the little apple is staying on the screen for longer periods of time. It was my little iPod's heartbeat! Come on, iPod! You can do it! We wait another minute or so and the apple is replaced with the familiar white screen that says, "Do not disconnect," and has the prohibited symbol. The little battery up top is completely empty but after a few more flickers, the little red bar starts to rise inside of it.

"Oh thank you, Jesus! It was just really low on juice. She's coming back!"

Donny shoots me a disgusted look. I ignore it, too happy that my iPod is finally breathing on its own.

"For one second there, I thought I would have to slit a hole in her neck and stick a straw down there. What? That's what they do on *ER*."

Panic Attack

January 9th, 2007

I usually freak out in the middle, or at the end, of a semester. "I'm going to fail!" Never at the beginning. Until this weekend. Two of my classes are online courses and the other two are on campus.

I logged in to the school's online portal yesterday to see if the online courses had been loaded. Holy crap! What the hell was I thinking? I took one online course my first semester, General Intro to Psychology or Psych 101, and it was horrible. Much more work than I expected. Well, academic woes are right up there with pregnancy pains. You obviously forget how bad they are, because in time you'll find yourself doing the shit again.

This semester's American Literature class? Oh, sweet heaven. It's like literature from the beginning of time. Ok, I'm exaggerating. But it's from, like, a REALLY long time ago. The first assignment? *A Model of Christian Charity* by John Winthrop.

God Almighty in His most holy and wise providence, hath so disposed of the condition of mankind, as in all times some must be rich, some poor, some high and eminent in power and dignity; others mean and in subjection.

Oh my fuck. I don't even know what that *means*! I don't go to church! I tossed *Norton Anthology's of American Literature to 1820, and 1820-1865*, under the computer desk. I don't want to look at those books again. They're evil.

Oh, and my American Government class? On the calendar for today he says, "Welcome to the first day of class. You should read chapters 1-3, 6, and 12. Also, read lectures 1 and 2."

Dude, I don't even have the book yet!

And his syllabus! *360 and higher is an A. Use the sheet below to mark your points as you take quizzes and exams. I will not do your math for you. Do not come to me asking how you're doing in the class. Deadlines are not to be missed. Deadline. You cross the line, you're dead. Simple.*

I'm not *even* making that up. I'm so screwed.

Nina Does Goodwill

January 13th, 2007

I was born without that gene that most women seem to have - the one that makes it so they love shopping and can do it for hours at a time. Well, I'm going to go one step further and say that there's some metaphysical, biological phenomenon that makes it *impossible* for me to catch a deal. Every other woman I know says shit like this:

EOWIK: "They were 75% off the original price, then marked down another five bucks, and I had a coupon, *plus* the 30th customer of the day got an extra $20 off their purchase and that was *me*! So, I got these Prada shoes for *four dollars*! Can you believe it?!"

Nina (with hate in my eyes and a fake smile): "How nice ... for you."

I've been hearing great things about Goodwill for awhile now. I have bags and boxes of stuff that I want to donate, but I never get around to sorting through them and dropping them off. In the past week alone I've had three friends gush about the great treasures they found at the Goodwill, so I took it as a sign that maybe today was the day I should check it out.

Right before I left the house, I was talking to my friend, Bertha, and she issued a warning.

"I'm headed to the Goodwill."

"Be careful."

"What do you mean?"

She proceeds to tell me how people can bring home all kinds of shit from Goodwill stuff: roaches, mothballs, cooties, elves, AIDS. I almost didn't go.

As I was on the way there, I called my Dad for directions because I was a bit unsure of where I was going. He wasn't there, but when I told my sister where I was headed, she kinda paused. No doubt thinking, "What have you done with my sister?"

My mother has been calling me a snob for years and the moment I entered the Goodwill I finally knew why.

I walk in wearing low rise jeans, high heeled boots, a black pea coat, designer bag and with my digital camera swinging from my wrist. I walk right past the shopping carts and stop dead in my tracks. There was furniture. Actual furniture. Like sofas, bookcases, end tables... you know, *furniture.* I actually turned around and looked at the entrance thinking that I'd mistakenly entered the wrong store.

Then the smell hit me. Does every Goodwill smell like old people house? I almost left, but I was determined to find a bargain. I wanted to be one of those women who find a miraculous deal. I went to the back of the store, straight past the clothes, and spent ten minutes looking at lamps. Then I looked at some framed paintings. I saw one that would be perfect for the baby's room. Then I remembered that my dumb ass doesn't have a baby, and that it would probably be years before I did, but damn, it was only two dollars!

The most interesting things I found were a cassette copy of the first LP I ever bought. Jack Wagner's (Frisco from *General Hospital*) *All I Need.* "All I neeeeed... is just a little more time... to be sure ... what I feeeeel." And I found an Amazing Shrinky Dink maker! I almost bought it, but I couldn't remember what a Shrinky Dink was. And I figured you couldn't find the necessary ingredients anywhere on *Earth.*

The most annoying part - besides the smell of moth balls, Geritol, and death - was the way they organized the clothes. It was like Infants and Children. That's it. No sizes, no gender specific racks, no age groups. And they were only categorized by color. There was a whole rack of red clothes, green ones, etc. And for patterns, well they just piled all that shit together. Polka dots, plaid, stripes, butterflies, didn't matter. Oh, and coats. They just lumped those together, too.

When I did find something cute it was always in smaller sizes. All of my nephews are younger than Kali and my best friend's children are as well. It's one thing to buy something for your *own* child from Goodwill, but wouldn't it be kinda tacky to buy something for someone else's baby at Goodwill?

Them: "You shouldn't have gone to all this trouble."

You (sheepishly): "I really didn't."

The Ballad of Connor and Courtney

January 20th, 2007

Donny and I were both knocked out at 9:30 in the morning when Kali came into our bedroom.

"Mommy, can you come downstairs and pour me some Kool-Aid?"

Without opening my eyes, I asked, "Don't you have juice boxes?"

"No, Daddy said he's not buying them anymore because I never finish them and it's a waste of money."

"Well, then Daddy should go pour the Kool-Aid 'cause Mommy would have bought you juice boxes."

I eventually gave in and groggily made my way downstairs. As I did, Kali starts telling me a story. "Remember I told you that Connor and Courtney are best friends? They've been best friends since the 1st grade. Well, they're not friends anymore. Wanna know why?"

I must have said yes or grunted.

"Well we were at recess the other day and Courtney started yelling in Connor's ear and he didn't like it. So, he started yelling back in her ear and they both got in trouble. Now, Connor is mad at Courtney and he's not talking to her. He said she doesn't even exist."

I thought that was pretty mean and figured Kali was exaggerating. I said, "I'm sure he's not that mad."

"Well, Connor and I were talking yesterday and Courtney came over and started talking to us and Connor looked at me and said, 'Do you hear anything? I don't. Do we even *have* a Courtney in this class?'"

As I listened, I realized that this is how it begins. This is when boys learn the appropriate way to argue with girls and how to treat people when you're not getting along with them. And at this tender age of eight, Connor is well on his way to mastering the art of douchebaggery. His parents must be so proud.

I Do Housework... Sometimes

January 25th, 2007

Lately, I've been putting off everything of importance to the last minute – especially school work and housework. Yes, I do housework... on occasion. Sometimes. Okay, let me keep it real. Recently, I went to vacuum and as I kept pressing the little pedal on the bottom of the vacuum with my foot all it would do was tilt backwards.

"Why won't this thing turn on?"

"That's not the power. You have to hit the switch on the handle." Donny said patiently.

"Since when? This has always been the power." I continued to tap the pedal furiously.

"That was the *old* vacuum cleaner."

"Well, what happened to that one?"

"It broke so I bought this one."

"When was that?"

"Like, a year ago."

Shut up.

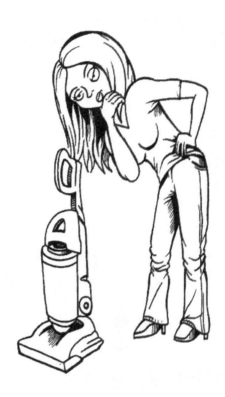

Because It's Never Too Early to Develop a Complex

February 13th, 2007

Yesterday I had *Oprah* on as background noise while I did my Spanish homework. Kali comes home from school and sits on the floor beside the couch. I can't see her, but I hear that she's keeping herself occupied with something on the floor. The show was about amazing kids who at ages like 8, 12, and 15 were opera singers, college students (and a surgeon), and CEOs respectively.

As the episode goes on, I can hear Kali getting more and more impatient with whatever she's doing. What was she doing? Practicing tying her shoes. Now, some of you may be thinking that at 7, she should already know how to tie her shoes. She does, but over the past few years all of her sneakers have been of the slip-on variety. Nike or Sketchers, they were always ones that require her to just slip her feet in and go. And even when we have bought her lace-up sneakers, I usually tie them for her because it's quicker and I know the tie will actually *stay* tied if I do it.

Because her mother is lazy and loves items of convenience, my child, at the age of 7, was trying to remember how to properly tie a shoe. She had it down except when it gets to the part where you pull each loop away from each other to tighten the laces. One loop kept slipping. At one point, she got so frustrated she exclaimed, "She's eight and she can sing in German and I can't even tie my shoes!"

I thought she was going to throw the shoe across the room. Like me, she has a horrible temper. Her frustration level gets so high she just lashes out. Last week, she threw the XBOX controller across the room which led to her weekend-long banishment from the console. On Sunday, she asked if she may be allowed to end her punishment a day early and play with the XBOX. I explained that the controllers were $50 a piece and that she was more than welcome to end her punishment a day early in lieu of a $50 spanking. Confused by the word "lieu" and terrified of a spanking worth $50 - whatever *that* means - she shook her head and went upstairs to read a *Juni B. Jones* book.

So, where was I? Oh yeah, I sat on the floor with her and we each took a shoe (new dress shoes purchased on Friday for the annual Father/Daughter dance which I would post pictures of if the internet wasn't full of scuzzy pervs because my daughter and my husband both looked dashing... did I really just say dashing?) and practiced tying until she got it right.

As we did, I explained to her that she shouldn't be jealous of those children on *Oprah* because they were all most likely late in life children whose mothers had to take all kinds of fertility drugs just to get pregnant, which also means that their genius is really some kind of disability which means they will be smart and accomplished, sure, but they will also suffer from social inadequacies and remain virgins well into their thirties. Meanwhile, she earned her brains the old fashioned way: through her brilliant mother and hard work. And she too will grow up to be smart and accomplished, albeit with sloppily tied shoes, but accomplished nonetheless.

Scary Dream

February 26, 2007

I had a dream last night that Donny finally snapped. We were arguing over some stuff he found and right in the middle of the argument he broke down. I could see the moment it happened. His eyes watered, his shoulders slumped, and then he pulled out a knife - a big ass, Michael Meyer's knife from thin air. I started backing up and reached for the phone. He didn't even care. And I knew I was in trouble. A sane person, once seeing you're calling the cops, would put the knife down.

"Ok, ok, ok, I was just playing. I'm putting it down. Put down the phone. We can just talk." But someone who has officially gone White Boy Crazy doesn't give a shit if you call the cops or not because he knows by the time they arrive *everyone* will be dead.

You know how dreams skip around? Well, the next thing I know he's showing me all the stuff he found that made him snap... while still holding the knife: a piece of paper that had some doodling on it by me and two male coworkers, made during a very boring staff meeting. Some pictures of me in a skimpy dress taken on the back deck of his mother's house - pictures *he* took mind you - and a myriad of other things that all had logical explanations behind them.

I remember thinking, "I'm going to be murdered over a *misunderstanding*!"

This all stems from the fact that I felt guilty last night. We watched the Oscars, showered, and got in bed around 1am. He had to get up at 4:30am and I was dead tired. We fell asleep holding hands, but I know he was thinking, "Screw this hand holding shit, let me put my penis in you!" I was too tired, people!

I feel really bad because this weekend he painted the family room. The only room left on the first floor that we hadn't painted. And I did nothing. So, tonight I'm going to make sure to give him some because I really don't want to have anymore dreams like that. It was freaky.

Black Circus

February 27, 2007

Did you guys know that Black people have their own circus? We do. It's called the Universoul Circus. Get it? Universal. Soul. Black people have rhythm, and everyone else... doesn't. I don't know. Anyway, my parents took Kali there two weekends ago with some other family members. Donny and I didn't go because Donny had to work, and I'm not really sure why I didn't go. Oh yeah, I hate leaving the house, and I don't like animals, crowds, or people in general.

So, before they go I tell my sister, "Don't let any elephants trample my baby." She assures me she'll do her best to avoid an elephant stampede. A few hours later she calls me from the parking lot. It seems my nephew wasn't enjoying his first trip to the circus so she took him outside for some air and a break.

"You should have come for the blog material alone."

"Why? Is it horrible?"

"It's just... black."

I crack up laughing. "What's that supposed to mean?"

"There are no lions and elephants here. Kali is sitting there looking mildly amused. She only seemed to get interested when one of the guys doing a high wire act almost fell."

That's my baby. She digs carnage.

I guess things livened up after the phone call because Kali came home gushing about how much fun she had. My father told me the next day that the finale included three elephants in wigs called The DreamGirls. The audience was encouraged to guess which were Beyonce, Jennifer Hudson, and the third girl no one pays attention to. My father said as one elephant passed, their eyes met and he saw the shame of years of humiliation.

"Are they real Grandpa?" Kali asked, slightly frightened.

He assured her they were real, but also reassured her that Grandpa knew where all the exits were in case today was the day the elephants snapped at having to wear wigs and sequins, and that although he didn't know how many nine millimeter slugs it would take to stop an elephant, he had enough on him to find out. That's how Grandpa rolls.

My Weekend as a Single Mom

March 12, 2007

Whenever Donny goes out of town I get a small taste of what it would be like as a single Mom. I say small taste because as a single Mom I doubt I would be able to afford a five bedroom house in the 'burbs, two cars, and an Xbox 360, but it's nice to pretend. Let's all just play along, shall we?

Donny left on a Thursday in the hopes that he'd get to Michigan in time to see his Grandmother before she passed. The doctors had sent her home the day before with the warning, "It could be days, it could be hours." Unfortunately, she died that morning while he was in the air on the way to Chicago. He called me at 1:30 in the afternoon as he waited for the flight to Michigan to board.

"I have nothing to do. This is a nice airport."

"Call James and tell him to come hang out with you."

James is a friend of mine who lives in Chicago. You may have seen him on two seasons of the CBS reality show, *Big Brother*.

"He'd only come hang out with me if you were here."

"That's because I'm awesome."

"I can always go see Oprah."

"Asshole."

I worship at the church of Oprah.

Thirty minutes later he calls me with the news. I felt so horrible for him. Let me tell you, my maternal Grandmother is 80 and I adore her. If when I got the news that she died I was in an airport in a strange city surrounded by strangers, Homeland Security would detain my ass with the quickness. Why? Because I'd act a damn fool, that's why. Fortunately for all involved my husband isn't as prone to theatrics as I am, and composed himself long enough to board the flight to Michigan.

Friday, I put Kali on the bus and spent the day watching movies (something I'm sure a single mother wouldn't be able to do, but we're pretending remember?) I watched *The Departed* and after dinner and putting Kali to bed, I watched *The Prestige.* I highly recommend them both.

Saturday, I woke up early and worked out on the elliptical while watching *Charmed.* Shannon Doherty died and I cried. A lot. So much so that I totally understand the judgmental snickering going on as you read this. I don't care. I made breakfast for me and Kali, and then we went to Blockbuster Video.

"Can I sit in the front seat, pleeease?"

For some odd reason, whenever Donny is out of town, besides getting a taste of what it would be like to raise a child alone, I also have this inexplicable habit of spoiling Kali. So, I said yes. I know, I know. I wasn't thinking.

Off we go and Kali is full of questions. She wanted to know what every light, needle, lever, button, and pedal in the car meant. Sadly, I could only answer a few of them. She points to the emergency brake.

"What's this?"

"If the brakes on the car don't work, I think I'm supposed to pull that, and hopefully we'll stop. You also use it if you park on a hill. I think it ensures the car won't slide."

"What happens if those brakes with your foot don't work *and* this one doesn't work?"

"Then we're fucked... but don't say that cause it's a bad word."

Silence.

"We're doomed. You should have said we're *doomed*, Mommy."

Little did I know, and I found out this morning, that the airbags could possibly break my poor baby's neck and that's why children under thirteen aren't allowed in the front seat. Great, just great.

We stop at Wal-Mart for groceries and *Charmed* season 4 DVD because I simply *had* to know how the Halliwell sisters dealt with the loss of their beloved Prue. Kali asks about eating in a restaurant that night.

"No, because I spent more money than I wanted to today. I bought that *Charmed* DVD set and..."

"Daddy will be mad?"

"Well, not really."

"Because it's his money?"

"Technically, yes, but it's really *our* money because we're married."

"So, you're going to tell him?"

"Well, no. I'm going to put it with all our other DVDs and see if he notices. If he doesn't...."

"You're so sneaky," she said in a voice tinged with awe.

Are you keeping count?

Endangering the life of a minor? Check.

Used foul language in front of minor? Check.

Taught said minor how to lie and deceive? Check.

So, I'm realizing by last night that this single mother business is kinda hard. I'm loading and unloading the dishwasher, doing all the laundry, taking out the trash, checking the mail, paying bills, cleaning, cooking, bathing the child, etc. No wonder I'm normally so lazy. Donny is here to do all this stuff for me, or at least help with the majority of it. In actuality, it's *his* fault I'm this way. Ok, so I realize that makes no sense, but it makes me feel better about myself and less ashamed. I've cooked more since he's been gone than when he's here. I can tell he's noticed as evident by the long pauses after I tell him how I've spent my day.

"I cleaned up, did some laundry, made lunch, now I'm studying before I make dinner."

Through the phone lines I can hear the gears in his head spin as he tries to figure out a way to get me to do this shit *when he's home*. Either that or he's contemplating whether or not the family can stand two funerals in two weeks as he surely wants to choke my ass by now. I don't know what's gotten into me! Friday night I made Ginger Teriyaki marinated chicken with stir fry veggies. Last night I bought a rotisserie chicken, made pasta with a light cream sauce and steamed broccoli. Kali wanted no parts of that so I made her a Kid Cuisine that came with the one food that she loves and I cannot stand: The corn dog.

I hate corn dogs. I despise everything about them and why I buy them for my child is beyond me. As I put it in the microwave, I hold the stick between my index finger and my thumb and scrunch up my nose. You would think I was holding a rat. Kali just shakes her head.

"Why do you hate them so much? You like hot dogs. You like corn. You should like corn dogs! Give me two good reasons why you don't like them."

"The way they look and the way they smell."

"Ok, give me *five* good reasons."

What a little smartass.

Yesterday was the funeral and it was hard on everyone. Donny's grandparents were married for fifty-four years. They did everything together. My heart breaks for his Grandfather. My mother-in-law called to ask if I would listen to what she wrote to read at the funeral. Somehow or another I have a reputation for being good with words. This was one time I wished it weren't true. Or at least that people didn't think it. I listened to my mother-in-law talk about her mother and she broke down several times as she read. She cried, I cried, and I told her it was perfect the way it was. I wouldn't change a word. It really was perfect.

Today, my husband went to his father's grave. He hasn't been to Michigan in years and I'm sure it was emotional. I haven't been able to reach him to find out though. I called his mother's cell phone when he didn't answer his and was told he was at a relative's house partaking of a little target practice. That did not make me happy. I don't know that Donny's ever shot a gun in his life. I don't need him coming home with any new White Boy Crazy skills.

So, now I'm tired from a day of cleaning, studying, washing and folding clothes, reading with Kali, playing with Kali, and cooking. She's bathed and in her bed probably watching T.V when she should be sleeping. I'm going to lock up the house, set the alarm, shower and put Kali into bed with me with the door locked, weapons near, and phone tucked under the pillow.

My husband comes on Wednesday. Not a day too soon. This single mother business is lonely.

School Bus Drivers, Unsung Heroes

March 21, 2007

Today I went with Kali's second grade class on a field trip. We went to a Japanese steakhouse for lunch. I know what some of you are thinking. Probably the same thing I thought when the permission slips came home. "Damn, what kind of field trip is that?" Well, it is the second of three scheduled to coincide with whatever her class is learning at the time. This trip was actually more sensible than say, the trip my 7th grade math class took to see Spike Lee's, *School Daze*. Yeah, I don't know how my teacher pulled *that* shit off.

Kali's grade just finished several weeks of learning all about Japan - the people, culture, language, etc. My child can now count to five in Japanese, say a lot of basic words and phrases, write and recognize a myriad of symbols for basic words, and tell you all about its geographic makeup. I can barely give directions from my house to the airport.

Seeing as how we live in suburban Atlanta there wasn't much to offer the children by way of Japanese culture, so the best the school could come up with was *Nagano's Japanese Sushi and Steakhouse*.

As we traveled by school bus to the restaurant, I wondered how the bus driver did this on a day to day basis, twice per day. I honestly would have driven the bus off a bridge, killing myself and the children on board just to be free of the noise.

I'm proud to say that the other class we were sharing the bus with seemed to be making most of the noise, but that's not to say Kali's class were on their absolute best behavior. I saw one little boy slap another girl in the face... twice. Then there were the ones who couldn't grasp the concept of keeping their legs out of the aisle. You could totally tell the difference between the way the teacher disciplined and I did.

"We do not use our outside voices inside the bus, boys and girls." - Teacher.

"Um, you need to sit down on the seat and I'm not telling you again." – Nina

"If you do that again, you're losing 5 minutes of recess." – Teacher

"Don't make me turn around." – Nina

And I wasn't even talking to my own child! When we got to the restaurant I thought it was cool that the bus driver ate with us. She had a Coke with her lunch, but I really wouldn't have minded if she had something stronger. Hell, she earned it.

Lunch was good, but then I really enjoy that Hibachi-style food. There were a few children in Kali's class that "acted like they ain't never been nowhere." Remember when your Mom used to give you that warning whenever you either went to a. a restaurant or b. someone else's house for dinner? My mother's main fear was people thinking that she didn't feed us at home. Even if times were lean, she didn't want people *to know that*. So, there would be no acting impatiently for food and no asking for seconds or eating off of someone else's plate. Therefore, you got the warning, "don't act like you ain't never been nowhere," before your ass even left the house.

After the waitress mistakenly gave some of the children Cokes when we clearly told her Sprite, there was one really overweight boy who managed to suck down *the whole glass of Coke* in the time it took her to run to the kitchen with replacements. I was embarrassed for his parents.

And speaking of embarrassed, don't even get me started on the little girl named Precious. Yes, you read that right. Precious. When Precious first joined Kali's class the conversation went like this:

"We have a new student. Her name is Precious."

"She's brown like Mommy, right?"

"How'd you know?"

"Mommy just knows."

Anyway, poor Precious was dressed in a red mini skirt that even she knew she had no business wearing because she kept tugging at it, a dingy white shirt, her hair was a hot ass mess, and she had on black, knee-high, pleather boots. To add insult to injury, her knees were so ashy I thought she'd been kneeling in flour before we left. Why, my people, why?

And as if to remind me why I don't like children, and why I'll probably not chaperone another damn field trip, here's a conversation on the bus returning to school:

"Kali's Mom, are you going to check Kali out of school?" asked a very cute little blue-eyed boy named Ben.

"No, she's going to stay and do her work with everyone else."

Kali asked, "Why?"

"Because I have a lot of homework to do and I have to study."

"You're in school?" Ben asked.

"Yes."

"I thought you couldn't be married in college."

Little bastard.

The Love of a Good Black Woman

March 22nd, 2007

Sometimes Donny gets offended when I say he may go White Boy Crazy. I don't care.

Well, I care enough that I don't push it. I don't want him to snap and kill me. Who needs to be right *that* badly, you know?

Whenever we talk about his past I am reminded of how white he is - the good old days of pharmacy parties where he and his friends would each raid their parents' medicine cabinets, and then get together to take whatever they found. It's a wonder he's still alive.

And let's not forget how he came home from Michigan last week, after attending his Grandmother's funeral, and told me about playing Beer Pong with his siblings and cousins. Huh? What? Beer Pong is officially the whitest activity in the world.

Between that and finding out that he was target practicing while he was there, I've been watching his white ass like a hawk since he's been home. At the first hint of WBC emergence, I'm just going to kill his ass *first* and claim self defense. My whole defense will be based off of the details of the Scott Peterson and Mark Hacking cases. I will just look at the judge and jury and be like, "Can you really blame me?"

Just when I thought I could rest easy, and with both eyes closed, we have a conversation like last night's. I'm doing homework and he's playing *Tiger*

Woods' Golf on the XBOX. I start to tell him a story about this girl whose ferret likes Starbucks. He had the same reaction the girl did when she told me the story which was, "Can you imagine a ferret hopped up on caffeine? Insane!" I was thinking more like, "Um, why would you give a ferret enough Starbucks to figure out that he likes it? That shit's expensive!"

So, then my husband says, "I used to get my ferret stoned."

I drop my pencil. "Excuse me?"

"I used to get my ferret stoned."

My mouth is wide open.

"What? It was funny."

"I can't even believe this. You mean to tell me you had a *ferret*? How white are you?"

"Shut up."

"What would even possess you to try and intoxicate a ferret? I hope you realize that you were very well on your way to being White Boy Crazy. *I saved your life* and the lives of God knows how many innocents. Donny, you were saved by the love of a good Black woman."

And then he says, very calmly...

"I know."

Sigh. I guess it's back to sleeping with one eye open again.

The Daughter Becomes the Mother

March 23rd, 2007

It's a scary moment when a woman realizes she's becoming her mother. Not that there's anything wrong with my mother. She's beautiful, strong, generous, and funny. She went from welfare to the NYPD. No, she wasn't arrested; she was a cop.

I'm not saying I'm a better mother. Sure, Kali's life is different than mine was at her age. She lives in a house now that is much nicer than any house I ever lived in. As a matter of fact, I wouldn't say I'm a better mother than anyone who loves, takes care of, provides for, and protects their children. We all do the best we can. And that's exactly what my mother did: the best she could. We were always healthy, happy, and safe. Everything else is just packaging.

I will say I'm a lot more fun than my Mom was with me. Then again, she also had four other kids, a house to clean, and a dangerous job. Hell, she wasn't having fun with us because she loved us less, her ass was just *tired.*

Imagine how scary it is to not only realize you are becoming your mother, but that your child is turning into you, *all at the same time.* Yesterday, Kali had a meltdown. The batteries in her DirecTV remote were dead and she couldn't change the channel to watch her favorite show. Yes, I know. First world problem. Back when I was growing up, I didn't have my own television in my room. If my mother was watching *Donahue* my siblings and I had to *imagine* what was going on with our favorite programs.

Nina: *"Then Rog says, 'You're not gonna tell Mama, are you?'"*

My sister: *"And Dee says, 'No. I won't tell... if you give me a quarter.'"*

(Canned laughter)

My brother: **"***Then Dwayne comes in, 'Hey, hey, hey.'"*

So, last night Kali storms past the study in a blur of pouty lips and wild hair. I hear her rummaging through the kitchen drawers. Donny asks what she's looking for. She growls a response. I barely make out the word "batteries."

"Here, Kali," I called out. I handed her two batteries from the computer desk. She stomps upstairs. Donny comes into the study, "That girl is so much like you it is scary."

"I don't act like that!"

I *totally* act like that.

As she reaches the top of the stairs I hear a thump and then a wail. In her huff, she managed to whack her hand against the banister. Here's what my mother would have said to me, "That's what you get for flouncin' your butt around."

I settled for the more succinct, "Good for you." Don't worry, she couldn't *hear* me. I was downstairs, remember? After we realized I'd given her bad batteries, and with her hand throbbing, what followed was about five minutes of pure hysteria. By the time I figured out a solution (we just gave her the DTV remote from our room) my child was a heap of quivering, sobbing flesh and tears on the floor of the formal living room.

I laid down with her, rubbed her back, and wiped her tears. I kissed her wet face. I explained that she couldn't react that way every time something went wrong. Donny was leaning against the wall with his arms crossed watching the whole thing.

"Hello, Pot. Have you met Kettle?"

Smartass.

The one thing that *all* parents have in common is that we ask our kids to lie. We teach them not to, and we damn sure make it clear that they can't lie to *us*, but all parents will ask their children to lie at some point. Anyone who says otherwise is, well, lying.

Kali's school is having a Fun Run fundraiser to obtain a new gym floor. For the next week the kids get pledges from family, friends, and local businesses. Every day they bring in their pledge sheet and get prizes. So, if I pledge $10 for every lap Kali will walk/run she gets a camera. A $3 per lap pledge gets her a ball. The prize for the $50 per lap pledge is an iPod Nano.

I explained to Kali that normally that iPod would cost about $150. I told her if I pledged $50 per lap, and she did one lap, we'd get the iPod she wanted for her birthday for $100 less, and we'd also help the school get a new gym floor. I then made her familiar with the terms, "can't beat that with a stick" and "win-win." The problem, of course, is that I have to trust that my child will not do more than one lap. She assures me she can handle doing one lap only and then sitting the rest out. We decide to practice to be sure.

"Ok, Kali. I'll be the Fun Run people, and you be you. You just finished running or walking one lap. You ready?"

"Wait."

She then proceeds to run through the kitchen, foyer, formal living and dining rooms, and back to me in the kitchen. She stands before me, huffing and puffing, leaning over with her hands resting on her knees.

"Ok, I'm ready."

Hey, my child's a *professional.*

"Hey, little girl. You only ran one lap. Don't you want to do more?"

"No, just one."

"Are you sure? All your friends are doing more. You can really help your school!"

"No, that's okay. I just want to do one because my Mommy said we can't afford an iPod the other way."

Yeah, so, we still gotta practice that part.

Burrito Armpits

April 19th, 2007

"Mommy, my armpits smell like old burritos!"

What?

You ask Kali how it feels to be eight, and she'll tell you it feels the same as seven. Of course, we know that having a birthday doesn't automatically transform you into some new, year-older person, but I have noticed a slight change in Kali each spring right around the time of her birthday.

One year, I happened to notice that her vocabulary seemed to expand. Another, I noticed that her eating habits and appetite changed - toys be damned, she was definitely eating more than a Happy Meal provides. This year I noticed something else.

Yesterday, I came into the study to check my email. Kali was sitting on the floor near the computer watching TV and Donny, who had been on the computer when I entered, moved to the sofa so I could get on.

"What's that smell?" I asked sniffing the air. "Is that me?"

"I don't know. Probably," replied Donny.

"What smell?" asked Kali.

I let it go. Hours later Kali was on the computer, and I leaned over her to type something on the screen.

"Oh, my God! Kali, that's you!"

"What?!"

110

Then I remembered that my child had P.E. that day. But still! I know it's been awhile since I've been in gym class, but I'm pretty sure "roll around in hot garbage" wasn't a school-approved activity.

If you've been reading this blog awhile you may remember the blog a few months ago where Kali informed me that her armpits smelled like old burritos. This revelation led to the purchase of her first powder-scented deodorant. It's not like it's something she needs every day. Just once in a while, after a particularly trying day I suppose, she comes home a little... tart. Poor baby.

What I don't understand is the fact that *Kali gets a kick out of it*. She was all, "Hahahaha, smell it, Mommy! Smell it!" And she'd proceed to stick her hands under her pits and shove them in my face. I all but threw her little butt in the tub.

I thought I had *years* before I had to worry about this! Then again, when most of the little girls at a recent pool party were already sporting little breast buds, or niblets if you will, I shouldn't be surprised.

Remorse

May 8th, 2007

Kali tells me she doesn't want to go to school tomorrow.

"Why not?"

"Cause I'm going to be in trouble."

"What did you do?"

"First you have to promise not to get mad and not to make an angry face."

"Fine. What?"

"I accidentally stole a piece of candy."

With great effort, I keep my face neutral as I put down the icing spatula and turn from the cake I'd been decorating.

"How, *exactly*, do you *accidentally* steal anything."

"Well, Stephanie took one from Ms. A's desk. So, I took one and I was going to put it back, but I forgot."

"Since when do you do something because someone else did it?"

"I was going to put it back!"

"That's not the point!"

"That's what the [substitute] teacher said."

"So, I guess she's going to tell your teacher when she gets back tomorrow?"

"Yes."

"Go right now and write an apology to your teacher, and understand that there will still be consequences when you go to school tomorrow... as well there should be. And don't you *ever* put your hands on something that doesn't belong to you. You understand me?"

"Yes." With tears in her eyes she writes this apology:

Dear Ms. _____,

I'm sorry I took candy from the jar. First, Stephanie took one then I took one. I was gonna put it back before recess, but we didn't have time and I forgot. It was in my pocket. Please don't let me get in trouble, PLEEEEASE!

From,

Kali

P.S. Stephanie didn't say sorry, but I did. :-)

"Kali! This is not an apology! Go write it again and this time I don't want any mention of Stephanie! And no smiley faces with big teeth."

I was secretly quite pleased with her punctuation and spelling. I don't have the new apology because she took it to school, but it went something like:

I'm sorry and it won't happen again. Ever! From, Kali

After she went to bed last night, my parents, Donny and I sat around the kitchen table talking and I showed them both letters.

My Dad said, "Aww, the first one had *personality!*"

"Fuck personality! I want remorse!"

Hit the Deck

May 10th, 2007

Last night, after a dinner of sage pork chops and parmesan rice, Donny and I were chilling in the family room catching up *CSI* episodes. I noticed a deck of cards on the coffee table. *Hit the Deck.* I called Kali into the room for a little family time.

I should have known that any card game whose instructions begin with, "All players should remove all jewelry from their hands," would be dangerous. The game plays pretty much like *Uno* with a few exceptions including the, "Hit the Deck with a Hand" card. Once played, the player must yell out that phrase and all players then race to slap their hand down on the discard pile. The last hand down has to pick up four cards.

The first time the card was played I thought I would need stitches from the cut I got thanks to Kali's claws.

"Owww!" I yelped.

"You gotta be faster," said my completely unsympathetic child.

Donny is probably the most competitive person I know. Even more so than me, and I *hate* losing. It doesn't matter if he's playing Jacks with cancer-stricken children or a card game with his own child. He goes for blood… which he got as I cut a scared glance at Kali and licked my wound. Speaking of licking, at one point Donny threatened to lick both sides of his hand so that we wouldn't want to place our hands near his when he played a Hit the Deck with a Hand card.

"I don't care," said equally competitive Kali. She was in the zone.

So, we're playing for awhile and I'm winning, much to the disgust of my husband and child.

"Mommy is cheating," declared Donny after one particularly brutal round.

"You can't cheat at this!" I responded.

"I bet *you* could figure out a way." I was almost offended.

Halfway through the game I was struck with really bad gas. I don't know if it was the sage, the pork chops, the parmesan, or the rice. I gave my family a warning and let one out. The funniest thing happened though. I was sitting Indian-style on the sofa and instead of going down, the fart went up! Like through the crack of my ass and out the top of my PJ bottoms. It felt so funny that I started to giggle, and the more I laughed, the more I farted.

My family looked at me as if I'd suddenly grown two heads.

"What's so funny?"

"It's...it's...it's...c-c-coming out...the back," I said breathlessly.

"It's coming out the back?" Donny asked, his forehead wrinkled in confusion.

"Of course it is!" said Kali. "Where else would a toot come from?"

Then they both exploded in laughter, and I was too busy laughing and farting that it took me a full minute to explain myself.

Ah, good times.

Gambling

May 23rd, 2007

My love of BINGO has gone to a whole new level. I am now addicted to these scratch-off BINGO cards you get from the gas station. Sometimes, when Donny comes home from work he has a few of the $2 cards for me where you can play four cards of BINGO at once. It's like he's bought me diamonds. I don't know whether to blow him, or cook for him, or both!

Monday night, he gave me three cards and I won a free card and $15. Kali came into the room while I was scratching away.

"Ooooh, can I do one?"

"No."

"Why not?"

"Because they're mine."

Turns out Donny had to run back out for something we needed for dinner and while he was gone he got more BINGO cards. Kali beamed as he tossed her one. I was only vaguely aware that we were allowing our child to gamble.

This morning, as we prepared to meet the school bus for the final time till August, I asked Kali if she wanted ice cream money and then realized I didn't have any cash on me.

"Where are the two dollars my friend Bertha gave you?"

"Oh, Daddy used that to buy my BINGO card."

Ok, I wasn't sure it was kosher to let my 8-year-old do a scratch-off card, but I'm pretty sure it's wrong to make her pay for it as well.

My Left Eye

May 24, 2007

"Mommy, look what I'm doing with my left eye."

"Uh huh."

"You didn't even look."

"Yes, I did."

"You barely looked... at my right eye. Mommy, *this* is my left eye."

"Girl, I know which is your left eye. I *made* your left eye."

Skinned Knees

May 29th, 2007

I am a knee snob.

Actually, I am a snob about several things knees being just one of them.

I am a nice person. I don't hold the things I'm snobby about against people. But I notice. And I suppose I judge. And sometimes I guess it would be fair to say I mock. What things are you snobby about, Nina? Glad you asked.

Well, for one, short people. Don't get me wrong: Some of my best friends are short people. Hell, my *bestest* friend is what some might call short. I don't treat short people any differently. They are completely welcome in my home and are treated with the utmost respect. I've even had sex with a short guy. Or three.

But when I'm in the presence of short people, which is quite often 'cause I'm tall, I notice. And I judge. Quietly. In my head. I think, "Wow, it must suck to be that short." And when short people, particularly women, stand next to me and do that thing where they stand on their tippy-toes and say, "I feel so short next to you," I think, "Yeah, sucks to be you," even as, out loud, I do that thing that all tall girls do. You know, we roll our eyes and shake our heads, "Oh, please. It's not all that."

And then we bore you with tales of the burden of being tall, of being teased as a girl, not being able to find jeans long enough, and having nicknames like Olive Oil and Beanpole growing up, blah, blah, blah, the usual tall girl bullshit, which really amounts to nothing because everyone knows that little girls who are tall and teased grow up to be 18-year-old women who are tall and no matter where you're from, that's hot.

Let's see, what else? Oh, public transportation. I'm a public transportation snob. That stems from having to take it most of my life because I had no choice. So, now when I'm in my car and I pass people waiting at a bus stop, I feel bad for them. It doesn't matter if the person is waiting for the bus 'cause their Expedition is in the shop. In my mind, waiting for the bus brings back memories of waiting, and then standing the whole ride because the bus is full, and turning up your walkman so you can't hear the guys behind you trying to hit on you, and trying to make your body as small as possible as the pervs squeeze by and accidentally on purpose rub against you. So yeah, I pretty much turn my nose up at having to take a train or a bus ever again.

And finally, I'm a knee snob. I think women should have nice knees. Notice I didn't say pretty. Cause, knees are knees. Well, except for those unfortunate few who have knees that resemble wrinkly, shaved vaginas. That's not cute. But for the most part, a knee is a knee is a knee. Except when they're scarred. Then they're a mess. And I judge. And I mock. Quietly, but still.

I didn't always have knee issues. In fact, I didn't pay my knees much attention at all growing up. When I was young, about ten or so, I had a crush on this little white boy down the block named David. And David used to hang out with my cousin Joey. One day, we were playing in the vacant lot next to our house. (Hey, it was Brooklyn. Don't judge me!) Anyway, we were playing and I fell and hit my knee on a pipe. I realize now it could have been worse. Like a dirty syringe. Anyhepatitis, I hit my knee and it hurt like hell, but I wanted to seem tough in front of David so I ignored the pain.

That is, until a short while later when I looked down and realized that my whole left gray corduroy-clad leg was covered in blood. So much so that the pant leg was sticking to me and was no longer gray, but rather a sickly shade of burgundy. The wound was cleaned to reveal a nice dime-sized hole. I spent the night in pain with my knee elevated by pillows.

Note to self: Call mother at completion of this blog and confront her with the possible drug and/or alcohol addiction by her and my stepfather. What were they thinking?

By the time anyone thought to take me to the hospital the next day, I was told that stitches would have been necessary but the statute of limitations had passed. To this day, I have a dime-sized scar on my left knee.

And I never cared until the day my father told me about a bachelor party he attended. I was in my late teens, maybe early 20's, I forget. Anyway, he had gone to a bachelor party a few days prior and was telling me about going to Scores, a NYC strip club. He was describing how pretty the strippers were, and how perfect their bodies were, and in doing so said the sentence that caused my current knee snobbery, "....I mean, these women didn't even look as if they'd ever skinned their knees as children."

And so it began. I became obsessed with making sure my knees didn't look raggedy. I remember being particularly peeved with an ex after a rigorous night of sex on the floor when I discovered rug burns on both knees! Note that I didn't give a damn about a similar burn on my lower back. You know, where the tramp stamp goes.

I realized this past weekend that my knee snobbery has started to affect my mothering skills. Kali fell off of her scooter last weekend and skinned both knees - the right one really badly. As I cleaned it off and started to apply Neosporin she had a fit. She was scared that the cream would hurt.

"No, it won't hurt. I'll be gentle. It will help you not have a scar later. And trust me; you don't want to grow up to have scarred knees." I was only marginally aware that I was quite possibly instilling the same knee snobbery/complex in my child.

Yes, "take care of your knees" has earned a place alongside other motherly sage advice like making sure you're wearing clean underwear in case you get hit by a bus and have to go to the hospital. Although, even though I've never been hit by a bus, I would assume that should it happen, and I survived, the condition of my panty crotch would be at the very bottom of my list of concerns.

Tonight, after a week of playing, baths, and basically being an 8-year-old kid, I noticed that every time the injury would start to develop a scab it wouldn't last long. Before bed I practically had to hold Kali down to apply more Neosporin and attach another band-aid.

"Mommy, it's fine!"

"Well, I just want to be sure."

"Nina, it's fine," seconded Donny.

"Why do you keep rubbing that stuff on there anyway?"

I sighed and replied, "Because, you don't want to have scars on your knees. Trust me. When you are eighteen, and tall, with legs that go on forever, and you walk into a room with a pretty skirt and cute shoes and everyone is looking at you, you'll thank me."

I gave it a generous rub of Neosporin, slapped a band-aid on it, and sent her little butt to bed.

"Just wait till we have a son. He's going to have all kinds of scrapes and bruises and you won't be able to Neosporin them all."

"That's what *you* think."

You may all think I'm crazy as you read this. I don't care. But I bet almost every woman that is reading this will have taken a moment to check out her knees. And the next time you see another woman in a skirt sans panty hose (I mean, really, do they even still *make* panty hose?) you will look at her knees. And you will judge. And maybe even mock.

Quietly, but still.

Colder Than a Witch's... Well, You Know
June 19th, 2007

For the past few months the temperature in my house has been a major issue. I'm not sure when it all began, but my earliest recollection would have to be February of this year when my friends Lacey and Brett came to visit. They complained that the guest bedroom on the second floor was really hot. Of course, my first thought was that maybe Lacey was going through *the change*, and the temperature upstairs was fine. Then I remembered she's like a month younger than me so that probably wasn't it.

When my Mom was here recently, everyone complained that it was still really warm in the house. I was always able to come up with an excuse like, "Well, we just finished cooking and the oven was on," or my personal favorite, "It's too many negroes in here. My house ain't used to having this many people in it and you know black attracts heat." Plus, it's possible my Mom really is going through *the change*.

But for the past few weeks I've been unable to ignore that my house is not as cool as it should be when the A.C units are on. Downstairs isn't as bad as upstairs. When you hit the second floor landing you can immediately feel the difference. It's stifling and this with the second floor thermostat set to 68 degrees. For the past week or so, Kali and I have been sleeping downstairs on the sofa and loveseat because it's so much cooler.

So, finally I asked Donny what he thought it could be. We didn't want to even think about how much it would cost to fix two AC units and were praying it was something small. Donny just kind of shrugged. Then for some bizarre reason I asked, "Could it be that the filters need to be changed?" This is bizarre because I know diddlely-squat about air conditioning units and I must have heard about filters on some TV show or something. Either way the question seemed logical to me.

"It shouldn't be."

That's what he said. Now, what do *you* take that to mean? That Donny has recently changed the filters, right? No matter what recent is, his answer basically said that no matter when he did it, the change occurred within a reasonable amount of time that our lackluster air conditioning should have nothing to do with dirty filters. Right?

The next day I'm on the phone with my Dad and we're trying to figure out what the problem could be. He said that he seriously doubted that the units were malfunctioning because what would be the odds that two units (one for each floor) would go at the same time? And then he asked me about the filters and I told him that Donny said that couldn't be it because he'd changed them recently.

"When?" asked my Dad.

"I don't know." And then I told him Donny's exact words and in the silence that followed I knew we were both thinking the same thing: The filters needed to be changed. Why? My husband has an uncanny ability to relay false information. That is not to be confused with lying. Donny is a horrible liar. He can come in from being in the garage and I'll ask....

"Were you smoking?"

"No," he replies as the single syllable provokes a perfect smoke ring that smells accusingly of Marlboro Reds.

No, it's not that he's *lying* when he says things like, "It shouldn't be the air filters." It's just that in Donny's mind, what may seem normal and logical to you and I gets all gobbled up. For instance...

126

Donny and I can watch the local news one night: *"A local man caused quite a scare on the streets of Cartersville today. Simon Jeffries was driving northbound on Old Highway 78 when his 1992 Toyota Camry went out of control. It was 15 terrifying minutes as Mr. Jeffries tried to get the car under control just barely avoiding any major accidents. Fulton County police deputies were alerted to the runaway vehicle by several 9-1-1 calls from frantic motorists. With the help of the officers, Mr. Jefferies was able to stop the car safely on the side of a secluded road. Thankfully, no one was injured."*

The *very next day* Donny will be on the phone relaying the story to someone else: "This guy was driving this big black semi on I85 and like had a heart attack or something. Anyway, he lost control of the truck...I think it was carrying gasoline, dynamite, and matches. The cops had to shoot out the tires to get it to stop. Four people were killed."

Huh?

When Donny came home from work the day of the conversation with my Dad, I brought up the subject of the air conditioning again. He asked me if I'd programmed them correctly. I assured him that I had. The upstairs thermostat was never set to heat or cool the second floor during times when no one would be up there to appreciate it. Like, Monday thru Friday during the day when we are all at school and work. Then I asked him the question I was dreading.

"Donny, when was the last time you changed the air filters?"

"It's been about... (pausing, lips pinched, eyes looking heavenward in recollection)... three years."

"Ago?"

"Yeah."

"2004 three years ago?"

He nods.

"Donny, if you don't take your ass to Wal-Mart right now..."

While he's at Wal-Mart I call my Dad and voice my frustration. Who does that? Who thinks three years was not long enough to cause an AC problem? Don't get me wrong. It's not like I was really upset with him. Like fight-worthy upset. Just annoyed. The air conditioning thing isn't really that big of a deal. It's just that I tell him all the time that I hate feeling like I have to get second opinions or verify the things he tells me. I should trust that when he says he has handled something, he has. It's my pet peeve with him.

You should all be pleased to know that after he replaced the filters and each floor took a turn having the units turned completely off for several hours to melt any backed up ice, my house is freezing cold. Seriously. Last night we were upstairs watching *The Shield* and after awhile my teeth were chattering and my nose was running.

"Oh my God! It's freezing in here!" I exclaimed as I dove under the comforter, "Turn the AC off!"

"Woman, you are impossible to please."

This is true.

Action Figures

June 20, 2007

As I tried to watch a *Dateline* I'd TiVo'd about a serial killer in Italy called, *The Monster of Florence*, I could hear Kali making explosion noises and squealing. From what I could gather, someone was trying to bust through a force field of some sort. She wasn't playing with actual toys, just her hands.

"Kali, shhhhh!"

"I'm playing Action Figures."

She waggled her fingers at me as evidence.

"Well, keep it down," I said as I rewound the TiVo to hear what I'd missed.

"Why? Daddy's all the way upstairs sleeping and you're not going to bed any time soon." She had a point. She continued in an excited and creepy voice, "Besides, I'm playing Action Figures and action is *loud*."

She had another point.

Weird Associations

August 7th, 2007

I make Donny laugh a lot more than he makes me laugh. That's not a diss to him. It's just fact: I'm funnier than he is. When he does make me laugh, though, he's so happy about it that he usually milks whatever he said or did till it's bone dry; hence, no longer funny.

Yesterday was my first full day on the *Sparkpeople* weight loss plan. It's very similar to *Weight Watchers* except it's free and their tracking tools are just amazing. I signed up on Sunday night after I'd already worked out for the day. When I read that following their program I'd only be required to work out on Mondays, Wednesdays and Fridays, I was tempted to not work out yesterday (Monday) because I'd already worked out the day before.

By the time the guilt of not doing it rolled around it was 10pm and I was ready for bed. I managed to pull on sweats and a t-shirt and then plopped on the couch eyeing the elliptical machine with open hostility. I felt tired, weak, and plain ole grumpy. When I noticed Donny heading upstairs to change his clothes, I asked, "Hey, can you bring me down a pair of socks? I forgot to grab some."

He came back down a few minutes later and pelted me in the back of the head with the rolled up socks.

"Ow!" I yelled. It didn't hurt, but I was shocked. They bounced off my head and hit the coffee table. He picked them up and threw them again, this time hitting me in the face.

"What the hell is wrong with you?" I asked, grabbing the socks and holding them to my chest.

"Keep it up and I'll do it again."

"Keep it up and I'll fuck you up."

What followed was a battle of epic proportions. I finally couldn't take the wrestling any longer and yelled out, "Stop it! I feel so dizzy my arms are burning."

Donny just stops grabbing for the socks and looks at me like I'm a complete moron.

"One has nothing to do with the other. That doesn't even make any sense!"

Then he starts laughing, and then I start laughing, and he sees this and decides to run it in the ground... all night. It started when he went to the kitchen to grab a drink for himself and a bottle of water from the fridge for me. I was climbing on to the dreaded elliptical when I glanced over my shoulder to see Donny sneeze into his hand.

"Ugh! What are you doing? Are you going to touch my water now?"

"Sorry. I couldn't help it. I had to sneeze 'cause my ass hurts."

It didn't end there. Before bed he confessed that:

His head hurt because his leg fell asleep, his toe itched because he had the hiccups, and my personal favorite: "I'm horny because my balls itch."

My Mother the Pet Killer

October 8, 2007

Last night I was on the phone with a friend and we were talking about her two gerbils that passed away this year. I asked her, "Why gerbils?" She explained that she wanted a pet, and considered a dog, but was afraid she'd kill it. I told her that I thought it took a whole lot to kill a dog. I mean, I almost killed a dog so I should know. Dogs will pretty much let you know, "Look, bitch. I'm hungry." I'm thinking you'd have to like, leave the dog home alone for *months* to actually kill it. You'd have to really put in some serious effort to kill a dog. Unless you're my mother.

My mother shouldn't be allowed to purchase a pet. No one should give my mother a pet. My mother shouldn't even look at a domesticated animal for too long. My mother is a pet killer. To be fair, she doesn't kill *all of them* - that we know of - but it's pretty accurate to say that she doesn't have a good track record with maintaining a pet for a very long period of time.

When I was nine, the first movie I saw on VHS was *Annie*. My Dad was the only one I knew with a VCR; one of those top-loading ones with buttons the size of baseball mitts and when you put the tape in, you had to push back and down. When you pressed the rewind button it sounded like you were trying to start an old Chevy. But, I loved that movie so when my mother got a tawny-haired mutt for us, I insisted on calling her Sandy. I have no idea how long Sandy lasted with us, I just know that one day my mother told me that

Sandy was homesick for her mommy so she had to leave. I bet if someone went digging behind the apartment building on the corner of Hendrix and Livonia in Brooklyn, they'd find some Sandy-sized bones.

Years passed and my mother once again found herself in the possession of a little mutt. A black, cute, little thing she named Sade. She loved her some Sade! I don't remember my younger sister, Naiemah's, reaction to Sade, but I know that my little brother, David, and I adored her. One day, my mother went to walk Sade after she'd gotten home from work. She came home a short while later without Sade.

"What happened?"

"I was at the corner by Key Food and this man saw her and said his wife would love her. He was just in love with her so I told him he could take her."

"You what?"

My mother had given our dog away. Leash and all. My brother and I sulked in my room. We cried and wished horrible things upon my mother. I mean, *who does that?* Who just gives away their kids' dog to a complete stranger on a whim? The only thing we had to remind us Sade ever existed in our lives was a half-eaten bag of dog food, two dog bowls, and a few piss stains on the carpet. It took us a long time to forgive her. Now, thinking back on it, I bet the man gave her some money. I wish I could remember if my mother subsequently got her hair and nails done after giving away my damn dog.

Years later, my mother brought home a white cat which she named Sade. I told you: She loved her some Sade! I was never a big fan of cats. I think they are sneaky and kinda evil and the thought of one walking on my kitchen counter and possibly jumping on my tables just drives me crazy. It's just downright nasty. Eventually, I warmed to Sade. She wasn't so bad. My mother had gotten her from someone in the neighborhood who had kept only one of the litter, Sade's brother named Snowball.

One day, my mother left the front door open and Sade took off. My siblings and I were pissed. *Who does that*, we asked. Who leaves the apartment door open when they have an inside cat in the ghetto? We didn't see that cat for awhile. I cried thinking of all the horrible things that were happening to her. When she finally showed up it didn't take long for us to realize what she'd been up to while she was out gallivanting. She was pregnant. By her brother. *Who does that?*

I never looked at that cat the same way again. I was like a disappointed mother who found out her daughter had been giving it up behind the school bleachers. She was no longer allowed on my bed, and I could barely tolerate her in my room. One night, while a friend of the family was over doing my hair, pregnant Sade came down the stairs and started mewing at my mother's feet.

"What's wrong with her?" the family friend asked.

"She's a dirty little whore pregnant with her brother's babies."

My mother slapped me on the forehead with a comb and followed Sade upstairs to the warm utility closet which was serving as Sade's labor and delivery unit. My mother stroked her back as she cried, and after a while came back downstairs.

"I think she's in labor."

"Ewww," was my response.

A few minutes later, Sade once again came downstairs, this time trailing blood on the linoleum and cried at my mother's feet. My mother followed her upstairs again.

"That's just nasty," family friend said. I agreed.

This went on a few more times until finally one of those times my mother was stroking her back little kittens popped out. Not her back, but you know, the usual spot. The blessed event was marred by the fact that two of them died the next day. We're not exactly sure what happened, but they were found with kitty litter spilling out of their little mouths. The third kitten was killed by Sade who'd eaten everything but the head.

"How is this *my* fault?" my mother asked when my brother, sister, and I gave her the stink eye as she buried the kittens in the yard. The answer was, it wasn't her fault, but we were somehow sure it was.

Then there were the birds that filled our house with song until my mother went to bed one night and forgot to cover their cage. And left the window open. In the winter. The next morning we found those birds in their cage, flat on their backs, legs up and as stiff as if a taxidermist had paid a late night visit.

Then there were the fish. My mother had a habit of buying fish without doing any research whatsoever. She just bought ones that looked pretty. There were the Japanese fish that were so gorgeous, but we found out the hard way that they couldn't occupy the same tank as one another. Seems they were also known as "Japanese Fighting Fish."

Then there were the little blue-speckled ones that ate all the other fish and my mother kept replacing them... till she found out the blue-speckled ones were in the piranha family, and also didn't play well with others.

My favorite fish adventure came in the form of a lizard with fins that swam in the tank with the other fish. He was a long, ugly fucker. One day, my brother went to sprinkle some fish food into the tank and noticed the lizard was gone. In a panic, we all searched the house. The lizard-fish was nowhere to be found. I couldn't sleep for days. Where could it have gone for God's sake?! It was a fish. It needed water to survive! Then one morning we were in the kitchen when something caught my eye. There, walking out of the bathroom like he paid rent, was the lizard. Walking and strutting as proud as he pleased totally devoid of fins. Again, my mother had failed to do research on her aquatic purchase, and didn't realize that after awhile the lizard-fish shed his fins and became more lizard than fish.

Over the years there were more pets that met calamitous ends. There were dogs that ran away or got sick and died. There was the Lhasa Apso fittingly named Dusty who, no matter how often you bathed him, had a perpetual look of filth about him. The last time she came to visit, to drop my sister Dina off at college in Atlanta, she brought with her a curious looking creature she swore was a poodle.

"That's not a poodle" I said.

"It is a poodle."

"It doesn't look like a poodle."

"Well, I had to give her a haircut."

My mother's desire and affection for animals sometimes outweighs her bank account and inevitably she will find herself in possession of a pet that she can't afford to take to the groomers as often as she should - as was the case with this pseudo-poodle named Mimi. So, my mother would call herself trimming the animal herself only to screw it up so badly, the only way to remedy the disaster was by shaving everything off and starting from scratch. Which is why the shaved, skinny, long-faced creature in my kitchen in no way resembled a poodle. She even caused Donny, who is really tolerant when it comes to weird looking animals to lament, "That's an ugly ass dog."

I know my limitations when it comes to pets, and Donny and Kali do as well. They realize that if we were to ever take on the responsibility of an animal it would primarily be *their* responsibility. I want very limited contact. Or, contact on my own terms. I like the idea of kittens, but not cats. And I detest cleaning a litter box. I like puppies, but not dogs. I'd want a dog that was guaranteed to get no bigger than say, a sofa's throw pillow. Donny loves Labs, but they get too big and any animal that can take a bigger shit than me can't live in my house.

Every time I start to weaken; when we see people giving away puppies in the Wal-Mart parking lot, we pass the pet store, or Kali and Donny start begging for a dog, I just think back to mother... and wonder if it's hereditary. And then I say no.

Ass Biscuits

October 11, 2007

The world doesn't stop when you're sick. I'm learning that the hard way. I want to write my professors and be like, "Dude, I'm dying. Give me a break." My bedroom smells like Vick's Vapor Rub and sick. There was another odd smell that I couldn't place until a few minutes ago. The other day I was baking and Donny ran out to get some stuff I needed. When he came back he placed a box I'd never seen before on the table.

"What's that?"

"Chicken in a Biskit."

"A who in a what?"

"You never had that before?"

"Uh, no."

They're chicken-flavored crackers.

"What does it taste like?"

"Chicken in a biscuit. Taste it."

After watching Kali and Donny munch on them I decided to give it a try.

"Agggh." I spit the chewed-up cracker into a napkin.

"You don't like it?"

"It tastes like ass in a biscuit."

Apparently, he brought the box upstairs and left it on his bedside table. I was tempted to stop using the Vick's vapor rub to keep my nose stuffed up just so I wouldn't have to smell them. Too sick, weak, and lazy to take them downstairs, I just closed up the box and tossed them over the landing to the first floor.

That aside, Donny has to be the best husband like, ever. He's been up for twenty-four hours, working. He came home two hours ago long enough to shower, change, grab coffee, and head back out. I kinda feel like a twat now. Maybe I should go get his ass biscuits and put them in the pantry.

Mortified

October 12, 2007

Let me set the scene:

INTERIOR; BEDROOM, EARLY MORNING:

We see NINA, an attractive, tall, curvaceous woman in her early 30's, sitting criss-cross-applesauce-style in the middle of a large bed. There are balled up snot tissues next to her (don't judge her!), a laptop in front of her, and various text books strewn about the bed.

She's wearing blue flannel LL Bean pajamas that are three sizes too big, but they cost like, $3, so what do you want from her? Her nose is as greasy as a bowl of fried chicken it's so lathered down with Vick's Vapor Rub. Every time she coughs it sounds like dogs barking.

Feeling a funny twinge in her belly she literally rolls herself off the bed and heads to the master bathroom.

INT; WATERCLOSET; CONTINUOUS:

We shall save you the gory details and just say that NINA'S suspicions that she was a baby killer in a former life were once again confirmed as it seemed that God saw fit to not only plague her with flu-like symptoms for four days, but to make sure she got her period in the midst of it all. Also, if her calculations are correct, it seems she is now getting her period earlier and earlier every month. Wondering if she is peri-menopausal she heads downstairs to make a cup of tea.

INT; 2nd STORY FOYER; CONT:

As NINA enters the hall she glances out the gallery window and spots a POLICE CAR parked in front of her home. The OFFICER in the driver's seat is making notes on a clipboard and consulting a small computer screen attached to the dashboard.

Having grabbed the phone before heading downstairs, NINA wonders if she should call her husband, DONNY, to make sure he's okay or if she should call her daughter, KALI'S, school. She heads downstairs, turns off the alarm system and is just about to open the front door when she notices the OFFICER approaching.

INT/EXT; FRONT OF HOUSE/FOYER; CONT:

OFFICER: Ok, this is about your lawn.

NINA glances at her front lawn which does resemble a small, South American jungle. Seeing the look of embarrassment and annoyance cross NINA's face, the OFFICER continues...

OFFICER: Yeah, we have better things to do, but they're really making us enforce this now. What this says is that you have till the end of the month to take care of the lawn and if you don't, you could face fines and/or imprisonment.

Extremely mortified for both the condition of her lawn and the copious amount of Vick's Vapor Rub around her nose - not to mention the state of her hair - NINA goes on a mini-rant against the Home Owner's Association that gets $500 of her, er, Donny's hard-earned money every year to do absolutely shit. She rants against her nosy-ass neighbors who can afford to have lawn care services come out once a week and whose husbands don't work two jobs so they're not dead exhausted on the weekends; therefore, able to mow their lawns then.

The OFFICER listens patiently, even nods a few times either in agreement or shock that someone who sounds as if they have two rolls of socks shoved up their nostrils can go on such a rant without taking a breath. Then, he asks her name to add it to the warning.

NINA: Nina Perez (insert German married last name here. Purposely left out to protect the innocent, lazy, and kinda broke.)

The OFFICER writes on the citation, signs it, and then hands NINA a bright pink copy. She considers balling it up in an act of defiance, but is suddenly overcome with the desire to sneeze and she does so right into the bright pink paper. Though unintended, it too serves as an accurate expression of what she thinks of the citation.

There's an awkward exchange of "excuse me," "hope you feel better," and "have a good day."

NINA plops down on the foyer floor and calls her DAD, a retired New York City police detective, who explains that though he understands her annoyance, and even has his own issues with his own HOA for his subdivision - which, by the way, is all custom-designed homes starting at $750k and going upwards of $2 million yet only charges about $400/year in dues - and they don't even have a pool or tennis court! - she is in the wrong. Not at all what NINA wanted to hear she makes up some excuse to get off the phone and calls DONNY.

They realize that they're going to have to, once and for all, make a decision on lawn care. If one, or both, of them aren't going to honestly commit to mowing the lawn at least once every two weeks, they need to bite the bullet and pay for a service. The latter is NINA's choice, but as her total contribution to the household funds this year has been about $1,500, she decides it's best to shut the fuck up and leave this particular decision making process to the breadwinner, DONNY.

As they talk on the phone, NINA peers out the sidelight window and admits to herself that the lawn does look pretty ghetto. It's not so much the grass as it is the weeds. It does have a certain "no-one-has-lived-here-in-months" feel to it. She's not sure, but she thought she saw Mowgli chillin' in her Japanese Plum tree. They end their conversation with NINA asking if DONNY could bring home some orange juice, Nyquil, and tampons.

As she continues to lie on the foyer floor she once again glances at the bright pink citation slightly damp with her nasal fluids. Being dead wrong doesn't stop her from imagining exacting all kinds of revenge on her neighbors. On her citation, under "Property Maintenance Violations" the box marked "Grass, Weeds, Uncultivated Vegetation" is checked.

She looks under "Miscellaneous Violations" and notices "Leash Law." She immediately thinks of at least five neighbors on her block alone who violate that law every day. Then there's "Overcrowding." The family across the cul-de-sac has had at least three full families living in there at once at any given time, NINA thinks to herself. "You don't see me calling the cops."

"Accumulation of Solid Waste." NINA wonders if her neighbor's no-good, teenage sons, who are constantly cutting, or getting suspended from, school counts. She also wonders if the mixture of shame/annoyance/indignation she is feeling will keep her mind off the body aches, stuffy nose, and menstrual cramps. More importantly though, she wonders if last night's episode of *Grey's Anatomy* is available on ABC.com yet, since her TiVo cut off right as George got home to tell Callie about Izzy. She heads upstairs to find out.

Third Grade Detective

October 13, 2007

I shouldn't be surprised that a child of mine has a sharp mind for figuring stuff out. I come from a long line of puzzle solvers, detectives, and mystery lovers. And it's a good thing that I don't believe in telling a child, "... because I said so" seeing as how my child simply won't take that for an answer.

"Everything has a why, Mommy."

She's right. Everything does have a why. And just like Kali won't stand for "because I said so" she hates, "I don't know."

The other night, before bed, Kali was going through her kindergarten yearbook. We had a good time looking at kids she got to know in later grades and seeing how little they looked in kindergarten. When we came across one particular kindergarten class, Kali pointed and said, "Hey, look. There's Mary."

Mary is the fictional name I'm giving the girl who lives across the street. (Sometimes I call her Twat.) The little girl that I don't care much for, but has grown on me as of late... only because she's now acting less twat-ish towards Kali.

I looked, and sure enough, there was Mary - first pic, first row, first column. Kali looked up at the ceiling thoughtfully then asked, "How come we were both in kindergarten at the same time, but now I'm in third grade and Mary's in second?"

It was immediately obvious to me that Mary's ass had been left back, but for some reason I didn't want to say that to Kali so I settled for, "I don't know." I guess I had images of Kali sitting on the school bus the next morning and saying, "My mom said you must have been left back." I may think her parents are making huge mistakes in some regards to her welfare, and I may think that she's a sneaky little liar, but that doesn't mean I want to hurt her feelings for God's sake!

Kali was not satisfied with my answer and several times before bed I would hear her muttering to herself things like, "She's eight and I'm eight... I don't get it." Or, "She must be a repeater."

"Kali, don't go asking that girl why she's only in the second grade. It might hurt her feelings."

Kali looked disappointed, but not deterred. The truth was, I kinda wanted Kali to find out because now *my* curiosity had been piqued. Obviously, the child was left back, but I wanted details. I'm nosy. Sue me. I wanted to know so badly that the next day when Kali came to me and said, "Mommy, I know why Mary's only in the second grade," my immediate and unashamed response was, "Really? Why?"

"She repeated kindergarten."

And without thinking I responded, "That's fucked up."

And without missing a beat Kali said, "Yeah, I know."

There was a moment of silence in which we were both pondering how one goes about failing kindergarten. I mean, every Mom I know worth her salt has taught her child everything he or she will learn in kindergarten before they go. Hell, Kali knew her alphabet, how to count to twenty, how to do basic addition, and her address and phone number, all before she entered *preschool.* For most kids, kindergarten is like, a free year. Suddenly, I had a new thought.

"Hey! You didn't ask her if she was left back, did you?"

"No."

"Then how do you know she repeated kindergarten?"

Kali runs to her room and returns with two yearbooks.

"Well, I thought about it and then got my other yearbooks. And when I was in first grade, she was still in kindergarten. See?"

Kali flips through one of the books and points to herself, smiling in her first grade yearbook photo. Then she flips back a few pages and points to Mary who is still the first pic, first row, first column, but in a whole new kindergarten class. Sad.

Kali looks proud of herself.

"You weren't going to let it go, were you?"

"I just had to know. It's like... I couldn't even sleep."

"Well, I'm just glad you didn't ask her. She might have been embarrassed."

"Yeah."

Silence.

"But... I still wish I knew *why*. I mean, how did she fail *kindergarten*?!"

Everything has a why.

The Opposite of Me Is Cock

November 17th, 2007

Last night, after Kali's parent-teacher conference, we headed to our favorite Chinese buffet restaurant. At about two that afternoon I was suddenly overcome with the desire to eat dinner there. While we waited for the waitress to bring our drinks, we checked out the paper on the table that tells you what year you were born in. You know, year of the dragon, monkey, etc. Donny is horse, I'm tiger, and Kali is rabbit. While Donny and I went to get our food, Kali decided to stay at the table to finish reading all the characteristics that come with being born in the year of the rabbit.

As I'm putting some steamed rice on my plate Kali comes up to me and says so loudly that I damn near dropped my plate...

"The opposite of me is the cock."

"Uh huh. Get a plate."

"Is a cock like a chicken?"

"Mmm hmm. Do you want fried rice or white rice?"

"No rice. I thought so cause the cock looks like a chicken on the paper."

Oh sweet God. I just really wanted to tell her to shut up, but if there's one thing I've learned about being a parent it's that you don't draw more attention to things than need be. If I made a big deal out of the word she'd be Googling "cock" the moment my back was turned. We sit down to eat and of course when it's about as quiet as it can get in the restaurant Kali says, "Daddy, do you want to know what the opposite of me is?"

"What?"

"The opposite of the rabbit?" She clarifies.

"Tell him later."

"Why?"

"Just eat and tell him in the car."

"But I want to tell him now? Why can't I tell him now?"

And she looked so confused and upset, and was looking at me like I was just being a meanie so I said, "Fine. Go ahead." And because there is a God my child simply reached across the table and pointed to the picture of the cock. And Donny looked down and choked on his Crab Rangoon.

All talk of cock was soon forgotten when Donny remarks, "I told the guys at work about that centipede and they all said they would have all reacted the same exact way."

Donny did a little girly dance the other day when a centipede he tried to kill fell off the wall and onto his shirt.

"That's because you work with a bunch of P-U-S-S-I-E-S."

As Kali scrunches up her face trying to decipher the word I quickly spelled, Donny continues, "That thing was like ten inches long."

"No it wasn't! Did you tell them that? You are so full of it. It was like three inches... tops!"

"What's ten inches?" Kali wants to know.

I demonstrate what I believe to be about ten inches with my fingers along the edge of the table.

"Daddy, it wasn't that long. It was about this long." Kali then demonstrates about three inches or so with her fingers.

"After I killed it and it curled up maybe, but when it was alive and crawling it was like ten inches."

"You are so exaggerating."

"I don't know what that means, but I agree with Mommy."

Will Smith and My Period

December 14th, 2007

Last night I dreamt that it was this evening and Donny and I had gone to see *I Am Legend*. I fell asleep before the opening credits were done. So, we went back the next night and the same thing happened. Fed up, that Sunday I decided we'd go to a matinee and I invited Ann Curry from *Dateline NBC* to go with us. She agreed, but only if she could hang out at the mall while we watched the movie because she had no desire to see *I Am Legend*. I woke up before we left so I can't tell you if I fell asleep for a third time.

I can tell you that I just spent $31.00 for two movie tickets. We have two tickets to the 7:10 IMAX showing of *I Am Legend*. For $31.00 you can bet my black ass will be wide a-fucking-wake through the whole damn thing. I'm gonna be able to tell you who the key grip was, the production assistant, costume designer, everybody. Fuck. That.

And for those who were concerned about whether or not I'm pregnant, I'm about 99.9% sure my period will come today. For one, it was a week ago today that I got this crampy feeling and that's usually how it starts. Also, I consulted my blog yesterday (Yeah, I track my period via blogs; screw a calendar) and I wrote about us going to that hibachi restaurant on Friday, November 9th. I remembered a very uncomfortable ride home that night as I got my period. And my period comes on the same day each month, not date. So, if it was the second Friday in November, it will be the second Friday in December, even if that means that's 35 days apart.

That also means that should it come today before midnight, I will be ovulating approximately two weeks from now on the 28th. Since sperm can live for up to three days they say it's best to start trying in the three days before and after your ovulation date. So, what that basically means is that I should be Fertile Myrtle between the 25th and the 31st.

Now, there are some that recommend you do it every day during that week. But others think that you're diminishing the potency of the sperm by doing that so they opt for the every other day method. I think I like that way better. The last time we tried, when neither method worked, in a fit of desperation we tried it every day of the month. EVERY DAY. After four days I wanted to kill Donny. After six I wanted to give my vagina away. All I got for my troubles was a urinary tract infection.

"It's best that you urinate immediately after intercourse," my doctor informed me. And I sat there on the examination table with the white tissue paper sticking to my ass feeling like that whore of Babylon.

"But... but... all the books say to lay there with your hips up in the air to help the sperm travel."

"If it's going to get there, it's going to get there," said my doctor, who looks like a young Denzel Washington, and suddenly I just wanted my antibiotics and to get the fuck up outta there.

Early signs of pregnancy are very much like getting your period anyway which doesn't help when you're trying and nothing is happening. Mood swings, bloating, sore breasts. In fact, when I was pregnant with Kali my period was only one day late when I found out I was pregnant and I was in complete shock.

"How could you not know?" asked my mother.

"I thought I was getting my period! My boobs are huge!"

Last night my boobs were *killing* me. They were sitting up saluting the sun, round and full and just *sore*.

"You look like you got a boob job. They're huge."

"Shut up, Donny."

We played *Halo 3* for awhile and then I could no longer take it. "Ooooh God! I just wish I could remove them for awhile. They're so sore and so big and they hurt!"

And what does Donny do? He reached over, cupped and squeezed one. Like a cobra, my hand lashed out and slapped his. Hard.

"Ow!"

"Are you fucking insane?! I tell you my tits hurt and you start twisting and turning like you're trying to get better reception. Fuck off!"

I regretted how nasty I was almost immediately as I realized I needed his help. I had to free my girls from my new bra before I popped a strap.

"Can you please take my bra off? I can't move my arms."

He reaches under my t-shirt, unsnaps the bra and watches as I slip out of it and pull it through my shirt sleeve. I toss it across the room.

"I hate that bra."

"I just bought that bra. It was fifty dollars!"

"Shut up."

Then I notice he's staring at my chest.

"Look at your nipples."

They were poking through my t-shirt like two little beacons directing lost war ships. I hate getting my period. I think I just want to get pregnant so as not to get my period for awhile.

I found out I was pregnant two days later.

WOWser

January 26, 2008

I have crossed over to the dark side.

When Donny called from Best Buy last night to say he'd found the laptop I wanted and asked, "Did you want anything else?" there was a part of me thinking, "Don't say it. Don't even say it. Wait till May when the semester is over and you have a few months till the baby comes to sit on your ass and do nothing."

But I don't even listen to myself.

"If *World of Warcraft* isn't too expensive, pick it up."

And so it began.

First of all, the game manual for this thing is thick. I've seen thinner bibles. I was thumbing through it when I noticed that Chapter 3 was titled *Getting Started*. What the hell are Chapters 1 and 2 for? I installed the game while I read this massive tome. When it was done installing I had to wait another two hours for an update patch to install. I fell asleep reading the manual.

At 4am, the baby decided that it was time to get up and once again remind me that for the next six months I am his bitch, and if he wants me to get up at 4am to pee, drink a glass of water, a glass of Sprite, and eat two granola bars, then that's what the fuck I'm going to do. I watched a few minutes of *Halloween 4: The Return of Michael Meyers* on AMC. Then I tapped Donny awake.

"I'm scared to go downstairs."

"Why?"

"Cause I watched this Halloween movie."

"What you go and do that for?"

He groggily goes downstairs consoled by the fact that after I give birth to his child he can proceed with his plan to smother me while I slumber and bury my remains in the backyard. I seriously feel like those being held captive in the movies who know they're only being kept alive because of the information they have. As soon as they give up the code or location, they're toast.

After I ate we couldn't go back to sleep so I decided to play the game. First, I had to create a character and pick a realm. Guys, I've put less thought into getting married, starting a family, and buying my house. There's so much to know and consider. Do I want to be Alliance or Horde? A human, elf, or gnome? Paladin, rogue, or warrior? It took me a good thirty minutes to decide. I finally went with an Alliance rogue dark elf because Mitt Romney said rogues like to fuck shit up from behind and I'm all about fucking shit up from *any* direction. It's how I roll. Then I had to name my character. I chose Nina and it was taken.

"Who the fuck would take my name?"

"Um, maybe the first of the other 9 million people playing it named Nina."

I dismissed that. I have never met another Nina; therefore, they do not exist. It is a fittingly awesome, beautiful, sexy name. I've only heard it in TV and movies for awesome, beautiful, and sexy characters. If someone in WoW land used it, their real name is probably something unfortunate like Eunice and they jumped on this opportunity to be known by something as awesome as me.

"Use Neeners."

"I'm not using Neeners in *World of Warcraft*! That's not badass."

"Neither is Nina."

"I beg your fucking pardon. Nina is badass. It's like an assassin."

I went to my old standby from my *Sims Online* days, Kalina. Taken. Well, fuck. I finally went with another hybrid, Kanina. Available. I let the game pick a realm because I was too overwhelmed to pick one. I start playing and everything was going well. I accepted quests and completed them. I was gaining experience points and leveling up nicely. Until I accepted a quest to find some dude near a spider-infested cave north of Shadowglen. No problem, I thought. I just headed north and kept my eyes peeled for caves and spiders. I finally found the cave, but no sign of old dude.

"He's in the cave."

"No he's not. It says near the cave."

"I'm telling you, he's in the cave."

Why I listened to Donny and took my ass in that cave is beyond me, especially considering a) He's never played *World of Warcraft* in his life and b) the directions clearly said NEAR the cave. But I took my ass in there and was promptly gang raped by a band of spiders. As my soul appeared in a nearby graveyard and I guided it in the direction of the cave to find my corpse, Donny said, "I told you he wasn't in the cave."

I found my corpse in the middle of a spider circle jerk. When they were done, I resurrected myself and got the hell out of the cave. By this time, my two inventory bags were full so I headed over to the merchants to sell some loot. As I was leaving, I ran into another live player, Elfinator.

Hey, Kanina.

Hey.

How'd you get to level four?

Uh, I just killed things and completed quests.

Oh. I'm so lost.

Just look for the people with an exclamation mark above their heads and accept quests.

Apparently, he hadn't made it to *Chapter 5: Fucking Shit Up.*

And go in this door behind me to sell stuff if you need money.

How do I do that?

Right click on them.

Apparently, he had yet to make it to *Chapter 4: Buying Shit.*

I knew it would be useless, but I asked if he knew where the guy near the cave was anyway. I was right, he was clueless. I left him and ran into another live player, Katy Battlemage, or something like that. She told me she thought the guy was near, not in, the cave as I thought. After some searching, I found his raggedy ass to the left of the cave entrance, up a hill, suffering from a bad spider bite. I'm guessing he took his ass in the cave, too.

Cheez-It Breath Chat

February 2, 2008

I'm having an icky day. Thinking I'm in my second trimester and therefore immune to this ickiness I was surprised to wake up feeling so sick and miserable. Then I read what's going on inside my body for week 13 and I realize that it's a wonder I'm able to function. My poor body is going through it! Of course I was also shocked to read that my second trimester actually begins *next* week. Ugh! It's all so confusing. Nine months of pregnancy, but you're really pregnant ten months. They don't count when the baby is conceived, but a few weeks prior when you got your last period. My head is spinning.

Anyway, Kali is home from school today and she comes in my room around noon. I'm lying on my left side and she crawls into my bed and lies facing me. She has a box of Cheez-Its and she's munching from it. But they're not ordinary Cheez-Its, but some special flavored ones that Donny bought and they're making me want to vomit.

Kali talks a lot. It's okay. She gets it from me. I know this. That girl will talk your ear off if you let her. So, she's talking up a storm about God knows what with the stinky of box of Cheez-Its between our faces. I yawn.

"Wanna take a nap with me?"

"Will you close up the box for me?" Gladly. I reach over, close up the box, and toss the offending crackers towards the foot of the bed.

"Let's take a nap."

"How 'bout we just chat instead?"

"Ummm, how 'bout we just lie here with our eyes closed and love each other?" I counter.

"We can chat and love each other."

I don't have the heart to tell her that her breath is making Mommy want to hurl all over her, the bed, and our chat because I try not to have the ill effects of pregnancy stop me from doing things with her.

"OK, for a little while. What do you want to chat about?"

Silence.

"Darn. Now I don't have anything to say. Let me think of something."

Silence.

Then she starts talking to me about some family in the *Sims 2* that has eight kids and how they just had another one. Finally she asks to play the Xbox 360 which is in my room.

"I'm watching TV. How about at 2 o'clock?"

"But you just said you're going to nap. How can you nap and watch TV at the same time?"

"I'm listening to it. I'm listening to the news now and at 1 o'clock I want to hear the beginning of *All My Children*. If I fall asleep before 2, you can play it."

"So, you're saying I can play it without asking?"

"Yeah, don't wake me up. Just go ahead and play. I'm TiVo'ing the soaps anyway."

A minute or so passes and I keep my body towards Kali, but turn my head facing the ceiling. Suddenly, her little face appears inches from mine. "I can't tell. Are your eyes open or closed?" Cheez-It breath all in my grill.

"Girl, if you stop talking I might just fall asleep and you can play that much sooner."

And you know what? She didn't say a word for twenty full minutes. She sat and watched the rest of the news. I slept for about that same length of time. Right as AMC came on, I woke up.

"Was I snoring?"

"A little." Pause. "You were drooling a little too." A few minutes pass. "Want to see me blow a bubble?"

"Sure. Want to rub my belly?"

"Sure, 'cause there's a baby in there!'

Now, we're just hanging out in my bed, watching *All My Children*, blowing bubbles and rubbing my belly.

Parent-Teacher Conference

February 15, 2008

So, Donny and I have a method of dealing with parent required school events. We take turns. It all starts with beginning of the year registration and alternates from there. This year, I did registration and the following curriculum night so I just assumed that Donny would do the next two things; parent/teacher conferences. He went to the first conference a few months ago and before telling me how our child was doing in school he just says, "She's cute." Huh?

He was talking about Kali's teacher, which threw me for two reasons. One, he hardly ever comments on another woman's looks. In fact, it's only through constant nagging and little hints that I know he finds Beyonce, Tyra, and Sarah Michelle Gellar hot. I think we should now add Alicia Keys and the girl who plays Lois Lane on *Smallville* to the list. And now we can add our daughter's third grade teacher.

Secondly, I was surprised because I don't find her to be all that cute. Well, okay maybe cute is accurate. She's really petite, white, with a short brunette haircut. She's from Texas originally and has this really thick drawl, but she has these huge bug eyes. Anyway, when it was decided that Donny would be going to last night's conference the conversation with like this:

"You know you're going to the conference on Thursday, right?"

Eye roll.

"Oh, come on Donny! I'm achy and having your baby and I have a cold sore. Also, don't roll your eyes like you don't want to go smile up in her damn face again. 'She's cute!' You thought I forgot? So don't even act like your ass don't wanna go see her. Just remember who's having your baby and will cut your dick right the fuck off."

So, that's pretty much how that went. Last night Donny came home with a new revelation. Kali's stalker has been revealed. Remember the other day she found a note in her desk that read,

Dear Kali,

I hope your grades are doing well.

Did I say that? I meant to say you have the prettiest smile in the whole world.

Or maybe it was "the most beautiful smile." I forget. Either way, I thought I was going to have to go choke a bitch. Donny thought he'd have to go kill the janitor. Turns out, the author was none other than... Rachel.

Yes, that's a girl. It's not some French boy's name. So now I'm wondering, "Just how early do people know they're gay?" What?! Come on! Don't look at me like that. I'm sure I'm not the only one with gay friends who say they knew they were gay as soon as they passed the vaginal walls. I couldn't stop thinking about the woman on *Oprah* a few weeks ago who said she would write love notes to her girl friends when she was a kid and she knew then.

I've only met Rachel once. Last year, when Kali was in the 2nd grade, she had some girls from class come to her birthday party. Rachel's identical twin, Amanda, was in her class and came to the party with her Mom and Rachel. I remember Rachel being really quiet and shy. Now, this year she's in Kali's 3rd grade class and they are apparently best buds. In fact, that was the teacher's only complaint about Kali: She and Rachel pass notes in class. Of course, I had a little talk with Kali last night letting her know she better cut that shit out. (Remember the good old days when parents could actually threaten to spank their child in front of the whole class... and often did?)

Well, who should call last night but timid-voice Rachel.

"Hello?"

"Hi, can I speak to Kali?"

"Is this Rachel?"

"Yes."

"Mrs. A told us today that you guys have been passing notes in class. Is that true?"

"Yes."

"You two need to stop with the note passing, okay? When you're supposed to be paying attention in class that's what I want you to do. You guys can talk at lunch and recess. No more note passing."

"OK."

"OK. I'll go get Kali. Hold on."

Good Lord. When did I become an adult? I was the queen of note passing. Until I wasn't and got caught passing a note to another girl plotting for us to beat up another girl... complete with cuss words. The teacher sent the note home and I got the biggest ass whopping. My stepfather was like, "Well, at least you spelled everything correctly," before he beat my ass.

Open Letter to White People

March 6, 2008

Don't be offended, white people. This comes from a place of love.

Today I was reminded of a long forgotten stereotype I had about white people growing up. A lot of black people did. *Black people want to live more than white people do.* Where would we get such an idea, you ask? Uh, how about bungee jumping, parasailing, hang gliding, swimming in shark-infested waters and getting your leg bitten off only to go on *Good Morning America* talking 'bout, "Diane, I can't wait to get back out there!", and the inability to keep your fucking mouths shut while in a perfectly good hiding spot when there's a serial killer/mass murderer/psychopath after your asses!?

After years of watching horror movies I feel as if I'm more than qualified to advise white people to stand up. Stand up, I say! Stand up, rise up, band together, and tell Hollywood screenwriters you're not going to take it anymore! They ain't got shit else to do right now (writer's strike), so why not listen to your long overdue and valid complaints? Tell them that you will no longer tolerate being portrayed as sniveling, stupid simpletons. (Side note: you promiscuous ladies may want to get in on this as it seems having a healthy, but not choosey, sexual appetite means that you are destined to be filleted.)

Now, I realize that this depiction of white folks is a little unbalanced since black peoples' history in horror films can be summed up as such:

1. For many years our asses weren't cast in any.
2. And when we finally were, we always died first.

If you've noticed, we are now represented more in horror films and when we are, we rarely, if ever, die first. Hell, it's not uncommon to see black people make it through the whole damn film and even through most of the sequel! And when we do die, we go out like P.I.M.Ps.

If you heed my advice and challenge these Hollywood writers to do right by you, here are some suggestions as to what you should address:

1. Why you all have to be so damn loud? I hate when the white girl being chased by the killer finds a good hiding spot and she gives herself away by whimpering and breathing all heavy.

2. If they don't answer you, they're dead. Every time a white person enters a spooky house, room, basement, etc. looking for someone, they gotta call out for the person six and seven times getting louder and louder. If Billy don't answer you the first time, Billy dead. Leave!

3. Shoot first, ask questions later. How many times have you seen a white woman have the killer at gunpoint only to stand there shaking and looking all confused? And how about when she tells the killer, "Don't move," yet proceeds to let him approach her dumb ass until he backs her up into a wall and takes the gun from her? I hate that shit. Girl, shoot his ass! Sometimes they try to explain it away by making the woman doubt whether or not the bad guy is actually bad. You don't want to shoot poor John and it turns out he was on your side. Solution? Shoot his ass in the kneecap! You can get away and if it turns out he was a good guy, bygones.

4. Stop leaving perfectly good hiding spots! Has anyone seen *30 Days of Night*? Why the hell would you be in a more than adequate hiding spot for like 20 days, and then leave to go hide in the grocery store with a shit load of windows and entrances?

And while we're on the subject, why is there always one white person in the hiding spot that just *has* to get out? He/she always messes it up for everyone. They're either claustrophobic or just plain too stupid to not freak out and ruin it. Kill his ass. And kill him early.

My favorite fucker-up-of-a-perfectly-good-hiding spot is the white girl that will run screaming from cover because she saw a rat or mouse, and right into the arms of the psycho zombie-vampire-rapist. Dumbass.

5. Whenever we watch horror movies together, without fail I will make Donny laugh by saying, "A time and a place, people. A time and a place." Why do I say this? Because white people always find the time to screw when faced with death. Now I can understand if you're in a room locked with a bomb and you feel like death is imminent, but while on the run and you find an abandoned house to hunker down in for the night, do you really want to catch an axe in your ass 'cause you just *had* to get your groove on? Does the threat of death and dismemberment really turn you on that much?

6. Is it too much trouble to ask that you make sure the killer is actually dead? Why do white women stab the killer in the *shoulder* then proceed to drop the knife, turn her back on the prone killer, and sob so loudly she can't hear that the fucker has just stood up and is about to, deservedly, stick a knife in her skull? Good rule of thumb? If you manage to incapacitate the killer, commence to cutting his head clean. the. fuck. off. And then his dick. 'Cause that's how you roll.

7. Ever heard of safety in numbers? Apparently white folks haven't. It can be like 12 of them stuck in a house with a killer and instead of everyone just sitting in one room and waiting for his crazy ass to come to them so he can catch a 12-man beatdown Brooklyn-style, they decide it makes more sense to split up into groups of twos, and sometimes solo, to look for clues, find an exit, etc. Inevitably, one of these groups will consist of a guy and girl who will find a room in which to fuck (see number 5.)

8. White girls, stop running up to the attic or down to the basement. For once I'd love to see one of you, I don't know, try the front door. Hell, even

jump out a first story window, but stop going to the places with little to no exits! And stop tripping and falling. For the first 45 minutes of the film, you are the most agile bitch ever, but as soon as body parts start flying, you suddenly can't run two feet without tripping over the wind. Learn how to run, bitch!

I can run in heels carrying a baby in my belly, my child in one arm, and my cell phone in the other while texting a blog. Surely you can dash 15 yards through the woods without stumbling twice only to fall on your back, all the better to scream perfectly into the camera while being slashed.

9. Listen to the black people! Even if it's the single, stoned brother, listen to his ass. Even if it's the brother sitting in the theatre. Listen to his ass!

10. Assume all urban legends are real. Stop trying to disprove them. Nothing good can come of it.

11. The killer is ALWAYS white. And always really, really, sick and twisted. If you are the last person standing, be prepared to run through an obstacle course made up of all the people he has killed before getting your ass. White killers think that shit is funny to watch you hurdling over poor Susie's head.

12. Stop taunting crazy people!

Family Portraits

March 25, 2008

I don't know when my hatred for family portraits began. I just know that the other day it occurred to me that they're pretty fucking lame. As Donny and I cleaned the kitchen Saturday morning I further expanded on what I found so irksome about them.

For one, people insist of dressing everyone involved exactly alike. Either they're all decked out in their Sunday best, or worse, they're wearing identical matching outfits: white button-down shirts with khaki pants, denim outfits, or hideous red sweaters at Christmas time. It *always* looks ridiculous. You have Mommy, Daddy, the three little kiddies, and sometimes, if they're really crazy, the family dog all decked out in matching Gap outfits. Why? *Who does that?*

Some families who do this will only do it once in a while. Their explanation being that it's rare to get the family together and it's a good thing to have a nice portrait together. First of all, by the time everyone gets dressed, drives to Sears, waits their turn, chooses from a plethora of hideous backgrounds, poses, and gets ass-raped for a $50+ package, they could have plopped their asses on the couch and set the timer on the digital camera placed on the fireplace mantle, wearing whatever the hell they happened to have on at the time.

I think what really bothers me is the fakeness of it all followed dangerously close by the dressing alike. The photographers make everyone look off to some mark over his shoulder, perhaps because if they looked directly in the camera we'd be able to see that Daddy is really miserable with Mommy, and Mommy is still disappointed that she didn't marry that guy she dated out of college, and that the oldest boy was conceived just to get Mommy off Daddy's back, and the youngest well, he was an accident.

I prefer candid shots. I like looking through our family albums and being able to say, "Oh, this was my Dad's surprise 50th party," or, "Remember going to Grandma's that weekend?" You get to see your family as they *really* were. Who rocked that unfortunate high top fade back in the day. Who wore those ridiculously tight pants back in 1998. Specific, obscure, yet wonderful memories can come flooding back by simply examining the backgrounds in each picture. "Wow, remember that old TV? Whatever happened to it?" "See that toy on the floor? Remember when Kali would play with it constantly... until that day she flushed it down the toilet?"

But back to the synchronized fashion. What up with that? How can a family of three or more dress in the same outfit, get in the car, and one member *not* take a moment to look around the vehicle and be like, "We look a damn fool?" Hell, even the toddler can look around, realize that for the first time his siblings and parents are all dressed like him and think, "Hmm, this is weird." And by weird he means stupid. What is that walk through the mall like? For every one person giving the walking Old Nay ad a look that says, "Aww, how cute," there is at least three of me going, "You've *got* to be fucking kidding me." You should never leave the house knowingly dressed exactly as someone else unless you're on a sports team, in a wedding party, or it's Halloween.

Do they think that the matching outfits somehow equal stable family? Are we supposed to look at those matching ensembles and think cohesive family unit? Above all, that they must really love each other in order for Mom (and you *know* it's always the mother's idea) to spend the time shopping to make sure everyone matched just so?

Finally, just what the hell are we supposed to do with these pictures? The only people who truly appreciate these family portraits are grandparents. Everyone else is like, "Why the hell? Where am I supposed to put this?" And you know what happens right? Eventually the grandparents die and you're gathering up their belongings and come across your own family portrait and realize that not even *you* want that shit because you already have your own copies *plus* the extras you couldn't unload because you let the young kid at *The Picture People* talk you into a big ass package you didn't need.

There are only two exceptions: children only photos...

Well, really that's the *only* exception.

Now, this is where you tell me how I just don't get it. And you're right. I don't.

I Actually Left the House

April 9, 2008

I know, I know. Pick your jaws up off the floor.

Yesterday I went with Donny and Kali to Wal-Mart for groceries. Donny means well, but when he does the shopping we usually run out of stuff in four days. I put on my maternity khakis but rolled up the legs a bit so they were kinda like capris, put on some flip-flops and a flowy shirt and a little make-up. I felt good!

I stopped to see my Vietnamese friends in the nail salon inside Wal-Mart. The owner, this man whose kids go to Kali's school, came up to me with his hand out to touch my belly and I immediately grabbed it and... placed it there! It's funny because I'm usually not a fan of people doing that, but when it's people you know, and who have worked on your feet, it's kinda okay. He rubbed and said, "That's a boy." I told him he'd be seeing me in a few weeks before my baby shower.

Can we take a moment and talk about how Hannah Montana's ass is ALL OVER WALMART? Every other step we took Kali could be heard squealing in glee. Donny said he saw her on a container of yogurt. I'm sure I saw her smiling up at me from a bag of flour.

We stopped at Dunkin' Donuts and I got a Strawberry Breeze Blast and drove home with the windows down. It really was a lovely evening in a Georgia suburb. When we got home I made arroz con pollo and we ate together in the family room while watching TV and chatting. It's been awhile since the three (four) of us had done that. Around 7:30 we all piled in my bed and watched TV still laughing and having a good time. Two funny things happened:

1. I was at *Ain't It Cool News*, reading this message board for *Battlestar Galactica* that started on the 4th (the day the fourth season premiered) and some people were really excited early in the day that they could view the premiere online at noon without having to wait for the 10pm premiere on TV. One guy's post said:

Subject: I have to wait till tonight...

I promised my wife I wouldn't watch it without her. I hate that frakkin' whore.

So I laughed and turned to Donny (who had sometimes been reading over my shoulder), "Did you read that?"

"Read it? I wrote it."

Oh, he had jokes last night...

2. The phone rang during *American Idol* and it was a local number that read *US Government* on the caller ID. Donny answered it and I heard him say I wasn't available. Donny listened for awhile and then pretended to write down a number.

"Who was that!?"

"An Army recruiter."

"For me?"

"Yup."

"Why did you pretend to take down his number? Why didn't you tell him I'm old and pregnant and I ain't going into the damn military to be shipped off to Iraq for God knows how long?"

"He said he can help you with your future goals."

"Unless he can help me with stretch marks we ain't got shit to discuss."

"That's what you think. As soon as you pop the baby out, I'm shipping you off."

Is Daddy Going to Touch Me?

May 6, 2008

The other night, while Donny was downstairs playing *Grand Theft Auto 4*, Kali and I were in my bed reading and trying to fall asleep. She had put her book down and her eyes were closed and her breathing even when Donny came into the room looking for lotion. He complained that over one eye was really dry and itchy as well as the area around his mouth (like goatee formation) and a small patch on his arms. He wondered whether or not working in the backyard earlier that day could be behind it all.

"Do you think it's poison ivy?"

"Who has poison ivy?" Kali's head pops up.

"No one. Go to sleep."

She didn't look convinced and laid there with her head propped up in her hand, dippin' all in our conversation.

"You're not going to sleep in here are you?"

We were both looking at Donny with the same look on our faces. Looks that said, "I love you to death, but I ain't tryna catch shit you got." No wonder he's so looking forward to having a son. Donny offers to sleep in the guest room or bonus room just to play it safe. He's gone from the room a few moments when I turn off the lamp and Kali whispers, "I feel sad."

"Why?"

"Cause Daddy has to sleep all by himself downstairs."

"Well, he'll probably sleep up here with us... just in the bonus room."

"Yeah, but he's still alone."

Sweet, huh?

Last night, while Donny slept, before I turned in myself, I decided to tuck Kali in, check the doors, make sure the alarm was set, etc. I push open her door and not only was the light on, but she was in bed watching TV.

"Kali! It's almost eleven! Lights out. Go to sleep!"

I tuck her in and toss in one last parting shot, "You know, I may sleep in and that means Daddy will get you up for school and you know he doesn't cut you slack like I do in the mornings."

She looked up at me with fearful eyes.

"Is Daddy going to touch me?"

"What?!"

She either repeated or clarified her question, but I'll never know which because I couldn't hear her over my own thoughts of, "Oh, great. Now I gotta go cut Donny's dick off." I had to ask her twice more what she said, mainly because her TV was so damn loud, when finally...

"Does he still have poison ivy?"

I laughed and sighed with relief. "No, he never had it."

She gave her own sigh. "Oh, good, 'cause I was going to say tell him not to touch me when he wakes me up, just call my name."

As I got into bed, Donny woke up and raised an eyebrow at the smile on my face. I explained what just happened in Kali's room. He just shook his head and rested his head on the pillow once more.

"Don't shake your head. That's how rumors get started. Kids mess around and say the wrong thing around the wrong person and next thing you know you got The People at your house investigating. 'I don't want Daddy to wake me up because he touches me.'"

Baby Busy

May 14, 2008

Lots of things going on. I warned you last week that I wouldn't be writing as much. I could feel it coming on. Blogging proves a nice distraction in between studying and taking exams, but now that the semester is over and my free time is truly that: free time, I am less inclined to spend that time on MySpace. Not that I don't have things to say because I do, but what usually happens is that I'll think of something interesting and funny and then end up writing the blog in my head, imagining the same responses from the same people, and then it's done. While not as satisfying as writing a blog, it certainly requires less effort. And being seven months pregnant, let me tell ya, you appreciate anything that requires little to no effort.

Yes, I'm now in my 7th month. Where did the time go? The baby's bigger which means I'm bigger, but apparently not big enough because he's constantly kicking, punching, rolling, and wiggling, as if he wants to get out. Long gone are the days when movement was sparse. He moves all the time, especially at night, and especially at night when I would normally be sleeping. I am awakened anywhere between 2 and 5am by kicking and wiggling. And there's no going back to sleep immediately. I just gotta ride it out. Of course, I'm hungry at those times so I end up snacking which means I'm pretty sure this third trimester will find me blown up and swollen. *Sigh*. I don't care. As long as he's healthy. I'll worry about weight loss later.

I find myself worried about all the things I forgot since having Kali. Everyone says it will all come back to me. I sure hope so. One thing I never forgot was the discomfort that comes with this stage of pregnancy, especially trying to roll over from one side to the other. Since you can't roll side to tummy to side, you have to roll side to back to side. And that's a bitch and a half. As I shift to my back I can feel the baby, the fluid, and everything else sloshing around in there shift with me and it's like a great wave moves upward and presses my already lifted internal organs even harder and closer to my lungs. Then I eventually roll to the new side only to have the baby and company roll with me. It's a chore.

Though the worst is when I'm lying on my side reading or watching TV and then suddenly I can't breathe. I don't feel him move, but I know he must have shifted in some way that is causing all kinds of pressure on my lungs. Depending on my mood I'll either ride it out or give him a little shake. When I go with the latter, he gives a little wiggle and finds a new spot. I'm sure he's thinking, "What up with that?"

He doesn't like the doppler. Every now and again Donny will say, "Can I listen to my boy?" And I never say no. I'll lie on my back and pull up my shirt and let Donny use the device to find the heartbeat. The moment he finds it, and it's nice and strong and loud, the baby starts kicking and wiggling. This usually causes a loud ugly noise on the machine. Then he moves to another spot. Relentless, and some might say annoyingly, we find him again and try to listen. And once again he gives a hearty, "Fuck you! I'm trying to sleep!" kick before wiggling away. We usually don't have the heart to try and flush him out a third time. Donny says he gets that attitude from me.

We've become obsessed with what he's going to look like. I've had dreams about him, but I learned from Kali that they never look like you imagine them to be. Donny says he hasn't dreamed about him once, and if he has he doesn't remember. Donny says he doesn't dream or never remembers them. I find that kinda sad... and weird.

Apparently, I waddle now. I caught Donny staring at me as I walked towards him the other day.

"What are you staring at?"

"You. You're waddling."

"Shut up!"

"No, I love it. I love it, I love it, I love it." And he wrapped his arms around me as I tried to wiggle free. Last night we were laying face to face about to go to sleep when I asked him once again, "What are you staring at? My fat face? Wondering how much fatter it's going to get?"

"No, I was thinking you're beautiful. And sexy. You're glowing."

I didn't feel glowy. I felt bloated and sleepy and knew I'd only get a few hours of sleep before the baby, literally, kicked my ass awake.

The big question of late is, "Will he have the Nina Lip?" My aunt brought it up on Sunday. She was saying that the baby will have lots of dark curly hair, Donny's dimples, and the Nina Lip. In all fairness, it should really be called the Cookie Lip because I got it from my Mom (that's her nickname) and then promptly passed it to Kali. And upturned top lip may be cute on girls, but on a boy... not so sure the Nina Lip will work. We'll see.

So, what else is going on? When we're not wondering what it's going to be like to have him here, we're getting the house ready for the baby shower next week. My mom gets into town a week from today and she'll go with Donny and me to our 29-week 3D ultrasound. We're very excited about that. We'll get a sneak peek at what he looks like. The next two weeks will be busy, but fun. We're expecting about 30 people to attend, my mother-in-law is flying in, and we're all really excited to see everyone and celebrate our baby.

Kali's List

May 20, 2008

When I got laid off back in 2005 I knew it was coming and made sure I stocked up on as many office supplies as I could. Don't judge me. For the past few weeks I've been using a small, lavender (that's how I roll), legal pad to keep track of, well, everything. Guest list for shower, to do's for school, the shower, Jack's room, July, etc. Kali came in my room one day and asked,

"Oooh, what's that?"

"My note pad."

"For what?"

"To keep track of stuff. My to-do lists and stuff."

"Oh. It's pretty," she said eyeing it longingly.

Last week, I was in bed when my mother called with a question about the shower. I went to consult my note pad, but couldn't find it. I'm at that stage in my pregnancy where if something isn't within arms' length of my bed in either direction, it ain't gettin' got. I told my Mom I'd have to get back to her. A few days later I was on the phone with Sophie and worried that I was disturbing Donny, who was in bed watching TV, so I took the call into Kali's room. As we are chatting, I spy my lavender note pad on her bookshelf. I snatch it up and find that she has began to use it for her own purposes.

There are *pages* of long division problems. She learned it this year in third grade and says it's her favorite kind of math. She will sometimes come into our room with a pencil and paper, toss them on our bed, and say, "Give me some division problems. Make them hard. I'm talking remainders."

There were two pages titled *To Do List*. The list read as follows:

1. Go in bonus room

2. Watch TV/play Sims

3. Go downstairs

4. Make food

5. Eat food

6. Go upstairs

7. Go in bonus room

8. Watch more TV

9. Get in PJs

10. Watch Juno

11. Go to sleep Watch Alvin and the Chipmunks

12. Listen to music

13. Go to sleep

14. Wake up

15. Choose clothes

16. Get dressed

17. Brush teeth

18. Go to school

19. Do stuff in school

20. Come home

21. Play.

At this point there's the word CONTINUE with a little arrow indicating you should flip the page.

22. Do the same thing all over again

Someone should tell her that To Do lists don't need to be so detailed. Then I flipped through a few more pages and found a page titled, *REPORT!* and it reads:

Did you know that the black people were slaves about 50 or 56 years ago? The black people were slaves to the white people. Also, if a black man would even look at a white woman they would be killed!? They would also be hunged in trees! If a black person tried to run away they would get caught and die! Or they could be sold to people like farmers and the slaves would for the farmers!

So, um, yeah... she may have not fully understood our conversation on slavery, segregation, the Civil War, etc. I can just imagine the look on all her little white friends' faces when she went to school with *that* little morsel of info... and their parents' faces when they went home with the news.

Anyway, today I've decided to eat as much as I can. I know it won't make a bit of difference when the baby wakes me up at 4am and I can't drink a glass of water or eat some buttered toast, but it makes me feel better mentally. See, I can't eat after 11pm tonight because tomorrow I have my glucose test at 8:30am.

After a Donny-made breakfast of scrambled egg whites, toast, bacon, and decaf I was hungry an hour later. "Can you get me a slice of strawberry cheesecake, one cold drink, and one hot drink?' He returned to the bedroom a few minutes later, placing a cup of coffee and a can of Sprite on the bedside table, and handed me a plate with a slice of cheesecake. My eyes lit up and I clapped and squealed with glee before accepting the cake.

"What am I going to do with you?"

"Love me," I responded, putting a spoonful of cheesecakey goodness into my mouth, "And feed me. What else can you do?"

Empty Nest

June 11, 2008

I don't know how parents who don't live with their kids do it. No judgment here. Well, I'm *definitely* judging the no-good deadbeats who aren't with their kids by choice. But I'm really talking about those parents who don't live with their kids due to break-ups and divorce. That has to be tough. It just seems so unnatural (and maybe that's a strong word) to go to bed at night, lock-up, and not have your babies in the house with you. Even when they're teenagers. So, yeah, I'll be *that* Mom who doesn't go to bed until Kali meets curfew.

When you're a city kid you don't mind your curfew as much 'cause there's always something to do, you're close to everything, and there's always a NYC train within a few blocks that can get you where you need to go, or a yellow cab if you're so inclined. But poor Kali. I don't know what she's going to do with us living out here in the 'burbs. I remember going to live with my Dad and Stepmom in Queens as a teenager and hating my 10pm weeknights - 11pm weekend curfew.

I had to walk like three or four blocks from their house to the bus stop. And I'm talking long blocks. Then wait for the bus, ride it to the subway station, catch the train into the city, and most likely transfer to another train that was taking me where I needed to go. By the time I got there, it was time for my black ass to turn right back around just to be home in time. It sucked. Hanging out closer to home wasn't an option 'cause there wasn't shit to do and all my friends were in Brooklyn or Manhattan.

I'm trying to imagine the kinds of teen trouble Kali will get into living where we do. I'm comparing it to the way I grew up and what I was exposed to. I'm not feeling like one is better than the other. When I grew up, I was dancing and partying in NYC nightclubs at seventeen. I was eating and hanging out in restaurants and bars with "grown folk" and celebrities. I was attending record release parties and movie premieres. I had an Oscar nominated heartthrob asking me back to his place cause I had the most beautiful lips he'd ever seen... this after he followed me to the ladies room. I would sleep on the train with my head on my friend's shoulder at 5am as we headed back to our apartment in Brooklyn, as most other riders were on their way to work. We had on last night's clothes smelling like last night's tequila. Once, I was courted by a female porn star.

I live in a different world now. I imagine Kali's teen years resembling a *Lifetime* movie. I have images of house parties in the suburbs where I gotta worry about little Matt slipping something into her red plastic party cup and not taking no for an answer. Then Grandpa has to go bust a cap in little Matt's ass.

When I think back to the way my friends and I just traveled *all over* New York City without a care in the world, wearing whatever we wanted, it's a wonder I'm alive. And yet the thought of Kali driving as a teenager scares me to death. The thought of her riding with a teenage friend scares me even more. Kids are stupid and it seems like every time we turn around there are reports that some kids around here were killed or seriously injured in car accidents that were their fault.

This isn't even what this blog was supposed to be about. I'm sitting here all mopey because last night my father and stepmother came to pick up Kali so she could sleep over and go with my stepmom and her kids at work to see *Kung-Fu Panda*. I thought I was over this, but every time they come to take Kali for overnight trips I get all... weird. You would think I was packing her off to war. I make sure to kiss her and tell her I love you a bunch of times before she leaves 'cause you never know, you know?

And I'm of the mind that no one loves your child like you and no one will watch them like you. So I get all paranoid, even when it's ex-NYPD detective Grandparents, when someone takes my baby anywhere. The Monday (Memorial Day) after the baby shower my mother and Donny's Mom took Kali and my little sister Bruklyn to Stone Mountain. Kali calls from my Mom's cell, "Mommy, I'm at the top of the mountain and I'm not even scared! We took the tram up!" I almost wet myself.

When she left last night I spent time in her room (mostly turning off lights and the TV) just touching her stuff. Call me old fashioned. I like having my children in the house at night. I thought it was just me, but I had talked to Kali while Donny was downstairs putting up dinner, and when he settled into bed he asked, "How was Kali? What was she doing?" Awww, we missed our baby last night.

So, she'll be home later tonight and I'm sure I'll feel better (and quite silly) once I see her, but I make no promises that I won't still feel this way when she goes with Grandma and Grandpa again... even if she's 12 or 15 or 18.

Dear Kali

July 8, 2008

Dear Kali,

I am writing this for you because there are things I want you to know. Things I want you to remember. I am going to tell you these things in person too, but I wanted to write them down so that you can have this to read whenever I'm not around.

Ready?

1. You know how sometimes, especially lately, you'll catch me staring at you? You'll be on my laptop at the couch or eating at the kitchen table and you'll look up to find me looking at you. You smile and say hi, or sometimes just smile, and I always just smile back. Do you know what I'm thinking?

I am always thinking how wonderfully beautiful you are. Absolutely everything about you, I find to be stunning. (Stunning means so beautiful all I can do is stare, in case you were wondering.) Yes, you're a pretty, gorgeous, beautiful girl with wonderfully long curls (No, you cannot get your hair cut!) and an adorable smile, and eyes that are so expressive. (Expressive means that I can see how you're feeling and what you're thinking by looking into your eyes. They hide nothing. And that's a good thing because they speak the truth. Although, you may not want to play poker for large sums of money. Just saying.) I sometimes watch how your eyes change with your mood and I can see already what kind of wonderfully complex (Complex means hard to figure out, and for a woman, that's a good thing.) exciting, brave, and smart young woman you're going to be. Watch out, world!

I have told you before that you have the most beautiful hands I have ever seen. They are lovely in shape. Your fingers are long and fluid. (Fluid means they move like liquid; soft and easy.) You have these delicate hands that make me smile. You're a funny dancer, kid. Watching you pretend that our new area rug is some kind of stage, or even better that mat those Olympic gymnasts use for their floor exercise, just cracks me up. You are so like me when I was your age. All long limbs (arms and legs), flying around, thinking all the world is a stage. It's funny that we bought the rug to protect the other carpet from spills and you took one look at it and thought, "Hmmm, what can I do with this? Oh, I know. I can dance on it! I can be a star!" It's a wonder you don't have wings. Like a fairy or an angel.

You are not beautiful because of the way you look only... which brings me to number 2...

2. *You are a good person, Princess Kali.* You make me smile. You make me laugh. You make me proud to be your Mom. You're kind. You're funny. You're incredibly smart. You ask a lot of questions, but you always ask the right ones. I love the way your mind works. I love to feed your mind as best I can.

You've been taking care of me a lot lately, you know, when I'm uncomfortable or in pain and you come to hold me and remind me to just, "Breathe, mommy. Real slow. In and out," it makes me feel better. You rub my back or my hair with those lovely hands and everything else melts away. When you were a tiny baby inside of me, I never imagined you would grow into this little person that you are, that loves me so much and takes care of me. It's supposed to be the other way around.

Yesterday, you were on the laptop with the headphones on. I was sitting next to you. Daddy was behind us, by the garage door, putting on his shoes, and preparing to head out to the store. I had to go to the bathroom, and for some reason I felt the need to tell you. I didn't want you to see him leaving, and me leave the room, and not know what was going on.

"I have to go to the bathroom," I said loudly tapping you on the shoulder.

"OK," you shouted back, "Do you need help getting up?"

That made me smile. I probably weigh as much as four of you, but just that you even thought you could, or would want to, help me up shows what a kind little person you are, Kali.

3. I have never, in my entire life, loved anything or anyone as much as I love you. Never, ever, not even once, not even close. Until this baby. I loved you before I knew you. Whenever I imagined having a little girl, I imagined someone just like you, but you're even better than my imagination.

I love you so much that sometimes it hurts. You'll know what I mean when you have kids of your own. It's this love that completely takes you over. It's a love that you could never feel for anyone else. That doesn't mean that I don't love Grandma and Grandpa, or Daddy, or any of my other friends and family. I do. But the love I feel for you, and for the new baby, is completely different. It's all consuming. (That means that it's a part of everything I do... all parts of me.) It's the most special love I've ever experienced and I'm so grateful that I have.

I worried how I would ever love another child. I love you so much, so hard, so insanely, wildly, *much*, that I thought some of it would surely have to go away in order to love another child just as much. I was wrong. Kali, a funny thing happened. I shouldn't have worried about not having enough love for the baby *because my heart got bigger.* The more he grew inside of me the more my heart grew and it was as if it said, "Here you go. I'm now big enough so you can feel just as much love for your son." Isn't that crazy? He's not even here yet and already I know that all the wonderful things I get from loving you, and having you love me back, are about to be doubled. And though I didn't think it was possible to love you more, I absolutely do.

4. I adore you.

5. I don't think I've ever told anyone this... not even you. But there have been many times when I thought, "Kali is my favorite person in the whole world. I'd rather spend time with her than with anyone else." It's true.

6. You saved my life. Having you made me a better person. It changed the way I see the world. It made me want more for myself, for you. My life is so much more full and special than it would have been had you not been born.

7. Thank you for being patient with me. I know sometimes, especially lately, I can be moody and snap at you. The other day I made you cry. I hate to hear you cry. Probably because you don't cry that often and mostly because when you hurt, I hurt. Even if I'm the cause of your pain, it still makes my heart ache to hear you cry. And when you came back into the room a short while later and you let me hug you and apologize, I hope you know that I really meant it. When we pulled away from our hug you said, "Rub noses?" And we rubbed noses like we often do. Like Eskimo do. Thank you for that.

8. Time goes by too quickly. Sometimes I look at you and I think, "How did she get to be nine already?! When did that happen?" But you're still my baby. You still sleep the same way you did when you were just a few weeks old. I'll peek into your room while you're sleeping... not in a creepy way, in a "she's too good to be true so I gotta keep my eye on her to make sure she's really mine" kinda way. Ok, so maybe that is a little creepy. But anyway, sometimes when you're sleeping you'll have your little fist tucked under your chin and you used to do the same thing when you were a baby.

You talk a lot... like me. And when you were a baby, after you were bathed and fed and burped and sitting in your bouncy seat, you would just start talking; baby talk that I didn't understand. But it was cute and it was loud. And I spoke back, to let you know you were being heard and loved. And to get you to continue because it was the sweetest sound I'd ever heard. And when you started talking that baby talk I knew you were tired because every time you did it you would just talk yourself to sleep. You still do that. When Daddy would work nights and you'd crawl in bed with me, you'd just talk, talk, talk till you feel asleep. And even when I would sometimes say, "Kali, will you please go to sleep?" I secretly loved it because it reminded me that my sweet little baby girl was still in there.

9. We are lucky. Not because of the things we have, but because we have each other. You said the other day, "Wow, I can't believe we have such a nice TV and I never even thought we'd have so many game systems." When we're sitting in the family room, like we tend to do a lot lately, we are not lucky because we are surrounded by nice things. We are lucky because we get to sit like that with each other and laugh and joke and smile. We are lucky because we are a family with a Dad that loves us and takes care of us. Because we have a new baby coming that is going to need us, and love us, and bring us more love than we ever thought we could hold. We are lucky, Kali, because we get to spend time with each other.

Try to remember this time, these few weeks before the baby arrives, because you'll be going back to school soon (Eek! Fourth grade! When did *that* happen?), and Daddy will be going back to work, and I'll be busy with Jack and taking classes again and we'll long for the weekends and evenings when everyone can take a breath, relax, and just look at one another. And talk to one another. And spend time with one another. It's going to seem like those moments are few and far between. (That means that it's going to feel like there aren't enough of those moments.) So, we should be thankful that we have them now. Let's soak each other up and appreciate each other. Let's appreciate not that we have lots of nice stuff, but that we have each other. There are plenty of people with nice stuff, but they don't have nearly as much love in their homes as we do.

10. It has been, without a doubt, the greatest joy in my life to be your Mommy. People have told me that I'm pretty, that I'm smart, that I'm funny,

and even that I write well. But the greatest compliment anyone could ever give me is to tell me I'm a good Mom. I try to be. I hope you think I am. It has been the greatest pleasure being your Mom.

When you call me Mommy I will sometimes pretend not to hear what you said just to get you to say it again. Sometimes, when you call me Mommy, I stop and think, "Wow, I *am* her Mommy." And I think how amazing and awesome it is. It makes me feel special. It makes me proud. It fills me with awe.

I love being your Mommy. *Never* forget that.

Love, hugs, kisses, and lots of nose rubbing,

Mommy

Donny's Not a Team Player

July 9, 2008

I hate playing tactical shooting video games with Donny. He just really sucks.

1. When we enter a room, he just enters the room. I peek around corners, lob grenades at bad guys if necessary, I watch my back and clear the room. Not Donny. He just waltzes in and usually ends up with a cap in ass for his efforts.

"Who taught you to clear a room?!"

2. He tosses out grenades all willy-nilly. I can't even count how many times I've been blown up by a Donny grenade.

"Sorry, I didn't see you there."

3. He doesn't follow directions. If we're going down a hallway and I say, "You take the left side, I'll take the right," I'll inevitably end up shooting him in the back of the head because he'll come wandering in front of my crosshairs.

"Stay on your side!"

4. He reloads out in the open. If there's a low wall around, it won't occur to him to crouch there and reload. Nope. Not my Donny. My Donny stands all out in the open, reloading, and taking shots.

"Push in the left joystick to crouch!"

"I know."

"Oh, cause I couldn't tell with all the non-crouching and dying you're doing."

5. He doesn't communicate. I'll be in the middle of a big battle and look on his side of the screen and notice it's all quiet and shit. Birds are chirping, the sun is shining, and no one is shooting him.

"Where the hell are you?"

"I'm at the bridge."

"What bridge?"

"Oh, I must have gone ahead."

"You left me? You suck!"

6. He's an ammo hog. If we come across ammo or health packs, I'll always ask before I pick any up, "How are you on ammo? How's your health?" Not Donny. I'll be running around saying, "Damnit! I need ammo." Donny's response?

"There was a bunch over here, but I got it.

Gee, thanks.

7. He's a horrible driver. He'll drive. I'll jump in the gunner seat and then he has the nerve to yell at me.

"Shoot them!"

"It's kinda hard to shoot when the Warthog's upside down!"

Last night we were playing *Halo*, and after about an hour I lied and said I wasn't feeling well just to not play with him anymore. I found that when it became more enticing to shoot him and lob grenades at his head than the enemy's, it was probably a good time to stop playing.

Kali the Morbid

July 10, 2008

I'm a little worried about my child. A few weeks ago, Donny and I were watching this *Dateline* about a woman who was raped and killed while out jogging and it turned out her body was dumped at the same spot another woman was killed on the anniversary of the first woman's death. So, Kali comes into our room, climbs into our bed between us as she is prone to do, and starts watching.

The *Dateline* narrator says something like, "Susan Smith's body was found later that night. She'd been sexually assaulted and strangled." Then they cut to an interview with the lead investigator. "I'll never forget the way she looked. It was one of the worst crime scenes..."

Kali asks, "How come they're not showing the body?"

I shrug. "They just don't show the bodies on shows like this."

She looked disappointed.

A few days later we're watching the local news, and once again she comes into our room, sits on the bed, and starts watching. They get to this story about finding a dead little girl in a house and apparently her body had been there for over a year. Her family just up and left to Mexico.

"They didn't show the body," Kali points out.

"They don't show bodies on the news."

"Well, that's not very interesting," she sniffed.

Donny and I exchange glances.

Cut to two Saturdays ago and we're driving home from dinner with my parents and sister. It's dark out. We're a few blocks from home when a small animal runs out in front of the car, thinks better of it, and turns to run back the way he came.

"Oh, man. Donny, did I hit it?"

"I don't think so. It was kinda small, but you still would have felt it."

Kali has had her iPod on during all this, but removes the headset to ask, "What are you guys talking about?"

"Mommy almost hit an animal... we're not sure."

"What kind of animal?"

"I don't know." Donny says, "It happened kinda fast."

I offered, "It kinda looked like a mouse, but that would have been one big ass mouse."

"Mommy, if you hit it, it will be all over the car or the tire. You can check when we get home. And if it is, I want to see it."

More exchanged glances.

Turns out, we didn't head straight home. That's the night we went to Wal-Mart to get the stuff we need for the hospital and grabbed an early edition of the Sunday paper so we could get a jump on the sales circulars. When we got home, I was bone tired and I could feel my hands and feet starting to swell. When I walked into my bedroom I noticed the TV was on MSNBC and the program seemed kinda interesting. I went into the master bath, turned on the shower, and called out to Donny, "Don't change the channel. When I come out I want to be able to rewind the TiVo to see that."

When I get out, I climb into bed with Donny, Kali's already in the middle, and I rewind the program. It's one of those caught on tape specials where you see crimes that were, well, caught on tape.

There was the grown ass man over six feet tall and two hundred pounds who starts kicking, hitting, and stepping on the fingers of a 18-month-old baby boy in a convenience store. At one point he purposely hits the baby with the door to a freezer as he opens it to get a beverage. When the baby cries and falls, he spanks him.

There was the 92-year-old man who is leaving a liquor store after playing the lotto and is attacked by a 20-something-year-old male who repeatedly punches him in the face before stealing the old man's car.

There's the skinhead looking guy who enters a supermarket one night and starts shooting people with a shotgun.

And on and on it goes. I realize that I've seen a lot of this stuff on other shows so I start paying less attention to the program and more to the newspaper spread out on the bed. It's not until a commercial comes on and Kali reaches for the TiVo remote to fast forward through the break that I realize she's more into the show than we are. When the commercial is over, she hits play, and Chris Hansen can be heard saying, "Now, back to *Caught on Tape...*"

And Kali says, quite excited, but very seriously, "See! Now *this* is what I like. Caught on tape! You actually get to *see* what happened exactly. This is better than the news. It's more *interesting* when you can see what happened... when it's caught on tape. *This* is what I like."

So, umm, yeah. At this point Donny and I are hoping that her morbid fascination means that she's going to follow in the footsteps of most of my Dad's side of the family: Law enforcement, detectives, avid readers of mysteries and crime novels, etc.

You know, hopefully that than... anything else.

Best Buy and Big Baby

July 11, 2008

I've been extra bitchy lately. I'm always kinda bitchy. And mean. And selfish. And moody. But when you're waiting to push a baby out of your body and the days seem like weeks and just entering his beautiful nursery makes your nipples leak... well, you get a little extra everything.

I had a routine doctor's appointment yesterday. I got up super early. Not out of dedication or preparedness. I just really had to pee. I pee about four times a night. Anyway, I got up around 6:30am. Donny got up then, too, and made me a breakfast of bacon, scrambled egg whites, toast, and juice. Then he went back to bed. It was decided that I'd be going to this appointment alone. I spent some time on the computer paying bills and then I got a bright idea...

We had picked out a camcorder and we knew we were going to get it from *Best Buy* online because their online price was cheaper. Since there's a store near the doctor's office, I thought I'd pay for the camera online (using the $50 gift card they sent us 'cause I completely bitched them out last week over the flat screen) and then pick it up in the store. They open at 10am and my appointment was at 10:30. So, at 9am I bought the camera and printed out the confirmation receipt needed for pickup.

Donny saw me to the car at around 9:30 like I was headed for Iraq and not the hospital 20 minutes away.

"I'll be fiiiiine."

"I know. Just be careful."

He says it's weird when I leave the house alone since I've been cooped up the whole pregnancy. Before, whenever he thought of the baby, all he had to do was look across the room, or find me upstairs to rub my belly. When I'm gone, so is the baby, and he said it was a reminder that he is truly *with me all the time.* I knew what he meant. The other day I went out to get some groceries, and I was cruising along thinking how nice it was to have alone time when he suddenly kicked as if to say, "Uh, no bitch. Not quite."

Anyway, I get to Best Buy about ten minutes before they open so I sit in the first parking spot reserved for internet pick-ups. Now, some of you may remember a few months ago I had a large disagreement with a friend on MySpace and it was over people with children and people without, and what she perceived to be unfair advantages given to people (women) who choose to have kids. I wonder what her reaction is to the Expectant and New Mother parking spaces popping up at some businesses.

To all the non-breeders out there who disagree, kiss my ass. Yeah, I chose to carry around a 6lb baby, 2lbs of amniotic fluid, 2 feet of umbilical cord, and to have my internal organs smushed and shifted. But that don't make this shit any less uncomfortable. If a few businesses want to hook my ass up with a cherry parking spot for my troubles, a-fuckin-men. I'm sure if everyone thought long and hard they'd find instances where they get over where others don't. It's called life. Sometimes it fucks you up the ass and sometimes it gives you sweet little perks simply for knowing how to use the damn internet.

As it gets closer to ten I notice others waiting in their cars with the AC on (too hot to be standing at the door) including this super old couple in a monster SUV in the handicapped spot directly in front of me. When I noticed Grandpa had some papers in his hand that looked suspiciously like an internet confirmation, I knew I had to act fast. At two minutes till, he opened his car door and I damn near broke my neck to get out of my car. I may be a weeble-wobble, but he's still old and I was pretty sure I could take him. By the time I got to the door there was a nice size group of folks waiting behind me. And it's not like it was a single door through which only one person at a time could fit. They were those big sliding glass doors that should they open, anyone could push past me to enter first.

I gave them all my best, "I wish a motherfucker would" face. Yeah, that's right; I played the Pregnant Card *and* the Angry Black Woman card. You know all that normal shit your bodies are doing? Digesting, pumping blood, etc? Yeah, well, mine is doing all of that... for two. I'm doing all that shit and growing a baby so, eat me.

I sail through the store the moment the doors open and head straight for customer service. The young black guy who greets you and checks receipts smiles hello. I know he's like, "Damn. You been here four times in two weeks and you always have on that same dress." Well, fuck you too, Greeter Boy. I ain't tryna buy anymore big girl dresses or drawers. I'm rocking the same two dresses until I go into labor. Then I shall burn them.

The pick-up was pretty uneventful though it did take a bit longer than one minute after handing over the receipt for the girl to fetch my order, and per their rules I coulda got $10 off because of that. But it was like a minute and some loose change and I had a doctor appointment to keep.

As I was in the waiting room, I decided to check out the new camcorder cause I didn't have shit else to do. There was a seal on the box that said, "There's a 15 percent restocking fee if this item is returned opened." The seal was placed so that it would have to be broken if the box was opened. I opened the box and realized that they gave me the wrong damn camera. I ordered the Sapphire Blue one and they gave me the Ruby Red. Motherfuckers.

I was furious and happy at the same time. I was going to go back there and get the fight I'd been itching to have for days now. I finally had someone to take out my frustrations on. I now had a legitimate reason to be a bitch to someone! And they betta not give me no shit about the broken seal or I'll beat 15 percent out that bitch's ass. But they shouldn't, I think, because I'm simply going to trade the camera in for another one, right?

Then several women in the waiting room start talking about recording the birth and most seem sure that the hospital doesn't allow you to film delivery, only the labor. Well, fuck me. That's the reason we bought the damn camera! We were scheduled to tour the hospital that night and I mentally kicked myself for not waiting until after *that* before buying the damn camera. Whatever, they still better not give me no shit, even if I return it.

I just knew that once I told the doctor how miserable I was she'd immediately hook me up with some magic medicine that would make me more comfortable, able to sleep at night, and hopefully something to make the next few weeks fly by. Uh, no. She, another young, black, cute thing named Dr. S, was like, "Yeah, um, that's how it goes. Nothing we can do. It will be over soon." I wanted to punch her in the mouth.

She measured me and then pushed and kneaded my belly like modeling clay. "Oh yeah, this is going to be a good sized baby."

"What do you mean?" my suddenly frightened asshole wanted to know.

"I'd say he's about 6lbs now. He could potentially be 8lbs by delivery."

Lovely.

I carry myself, and my juicy baby, back to Best Buy and explain the mix up to the girl behind the counter. "Oh, let me see what happened." Bitch, I just told you what happened. I ordered blue, I got red. Simple. Never mind the fact that on the fucking box is a big ass picture of the camera in red or that it says Rouge/Red on the side. I didn't see that because when the heifer gave me the camera, it was already in the bag and no, I didn't bother to check because well... I didn't. Look, I'm pregnant, I outweigh you, and I really want to beat someone's ass so if you're volunteering, fine by me. OK, so I didn't say *all that*. But it was *all over my face.*

While she's off "investigating" I start to feel sick. My hands start shaking, I get all sweaty, and I think I'm going to pass out. And I'm thinking, "Please Lord, don't let my big ass hit this floor. That would be embarrassing as fuck." She returns with the right camera, apologizes, and I give a look like, "Better had," but I think it lost some of its bite due to the whole pale and sweaty thing I had going on.

I knew what was wrong. My ass was hungry. It had been a good five hours since I'd eaten. I make a quick stop at the temptation items they have by the exit. I require the assistance of a manager to reach the Sprite, Snickers bar, Twizzlers, and pretzels because they were all really low and I can't bend. Don't judge me! I think half the Snickers bar was gone before I cleared the parking lot.

Big Poppy and Blue Eyes

July 14, 2008

Last night Donny was watching some home run derby or something or other on ESPN. I was on the laptop playing *Slingo Quest* when I happened to look up and notice this black guy in the stands that the camera kept focusing on.

"Who's that?" I asked.

"Big Poppy."

"What?"

"That's his name."

"Don't call him that."

Then a woman starts interviewing him and the caption has his name listed as David Ortiz (I *think* it was David, but I'm positive it was Ortiz.)

"Oh, his name is David Ortiz." I said.

"Yeah, I couldn't remember his name."

"Well, remember it from now on."

A moment later a commentator refers to Mr. Ortiz as Big Poppy.

"See, he just did it." Donny said.

"I don't care what *he* just did. *You* never call him that again. I just don't want to hear my husband refer to another grown ass man as Big Poppy. Biggie never had men calling him Big Poppa. Only bitches and hos. It just wasn't done."

A bit later...

We were watching Sunday night's *Big Brother* when the black girl pointed out that her children are biracial (her husband is white) and that her five month old twins (a boy and a girl) are very different. Her daughter has blond hair, blue eyes and white like the father, and the son is brown like her. Donny asks...

"What if the baby has blue eyes."

"He won't."

"How do you know?"

"Remember a few weeks ago I asked if any of your siblings had blue eyes or anyone in your family that you could think of? I was looking it up on the internet. The possibility... and there is none. I don't remember the details but it's something about a gene that at least one of us has to have and neither of us do."

"Yeah, but I don't know anything about my Dad's side of the family and he was German."

Donny's Dad was killed by a drunk driver when Donny was a small boy.

I sighed. "Donny, I already have one child that makes people look at me like I'm the nanny. Can I just have *one* chocolate drop of a baby?"

"Sure. A chocolate drop with blue eyes."

This conversation was particularly weird because earlier that day, all out of nowhere, Kali asked me, "Mommy, what if the baby has blue eyes?"

"Then Mommy got some 'splainin' to do."

"Huh?"

"Never mind."

I Have the Worst Poop Luck

September 5, 2008

Since this blog is going to be about poop I might as well address something I've been meaning to write about for months now.

I hate pooping.

Intellectually, I know *why* we need to do it. But emotionally, it bothers me. I hate everything about pooping - The way it feels, the way it smells, the time it takes, and the way a particularly nasty one can leave you feeling like you need a shower. You know what I mean. A poop so bad wiping ain't enough. You might as well jump straight into the shower when you're done.

Back when I used to smoke, and work at MCI, I would go out to big lunches almost every day. And without fail, as soon as I got back to my desk, my friend Shay would shoot me an IM and ask if I wanted to go out for a cig. We'd go smoke and when we were done, she'd head for the bathroom. She said after a meal and a smoke she always had to poop and she looked forward to it. It was her afternoon delight. I thought it was absolutely disgusting and preferred to do all my pooping at home. My stepfather had to start everyday with a hearty poop. He looked forward to it. If I had to begin every day with a dump I'd be one depressed bitch.

Remember the poop blog where I got poop *on* not *in* my hand? Remember that it got all over my platinum and diamond wedding rings and I was torn as to what to clean first, my hand or my rings? And I chose my rings cause that's how I roll? Remember the blog where I got so drunk I had it coming out both ends and I actually took a moment to ponder should I shit in the tub while vomiting in the toilet or vice versa? See? I tell you all my poop stories. Well, except one. I never told you the Poopy Pillow story. I know this because after it happened Donny laughed so hard with tears in his eyes and said, "You need to blog about that!" And I responded, "Shut the fuck up. No I don't."

Well, here's another... that just happened like five minutes ago.

I've been wearing glasses since the beginning of my pregnancy. I can't wear contacts while pregnant because they irritate my eyes. Also, I've been wearing green contacts since I was 17 and just like when Kali was born, I felt it kinda weird to have your newborn get to know you, look you in the eyes, and not see your *real* eyes. So, I wear glasses now except when I'm up close with Jack and then I take them off because I want him to *really* look into my eyes. Anyway, my point again, is that I wear glasses.

A few minutes ago I went to the bathroom. I had to poop and pee. I took my new book, *Twilight*, because I can't put the fucker down. I'm serious. I'm thisclose to scrawling Edward Cullen all over my Trapper Keeper with little hearts and arrows. So, I'm on the bowl reading and doing my thing. I wipe and then notice there's a dead spider on the floor. Great. Either Kali or Donny killed the spider, but didn't bother to clean it up. I grab another wad of tissue and deposit the corpse in the toilet. Then, I'm not really sure what happened.

I blame the damn book. Instead of just putting the damn book down so I could pull up my pants, flush, wash my hands, etc., I'm trying to still read and do all those things and somehow my glasses fell off my face and into the pissy, poopy, spidery carcass water.

GROSS!

If I'd stopped to think about it too much, I might have just tried to flush those fuckers down the toilet with everything else. But instinct kicked in, and before I could think of the nastiness of my actions, I reached in, grabbed the glasses, and tossed them in the bathroom sink. I activated the stopper and filled the sink with hot, scalding water. I added some hand soap, and a healthy shot of Mr. Clean.

See? I have the worst poop luck!

I would share the Poopy Pillow story, but it's bad. That's between me, Donny, the pillow, and God.

The Day Donny Has Been Waiting For

September 18, 2008

As of this Monday, Jack is six-weeks-old. Six weeks is the length of time given for a woman to recover from a vaginal delivery. Now, I can take baths, use tampons, have sex, and lift objects heavier than my son. I know I've been all judgmental towards women who had sex before the six weeks were up. And I felt bad about that. Until I gave birth to Jack, and realized three weeks later that I definitely didn't want anyone going near my vagina. Hell, I could barely walk down the stairs. I'm still feeling kinda unsure on my feet at times, and my pelvic bones aches, but I think it's my body getting used to all this damn weight!

But, I'm not alone. Over the past 11 months Donny has put on sympathy weight. He's 20lbs heavier. He hates it. I love it. I feel like he evened the playing field. Besides, he was skinny before so 20lbs ain't gonna kill him. I think he looks great. Then again, I can't remember the last time I had sex so everyone looks good to me. I'm watching *School for Scoundrels* now and having dirty thoughts about Billy Bob Thorton.

We've been working out together on the *Wii Fit*. We were both skeptical as to whether or not it could provide a real workout. It does. I was using it before Donny so he wasn't aware of all the features. That damn *Wii Fit* can be mean! First of all, when I step on the balance board it will sometimes exclaim, "Oh!" Like, "Oh, it's like *that*! You're bigger than I expected, but that's okay. That's why I'm here; to get your big ass in shape." Last night we worked out even though we usually try to work out between 5am and 6am. When I did the daily body test it told me I'd gained a pound since the day before. Then it suggests that I think about why that is. THEN, it makes you choose from a list as to why your big ass is still big. Donny nearly rolled off the couch laughing.

"That's cruel."

"I know," I sighed as I pointed the controller at the screen and chose, "Eats too much."

Another thing I'm able to do is resume my wifely duties of cooking every night. In preparation for this, I made my first serious grocery shopping trip since getting pregnant. Donny and I headed out to the Super Wal-Mart this morning with Jack. People would take one look at Donny and me, and want to peek in the stroller. Almost everyone we encountered. I don't know if it's 'cause we're an interracial couple or I'm so fine. Either way, they just had to see what we produced and they were never disappointed.

"He's so handsome!'

"I know, right?!" I kid, I kid. I would just respond with a humble, "Thank you."

It's funny watching the new Donny shop. He wanted to buy the worst foods. I had to remind him that we're both trying to lose weight so we needed to keep the snack foods to a minimum. Donny wanted to buy Halloween candy *now*.

"Let's get some Caramel Apple kisses."

"Let's not."

"Why not?"

"Donny, that candy will be gone before October gets here."

Then...

"Oooh, Chicken in a Biskit."

"No."

"Come on, they're fat-free."

"Yeah, too bad they're not nasty-free."

Anyway, not only is life getting back to normal since Jack was born; it's a better kind of normal. We, of course, have our moments. Sometimes we're a little sleep deprived and we'll snap at each other, but for the most part we laugh and smile a lot more than we ever did. And sometimes it's just the simplest things that will set us off, like pulling out of the Wal-Mart parking lot today.

"What's that guy doing?"

"Which one?"

"Donny, the guy right there with the cigarette."

"Nina, that's a woman."

"Nuh-uh," I say, craning my neck from the back seat to get a better look.

"Nina, I'm telling you, that's a woman. She's a manager here."

"But... but.. look at the rat-tail."

An Answer to an Age Old Question

September 22, 2008

The answer to "If a tree falls in the forest and no one is around to hear it, does it still make a sound?," is the same as the answer to, "If you do something humiliating and there's no one around to witness it, do you still feel like a fucktard?"

Yes. Absolutely, yes.

Last night, I did something I hadn't done in many, many years.

I dreamt I had to pee really badly and was so relieved when I was finally able to sit upon a toilet and, well, relieve myself. Only to find that as I pissed in my dream, I was actually pissing in the bed.

And though Jack and Donny slept through the ordeal, I still felt like an asshole. When I told Donny about it today he asked, "Are you going to blog about it?"

"Uh, no."

"Ha! I'll blog about it."

"You will not. You don't have a blog."

"I'll get one."

Bastard.

So, I come clean (so to speak) myself.

My name is Nina. I am 34-years-old. And last night, I peed the bed.

Balls

September 24, 2008

Donny and I are very sarcastic with each other. Kali quickly learned that Mommy and Daddy aren't fighting when they're being rude, sarcastic, or even yelling at each other. She's used to it. It's how we roll. It's all in fun. We sometimes forget that other people may not realize that we're not serious when we call each other jackass or threaten a beatdown. A perfect example would be us in the aisle at the supermarket.

Donny may ask, "Why are you walking so slow? You move like an old lady."

"Yo mama moves like an old lady."

Anyone within earshot may think dems fighting words. But they're not. I like my mother-in-law. I just like the way "yo mama" flows off my tongue. It's my standard comeback to Donny. I can honestly say that when I say it, his mother is the furthest thing from either of our minds.

But I've noticed that Donny has gotten a little *extra* smartassy lately. His threats have taken on an air of... certainty. There are threats of backhands, feet up my ass, and ass beatings. And now, I think I know why.

We were in the car leaving the pediatrician's office the other day.

"What do you want for lunch?" he asked.

"I don't care."

"Yes, you do. You always say you don't care and then I pick something and you don't want it."

"Whatever you want is fine with me, Donny."

"Woman, just pick something before I come back there."

Pause.

"You know, Donny. Jack's balls are not your balls."

"What?"

"I mean, just cause Jack has balls doesn't make your balls bigger. You can't just be acting all like you actin' 'cause there's an extra set of balls in the house. 'Cause, you know, I'll still fuck you up."

"You can try."

He laughs, is silent for a moment, and then says...

"Those are my backup balls."

I've Gotta Find My Groove
October 20, 2008

Today is Donny's first day back to work. Kali's in school. It's just me and Jack.

As I type this I am topless, in panties, with Jack falling asleep against my left boob and a burpee pressed against the right one to catch any milk drippings. I disrobed because I thought I was going to be able to jump in the shower, but Jack had other plans. After I post this I will lay Jack on my bed. If I'm lucky, he'll sleep long enough for me to shower and run downstairs and grab a cup of coffee and some type of breakfast.

Though I technically can't diet, today is the day I start... well, scratch that. Today is the day I STOP eating a bunch of crap. I gave myself six months to lose baby weight and I've wasted two of them just eating anything I wanted and working out sporadically. Today is the day I get serious. I can't eat less, but I can eat better. (I went shopping yesterday and stocked the house in preparation.) During his afternoon nap I plan on hitting the *Wii Fit* and elliptical machine.

But first, I need to wash my ass. So, if I can just... place... him... down... quietly...

You know, it struck me last night as I loaded the dishwasher that I am going to be a stay-at-home Mom for the first time in like five years. I stayed home with Kali until she started Pre-K. After getting laid off from MCI, I went back to school, always making sure that I took classes that allowed me to put Kali on the school bus and be home by the time she got home.

I'm not knocking mothers who can't do it, but I feel like it's so important to be home when your kids get out of school. I can't explain it. Maybe because I didn't have that. But, I think it sets a good familial tone when at least one parent is home when the children get out of school; to be there to ask about their day, prepare a snack, and supervise homework. And for the past few years my stay-at-home momminess (just made that up) was really just doing that. It's not hard to be a stay-at-home Mom when your kids aren't at home, but rather in school all day.

Now, though, with Jack I *am* a stay-at-home Mom. I'm scheduling my classes around being home with him ALL day which means online classes and/or evening classes.

Boy, I gotta get back on track. The old Nina, who stayed home with toddler Kali, would not be sitting here at 9am with her titties hanging out, hungry, thirsty, and smelling like breast milk. The old Nina would have had breakfast, showered, and knocked out at least one chore.

I'll find my groove. I'm just a little out of practice.

Bagel Outrage
October 26, 2008

I'm not one of those Yankees who move to the south and constantly bashes it. I'm not going to rant about how the people can't drive (they can't) and how if there's the tiniest sprinkling of moisture in the air they drive slower than my grandfathers (they do; who are both dead and one was legally blind), or how you can't find a decent slice of pizza to save your northern heart (you can't), or how there are still pockets of racial intolerance (there are.)

Why? Because the south has several redeeming qualities that make all of the above tolerable. Two of which are sweet tea and great houses at reasonable prices.

But I've come across a greater atrocity that cannot be ignored any longer: the inability to find a decent bagel in the state of Georgia. Newsflash: Lender's bagels aren't bagels. Thomas' Bagels aren't bagels. I need a New York City deli bagel. Think a massive hunk of carbs that makes your jaw hurt when you chew it. Slather on some cream cheese and that's a meal. Add a cup of steaming coffee and that's heaven. I can't find that here and after 15 years, I can't take it anymore!

Wanna know the the final rape of the fine delicacy that is a bagel? The Olsen twins revealed on *Oprah* that one of them (I don't know, nor care, which) scoops out the inside of a bagel and adds cream cheese to it before she eats it. Let me repeat that. She scoops out the inside of the bagel. What the fuck? What's the point? That's like eating a pizza without cheese. A hot dog without mustard. It's pointless. And un-American. Michelle Bachmann should be calling an investigation of *that*.

How Donny Almost Died

October 27, 2008

Let me start with a little back story leading up to Sunday so you may all better understand my state of mind.

Kali stayed home Thursday and Friday with a bad cough and cold. If there's one thing I hate about this time of year, and it probably is only the one thing, is the return to school means the return of catching cooties. I was trying to take care of her *and* Jack while keeping them separated. On Friday, around 11am, Jack threw a holy fit. He was fed and changed, but no matter what I did he continued to cry and squirm. I knew he was getting sick.

By Saturday he had a stuffy nose and slight cough, but never a fever. Sometime Saturday early evening, he was being particularly fussy when Donny said, "I wonder if he has a sore throat because I do."

WHAT?

When was he going to tell me this? I was pretty pissed. For the first time in nine years together, I made him sleep in the guest bedroom. So, he's all knocked out downstairs and I'm left upstairs with a sick, cranky baby. And I was hungry and thirsty. By the way, since I'm breastfeeding I'm ALWAYS thirsty. Seriously. When I get something to drink I usually down the first glass right away and then settle with a second. Anyway, I'm hungry, thirsty, sleepy, but I don't want to leave Jack alone and I don't want sick ass Donny and Kali around him either... though he was already sick.

Donny must have known he was creeping up my shit list because when Jack and I woke up on Sunday, Donny brought me breakfast in bed. So

Sunday, yesterday, we're chilling in the bedroom. We're watching stuff off the TiVos because they're all getting backed up. While watching one show we'd be transferring another from another room into the bedroom so it would be ready to go. I was on the laptop playing Scrabble. Occasionally, one of us would leave the room to go switch out a load of laundry, go the bathroom, etc.

I'm watching TV and playing away when suddenly Jack starts screaming. I hadn't noticed, but while he was laying on his back on our bed, minding his own damn business, his father decided to take the baby nail clippers provided by the hospital to clip his nails. Now, you all should know that I have asked/told Donny not to use clippers on Jack until he's much older. With Kali, I would either bite or file her nails down. All the baby books recommend holding off using clippers because it's easy to clip too much and possibly hit a nerve.

Everyone thinks I have the perfect husband, and most times, like 99.9 percent of the time I do. But Donny. doesn't. fucking. listen. I know this about my husband. Maybe because I'm so controlling he has to find little ways to exert his own power, but he picked a bad fucking time to do it yesterday.

He immediately scooped Jack up and started pacing with him trying to calm him down. I'm cussing his ass out. Not only was he doing what I asked him NOT to do, but it was dark as hell in our bedroom. I keep the door to the master bathroom closed and the door leading out to the hall closed because I hate sunlight. So, if he was going to be a jackass and clip the baby's nails, one would think he would at least do it with decent light.

Jack settled down pretty quickly and Donny assured me he was fine. I'm thinking he probably pinched his skin. So, we're back to watching TV. Jack is lying on the bed in front of Donny, on his back, and falling asleep. I remember we were watching *The Unit* and a loud explosion on the screen startled Jack, but he quickly went back to sleep. I'm not sure how much time had passed - maybe ten minutes - when I looked and realized that both Donny and Jack were gone.

I thought that was odd. The only places Donny could have gone were downstairs to get something to eat or drink, or down the hall to switch out a load of laundry. None of those things required Jack's presence. So, I paused the TiVo and headed downstairs calling along the way, "Donny?"

"Yeah?"

"Where's Jack?"

"Right here."

"What are you doing?"

And then Kali calls out, "Cleaning him up."

Now, at first I thought they were giving him a bath, but why would he be doing that now and without me? I enter the guest bedroom and there's my baby on the bed, in nothing but a diaper, Kali's rubbing his head and Donny is putting a small band-aid on his finger. Kali says, "His finger won't stop bleeding."

I literally saw red. I snatched him up.

"I'm taking care of it, Nina," Donny said. And to his credit he sounded heartbroken, but I didn't care.

"Yeah, you're doing a real good job taking care of him. Give me my son."

And I stomped upstairs. Donny followed and I slammed the bedroom door behind me. I sat on my bed trying to assess the damage, but I couldn't tell how bad it was because of the blood. Donny sat next to me and I allowed him to put the band-aids on. Jack is now screaming and I start to nurse him to keep him calm. All is well until I glance down at the band-aid put on not fifteen seconds prior and see that it is SOAKED with blood.

I yell at Donny to take it off. I take some gauze and apply pressure to try and stop the bleeding. Every time I checked, it would spill blood and I couldn't tell what the problem was exactly. The whole time, by the way, I'm cussing Donny's ass out. I don't even remember all I said. I know at one point he said something like, "I feel horrible. I feel like the world's worst father and you're making me feel worse."

And I replied, "Good. You should. Because I fucking told you not to use those things on him."

And so you know, I'm not downplaying my words so you will all think better of me. No. I fully admit I was a cussing, evil, pissed off mother bear yesterday and I was cussing his ass out. I'm downplaying it because the more I think about it, the more pissed off I get and for Donny's sake I need to stay mellow. He doesn't want to come from work today to death.

I called my Dad and asked if he'd come sit with Kali while we took Jack to the pediatric ER and filled him in on what happened. He said we should keep applying pressure and he'll meet us at the ER and take Kali back to our house, but he thought it would be best if we got going and not waited for him to get to our house.

So, off we went. We were signed in and there only about five minutes before I saw my Dad pull into the parking lot. Holding Jack, I met him at the automatic doors. I'd just recently gotten the bleeding to stop and showed my Dad the damage. A crescent shaped piece of nail was missing from Jack's right thumb. The skin underneath was exposed and raw. Just thinking about it makes me want to call Donny now and cuss his ass out.

We sat down and waited to be called. Donny was across the waiting room with Kali. He knew to give me space. My Dad whispered that when he hung up with me he told my stepmother, "She sounds amazingly calm. But I know she's pissed." My stepmother had the same response, "What was he thinking?" She'd been around during one of our conversations about how it's best to file the baby's nails.

While we were in triage, the nurse kinda tsk tsk'd Donny for using the clippers, but told me not to be too hard on him. Too late. While we waited to be called to the doctor, Donny went to get Kali something to drink from the vending machine. He came back with something for her and him, but not me or my Dad.

"You know, did you decide you weren't high enough on my shit list? Do you want to take Kali out to the parking lot and push her in front of a moving car?"

A short while later Kali was hungry so he took her to Wendy's and of course, that's when we were called. My Dad went back with me and the doctor told us that Jack didn't need stitches and that it was best to keep it clean and uncovered. As for the cold, she told me what I already knew which was that without a fever, there's nothing to do but to let the cold run its course and she agreed with the saline drops and suction in his nose we'd been doing already.

It was a two and a half hour ordeal I'd rather not have gone through. I know Donny feels bad, and I'm less pissed than I was yesterday, but I'm still upset. There was a moment when I was holding Jack, trying to nurse him and keep pressure on his thumb, and he kept moving his hand and blood would get everywhere (his face, my boob, my bra, etc.), where I came thisclose to punching Donny in the face. Seriously. And in the few seconds it took me to think it (just put Jack down on the bed in front of you and haul off and punch him in the face), I just as quickly realized how wrong it would be. But I was *that* angry.

And it's not because I don't expect there to be accidents, but this one could have been avoided. There was no good explanation, and he didn't dare offer one, for using those clippers after I'd repeatedly asked him not to.

When we got home I called my friends Lacey and Brett who I knew would be worried. When I told them that Donny was downstairs making dinner and pretty much walking around like a puppy who knows it did something wrong, Lacey said, "Whenever Donny sees you coming he's just going to piss on the carpet."

When my Dad and I were in the exam room waiting for the doctor to come in, my Dad told Jack, "You can milk this thumb for video games and bikes, Jack. Get caught playing hooky from school? Just tell your Dad you skipped school 'cause your thumb hurt."

Well, When You Put it Like THAT

November 25, 2008

The other day I was talking to one of my single, childless girlfriends and she was going on and on about the things that I used to think were so important back before I found "the one," got married, had two kids, and a mortgage. I tried not to get frustrated as I listened to her, keeping a watchful eye on my sleeping, beautiful, precious baby boy. I was worried about his upcoming physical therapy appointment, stressed over an issue with Kali and some little boy on the school bus, and about ten other things.

I listened as she pondered why some guy hadn't called. Had she been a little too easy? I wanted to say, "Yes, you probably were. And if he doesn't call, fuck him. Not literally. You already did that. But figuratively. Just get over it." Because in my mind I'm thinking there is more to life than this bullshit. And I smugly thought how wonderful it was that I didn't have to worry about such nonsense anymore. I have real, grown-up problems, damn it! I'm responsible for the lives of two people!

Finally, I couldn't take it any longer. In the spirit of Thanksgiving, I felt the need to point out all that she had to be thankful for, and that she shouldn't be wasting time on silliness when the rest of us have real worries that go beyond what some random guy thinks of us after giving up the butt. I pointed out that she was independent, attractive, smart, and made decent money. And though I don't regret my life at all, I wouldn't mind having some of her "problems" for a couple of days.

Then she said, "Yeah, but you know what? You get more love in a day than I get in a month."

And I didn't know what to say. "Um, there are your parents..." I offered this up lamely.

"True, but that's different. I want someone like Donny. I want someone to love me who doesn't have to. You are so lucky that a good man decided he wants to spend the rest of his life with you. He *chose* you."

Well, when you put it like *that*.

I guess when you're so busy living your life you don't realize how lucky/blessed you are. This time last year I wrote a blog about the things I was thankful for. It is because of that blog that my friend Emily was able to help me pinpoint the exact night our son was conceived.

I usually stay up later than Donny, like now, writing or watching TV. When I'm ready to fall asleep I'll turn out the light and cuddle next to him. Most times I'll wake him up just long enough for him to spoon me. That particular night, a year ago, I remember thinking, "If I wake his ass up he's gonna want some. Do I want some too or do I just want to sleep?" I woke him up. In the blog I wrote something like, "I am grateful for my husband who, when I woke him to spoon with me made love to me instead and then replied, 'Oh. Sorry' when I later said, 'That's not why I woke you up.'"

So, this year my list goes a little something like this:

- I am grateful for my husband who works hard and loves me and our children so much he looks forward to the weekends, not so he can go hang with friends, but because he gets to spend full days with us.

- I am grateful for Kali who remains sweet and funny, who loves her little brother so much. She is so protective of him. If she's holding him and I go to give him his pacifier she always says, in a cute baby voice, "No, no. He don't need it. He don't need it. Tell her, Jack. Tell her you're fine. You're not fussing." And then there are the times when she looks at him, he smiles back, and then she coos, "Look at those big brown eyes. They're just the biggest brown eyes." I'm proud that her parent/teacher conference revealed that she's a talented writer who comes up with stories well beyond her years. My daughter rocks.

- I am grateful for Jack who is dubbed by everyone that meets him, "the happiest baby ever." He smiles at you when you look at him. He is just starting to belly laugh which makes us laugh because what does he know about belly laughing?! I love that whenever he wakes up he looks around confused for a second until he catches my eye and I say, "Hi, my handsome boy. Did you sleep okay?" and then he smiles and puts his head down like he's shy and the popular girl just looked his way. And then I melt and scoop him up for wake up kisses which are just as sweet as the million other kisses we share throughout one day.

- I am grateful that this Thanksgiving the four of us are staying home for our first Thanksgiving as a family of four. Just us. Lots of food. Lit trees. Lit fireplace. Some movies, naps, Guitar Hero, and love.

- I am grateful that the words, "I love you" are spoken amongst the four of us *every single day*. Kali and I say it before she leaves for school, and Donny and I tell her again before bed. I tell Jack all day long and he tells me with those big brown eyes. Donny and I say it every day when he calls around 11:30am to check on us.

- I am grateful for my family and friends who tolerate my crazy ass. Especially Sophie who knows me. Everyone needs a friend that *knows* them.

- I am grateful for my education, for my drive and determination to spend 2009 chasing my dreams.

And you all; I'm grateful for every one of you.

Like Pulling Teeth
December 2, 2008

I have never had the desire to hit my child until last week. And then I wanted to kill her. Kali has had a new tooth growing in behind a baby tooth that wasn't budging. We were advised to leave it alone, and that the new tooth would eventually push out the old one. Well, that didn't happen. She'd been complaining that the old tooth was pushing into her bottom lip. I made an appointment for her to go to the dentist on Thursday morning.

She was very nervous over the possibility of having a tooth pulled. I understood this, and tried to display the appropriate patience. My father agreed to take us to the morning appointment so that Donny wouldn't have to take any time from work. While Kali and I went into the back, my Dad stayed in the waiting room with a sleeping Jack.

The dental assistant explained that first they would be taking x-rays of Kali's teeth. She seemed to handle this news well – she had x-rays of her hand and foot before. The assistant placed the tabs in Kali's mouth and asked her to bite down. Kali began to cry.

"What's wrong with you?" I asked.

"It hurts."

"It's not doing anything but sitting in your mouth."

We finally get her to bite down and then we both scoot out of the area so that the x-ray can be taken. Just as it's about to, Kali starts to gag and spit out the tabs. The assistant and I go over to her.

"What happened?"

Kali now has tears streaming down her face, she's breathing all heavy, and her bottom lip is quivering.

"I… don't… want… to… be… here. I… want… to… go… home."

Through clenched teeth I said, "Kali. Cut it out. They're just taking a photo of your teeth. It's not going to hurt you."

She was being a TOTAL drama queen. And to make it even worse, I guess the assistant didn't like the way I chose to handle it because she kept being overly nice about the situation any time I said anything.

Bitch, this ain't good cop bad cop. This is, I'm the Mommy and you work here so just shut the hell up and let me deal with my child.

We tried to get the x-rays a few more times, but the machine was broken so she said we'd do it when Kali goes back next week for a cleaning. By this time, Jack was awake so he and my Dad joined us in the back.

The dentist finally comes in, takes one look at the tooth and declares that it needs to come out. She said we could do it now or later. I chose now. And Kali lost her shit. She was crying and heaving and acting like we'd just sentenced her to death. When she said she had to go to the bathroom, I said I'd go with her. Part of me was afraid she'd pass out and crack her head open on the sink, but mainly I was concerned that if there was a window in the bathroom, Kali's ass might be ghost.

When the dentist applied the numbing gel to her gums, Kali had the nerve to ask, "How much more are you going to put on there?" The dentist and I replied at the same time, "Oh, you *want* this." I'd forgotten about the numbing gel before the actual needle. When it was time for the needle, from my position at her side and holding her hand, I told Kali to close her eyes. But because other people were talking, she didn't hear me so she saw the needle coming.

"What's that? What's that?"

"Remember that stinging little pinch I told you about? Well, that's it, but it won't hurt 'cause of all that gel, okay?"

Thankfully, she didn't even react when the needle went in. By the time the tooth was actually pulled, Kali was a trooper. She didn't even know it was out until she was sitting up and asking what the gauze was for.

"The blood," I said.

My father said I shouldn't have mentioned the blood.

"Why? The tooth is already out. She's gonna see the blood eventually."

"Wait. My tooth is out?"

All that drama for nothing. They put her tooth in a plastic pouch which she insisted on playing with later that evening.

"Girl, go put that tooth under your pillow before you lose it."

"I'm gonna put my tooth under a different pillow to see if the tooth fairy can guess which pillow."

"Listen, she ain't got time for games."

Later that night, before bed, I said to Donny, "I got twenty dollars cash back when I bought groceries earlier and the machine gave me four five dollar bills. I meant to stop at Starbucks or something and use the change to put under Kali's pillow, but I didn't have time. Before you leave for work, can you get one of the fives out of my jeans' pocket and put it under her pillow?"

He agreed.

That next morning, I woke up about ten minutes later than usual and Jack was up as well. I was nursing him when I realized that I couldn't put off waking up Kali any longer, or she'd run the risk of missing the bus. I was cradling/nursing Jack and headed towards Kali's room when something told me to check my jeans. Sure enough, all four five dollar bills were there. Damn, Donny.

I grabbed one, and still holding the baby, I made my way to Kali's room. I'm standing over her bed, watching her sleep, and trying to figure out which pillow the tooth is under without waking her up. I squat down and try the obvious; the one her head is on. I pass my hand under the pillow and I don't feel the bag with the tooth. Damnit, Kali! I try searching under the dozens of other pillows, but holding Jack is making it difficult. I place him on the bed next to Kali, and begin to search again. No luck. And then...

"Hey! Hey!"

Yes, that was Jack saying the only word he knows in an effort to wake up his sister. And it worked. I was wearing a pair of panties and a t-shirt so I quickly stashed the five dollar bill in the back of my panties.

Kali wakes up and for one moment I thought, maybe she forgot. No such luck. The first thing she did was lift the pillow her head was on and because I don't see the bag with the tooth, I'm wondering if maybe it fell behind the bed. Maybe I can just hand her the five dollars saying I took it from under her pillow moments before she woke up, and I can worry about finding the tooth later.

"She didn't take my tooth!"

"What?"

"It's right here!"

"Right where?"

"Here!" And she points to this tiny tooth, not in the plastic baggie, that blended in perfectly with the design of her sheets.

Son of a bitch.

"Well, why did you take it out of the bag? Maybe she couldn't find it. Maybe it was hard to see. Maybe you shouldn't make it so hard on the tooth fairy. Leave it there, she'll come back tonight."

I made plans to make the switch while she was at school and then claim that she must have come while Jack and I were napping.

Later that morning, after she left for school, I went to the bathroom. And I was just pulling up my panties and about to flush when I remember the money. I didn't feel it in my panties… and looked down to see it floating in pee water.

Perfect.

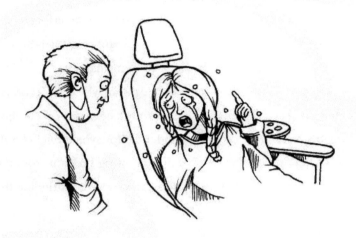

A Penis by Any Other Name

December 8, 2008

The other day Sophie and I were on the phone and Jack, who was lying across my lap on his belly, farted.

"Aww, Jack tooted." I said.

"Tooted? What's that?"

"He farted."

"You guys have names for everything. A pacifier is a bo-bo, bowel movements are poo-poo, and fart is toot."

"That's right. We call his penis a wee-wee or a worm." I added.

"What?"

"Yup. What do you call it?"

Sophie has a son, Leo, who's about to turn 2, and a daughter, Zoe, who's 5. "We call it a penis and a vagina." She said.

"That's weird."

"Why is that weird? The other day Leo and Zoe were sitting on the floor with their legs open rolling a ball back and forth and the ball hit Leo in his diaper. He said, 'That's my penis!'

I laughed. "Sophie, that is weird. Your children are going to grow up sexually repressed."

"Why?"

"Because no one uses those words."

"What's wrong with saying penis and vagina?"

"Uh, the words are PENIS and VAGINA. They're so clinical."

"There's nothing wrong with Leo knowing the proper word is penis."

"If you want to make sure he never gets laid, sure."

"Nina!"

"Think about it. When we're kids, we have cute names for it, when he's a teenager he'll call it dick, cock, johnson, etc., and when he's an adult having sex he'll come up with even filthier names for it. No one says penis or vagina except doctors."

"What do you use for vagina?"

"Poo-poo or cootie cat."

"Example."

"'Kali, go take a bath and make sure you wash your poo-poo.'"

"So, let me get this straight. Poo-poo means both shit and vagina?"

"Yup."

"See, this is why kids should know the real names for their body parts. If Kali were molested, God forbid, and had to testify and said, 'He touched my poo-poo,' they'd throw it out of court!"

"No, 'cause I'd know he either touched her shit or vagina. Either way, I'm fucking him up. Also, I didn't say she doesn't *know* the correct names, we just don't *use* them."

"Why not?"

"Because! They're *penis* and *vagina* and it just sounds weird."

"What do you call your boobs?"

"Boobs."

Silence.

"Or ninny-jugs." I add.

"What? Nina! What are ninny-jugs?"

"The jugs from which he gets his ninny, ninny being milk."

"That makes no sense."

"Why? What do you call them? Lactation orbs?" I snorted

"You're not funny. What do you call pee?"

"Pee-pee. Why? Do you make your kids say urinate? 'Leo, come urinate in the urination vessel.'"

"Shut up. I guess I'm just sensitive because I told you what my mother made me call my vagina when I was a kid, right?"

"You did, but I forgot. Tell me again."

"Munchie."

"Oh, she was just setting you up to be a lesbian, huh?"

"I hate you."

Taking Jack to the ER

December 9, 2008

I'm a good mother. I know I am. I adore my kids. I would do anything for my kids. There's not an ass born yet that I wouldn't kick for my kids.

And I know my kids. The other day Kali got off the school bus with her head hunkered down under her coat's hood. It was rainy and cold. Like a mother out of a freakin' commercial I greeted her at the door and asked if she'd like some chicken noodle soup. I'd recently bought a huge case of *Campbell's* from Sam's Club. You'd have thought I was stocking a panic room. Kali declined the soup as she kicked off her sneakers, but kept on her coat, claiming fatigue and slowly made her way up the stairs. I paused for a moment then followed.

By the time I reached the second landing she was already in her room at the top of the stairs, closing the door behind her. She left it open a sliver, peeking at me through the crack.

"Well, if you change your mind..."

"Okay," she said and closed the door.

I stood there for a moment and realized that my child was hiding something from me. I opened her door to find her taking off her coat by her bed. I expected to find that she'd left her sweater in school or something and was afraid she'd get in trouble. But she had the sweater on.

"Are you hiding something from me?"

"Well, I did take my hair out in school and I lost my scrunchie."

Ah, I then realized her raven, curly, long hair was free flowing and not in the neat ponytail I'd put it in that morning, and every morning before that.

"Well, if it's tangled tonight when I brush it, I don't wanna hear your mouth."

I suppose I should have yelled at her for trying to be sneaky, but Jack was sleeping and I didn't want to wake him as I saw a nap in *my* near future. See, a good mother.

And though Jack has only been with us for four months, I know him too. My baby isn't a constant crier or whiner. So, when he was downright inconsolable last week, I knew his slight cold had taken a turn for the worst. I took his temperature under his armpit and it was 100.2. I called the doctor and was told that to get an accurate reading I'd have to take his temperature rectally.

"Can you hold on one sec?"

"Sure."

"DONNY! Come take Jack's temperature."

I don't think anyone should be sticking anything up anybody's booty hole at any time for any reason. But being a good mother means that I will not think about myself and always do what's in the best interest of my children. And by "do" I mean, "have Donny do."

The doctor instructs, "Just stick it in until you can no longer see the silver tip." I relay this to Donny and he does. 101.2. I'm told that for his size and age that I shouldn't bring him in until it's 102.2 or higher. Also, just keep giving him Infant's Tylenol every four hours. We took his temperature rectally for the next few days.

Just yesterday I told my Mom about it and I told her how calm Jack was when we took it. Totally unlike the first time it happened to him: He was just a few minutes old and past that just entered the world crying jag. He was lying in the warmer calmly staring at his sister while a nurse cleaned him up. Then she stuck the thermometer up his ass and Jack lost his shit. My Dad has the whole thing on video. Anyway, back to my Mom...

"Yeah, you don't stick it in much and most babies do just fine. Just put some Vaseline on it and they're okay."

Silence.

"You did put Vaseline on it, didn't you?"

"Hey! Donny took it, not me!"

See? A good mother.

"You ask Donny how'd he like it if I came down there and stuck a dry stick up his ass?"

Better him than me.

When Jack woke up crying at 1am this morning I wasn't surprised to feel he was also burning up. He'd been fussy all evening and almost impossible to get to sleep. I lubed up the thermometer and took his temperature. 102.7. If Donny was fully awake he'd have probably come up with a better plan, but he wasn't and agreed that he should stay home with Kali (who was sleeping) and I'd take Jack to the emergency room.

I nursed Jack, gave him some Tylenol, and Donny got him dressed while I threw on some clothes. I tossed a yogurt, spoon, and bottled water into his diaper bag along with a book and we were off. Halfway there, I realized I hadn't brushed my teeth. I told myself I'd scarf down the yogurt as soon as possible to cover any possible funk. I was carefully scanning the road for deer, possible kidnappers, and murderers. I'd been thinking a lot about mortality and bad luck lately as a 19-year-old died right outside the entrance to my subdivision Friday night. Car crash.

I got to the hospital at 2:20am, bummed to find that the Pediatric ER closes at midnight, and I had to wait with the sick adults, of which there were two. There were also two sick infants before me. Jack wasn't triaged until about 3:40am and this included another well-lubed stick up the butt.

Jack's poor booty hole.

His fever had already gone down and I felt kinda foolish. And sleepy. I really wanted to go back home, but I figured I might as well wait since I was already there. I wasn't called back to see a doctor until 4:30am. I'd nursed Jack while were in triage and he'd fallen back asleep in his car seat while I watched *The Fresh Prince of Bel-Air* repeats once back in the waiting room.

A very handsome, bald, Indian doctor examined Jack. He would ask me questions and while I answered, cooed and played with Jack so loudly I wasn't sure he could hear the information I was trying to give him. At one point he said, "I'm so jealous of all your hair, Jack!

Um, okay.

Turns out Jack has a very slight ear infection in his left ear. At 4:55am the doctor told me he'd be back with a prescription for antibiotics and I could go home. I called Donny and told him I should be home shortly and that he wouldn't be *that* late for work. At 5:20 I was still waiting. How fucking long does it take to write a 'script on a notepad? At one point the doctor walked by and assured me he was going to fill out the prescription. He returned a moment later to confirm it was the left ear and then walked away again.

I'd noticed no one from Admissions had come to check our insurance, but I figured we were in the system so maybe they didn't need to. As I paced in the exam room I left the curtain open so people passing by could see how annoyed I was getting. Jack was getting sleepy and cranky again and he kept spitting up all over my shirt. I was tired, hungry, and starting to get shaky. A big fat black dude down the hall sat behind a desk sipping coffee, chit-chatting occasionally with nurses and a father of a sick child.

He finally looked my way, looked down at his desk, and looked at me again. He picked up a clipboard from the desk and waddled his fat ass towards me. Then my suspicions were confirmed: the doctor was waiting for the Admissions people to get payment information and the Admissions dude was sleeping on the job. I was pissed.

"Did anyone get you to sign these?"

Motherfucker, do you see my signature on there? That clipboard has been in front of you for God knows how long. Did you think I signed them when you weren't looking and returned them to your desk? Oh wait, that would be impossible since your big ass has been sitting there for 40 fucking minutes!

"Uh, no" I said instead.

He gets me to sign and initial a few forms, confirms my address and such in a computer in the room. I glance at the clock and finally ask, "Is this what the doctor was waiting for? I mean, he told me almost 40 minutes ago all he needed to do was get my son's prescription."

"I don't know."

Fat fucking liar. I wanted to karate chop him in his hot dog package looking neck with the clipboard. After he waddled his ass outta there, a nurse returns within three minutes with a printout prescription for Jack. It was 5:55am. I was beyond pissed. They all ought to be ashamed of themselves. A sick child waited there for almost an hour for no real good reason other than, someone wasn't doing their damn job properly. Then his ass tried to be all extra helpful when I was walking out, carrying the heavy car seat (with Jack in it) in one hand and his diaper bag in the other - he hits the button for me to open the door to the exit and wishes me a safe ride home.

Fuck off, big boy.

It's still dark and cold out. I hurry to get Jack into the car and lock up as soon as I'm safely inside. I call Donny and vent. Then I bitch as I drive by a bunch of closed pharmacies. What happened to 24-hour pharmacies?

When I reached the entrance of my subdivision I pulled over across the street near the scene of the accident. It's still dark out. At this point I didn't know the details of what had happened. All I knew was that around 2am

Friday night/Sat. morning Donny heard sirens. When we went out Christmas shopping the next day there were a bunch of people (mostly teens) standing around a big tree with stuffed animals, cards, and candles around it. A big chunk of the wrought iron and brick fence that separated the tree from the road was missing. We couldn't find anything on our local news all weekend.

I got out of the car this morning and went for a closer look. The skid marks from the road continued into the brown grass and disappeared into the tree. It was too dark to see the picture taped to the tree from where I stood and the lone lit candle provided insufficient lighting. I didn't want to leave Jack alone in the car any longer to investigate further so I got my ass back in the car, U-turned, and then drove across the street to my subdivision.

There was a group of high school students waiting for the school bus at the first intersection of the subdivision. I stopped, rolled down the passenger window, and asked the group as a whole if they knew what happened across the street. Three black girls told me that a 19-year-old boy, who didn't live in our subdivision, had run off the road and hit the tree and died. I thanked them and continued to my house. It wasn't until I was pulling into my garage that I realized two things.

1. High school kids are going to school way too damn early!

2. One of them heifers was smoking!

Donny helped me bring Jack in and then went out immediately to fill the prescription and get me some coffee. I crawled in bed with Jack, nursed him, and then we both fell asleep. I was vaguely aware of Donny entering the bedroom at some point with coffee I could smell, and a bag of medicine I could hear as he placed it on the bedside table. He left and ten minutes later the alarm went off. I had to get up to get Kali ready for school.

I filled her in on what she'd missed throughout the night. We kissed, exchanged "I love yous" and "have a nice days" and she left for school. When I crawled back in bed with Jack, I found myself thinking about the boy killed in the accident. Actually, Donny and I had been thinking about him since Saturday when all we knew was that his name was Tyler (one of the signs on the tree.)

As I stroked Jack's hair while he slept, I cried. Losing a child at any time is unacceptable, but right before the holidays just seems extra *wrong*. I found myself wondering if his parents had already purchased presents for him. I kissed Jack's cheek and wondered how many times Tyler's Mom had done the same. How many times had she been a good Mom and driven him in the middle of the night to the hospital because she worried about a fever? Did she also blow in his face to get him to swallow medicine and then laugh when he dribbled it out with a "what the hell is that, woman?" look on his face? Or was Tyler one of those babies that liked to take his medicine?

If someone told you that you had to work on a job for 19 years that might seem like a long time. It is a long time to wait for money or a long time to see yourself married to someone. But if someone told you, when you were caressing their newborn hair, that you were only going to get 19 years with your child, you'd say that wasn't enough.

I drifted back to sleep grateful that while on the road at 2am with my boy, I made it where I was going and home again safely and my biggest complaints were a minor ear infection, closed pharmacies, and a fat man who didn't do his job properly.

As always, life could be a lot worse.

While pregnant with Jack, I began to title some of my blogs under the heading, *Blog It Out, Baby.* This was done so that my readers who weren't interested in tales of morning sickness, stretch marks, and lactation could easily skip over them and not accidentally find themselves reading about leaking boobs or episiotomies. Much to my surprise, most people really enjoyed these blogs and I received many emails from women who said they helped them laugh through their pregnancies. Here are those blogs.

Blog It Out, Baby

NINA PEREZ

Strawberry Banana French Toast

December 17, 2007

Clue 1: For two weeks I couldn't study for more than 30 minutes without falling asleep on my textbooks. I'm talking passed out, drool stains, sleeping on the books.

Clue 2: Large, achy breasts.

Clue 3: I almost threw up in Wal-Mart.

Clue 4: I would only think about eating because it seemed I should. Like, hmmm, it's been four hours since I ate last, I may wanna do something about that. But then I wouldn't because the thought of actually eating made me ill. So, I'd wait until the hunger pains were so severe I thought my stomach was touching my back. Then I'd eat like a mad woman only to think about dying as soon as I was done.

Clue 5: Saturday morning at IHOP I just *had* to have the Strawberry Banana French Toast. And I HATE French Toast. I resisted. I had the T-bone steak with scrambled egg whites, three buttermilk pancakes and a side of bacon with a large orange juice.

Sunday morning I couldn't take it anymore. We agreed to take a home pregnancy test on Monday morning (today), but I just had to know. Sure, there were clues, but I felt like my period was coming at any moment. So, I tip-toed out of bed and went into the bathroom. I locked the door and turned on the water so Donny wouldn't hear the wrapper of the home pregnancy test left over from our days of trying years ago.

I peed on the stick and within ten second saw two pink lines. *I knew it. I'm not pregnant.*

I check the instructions to be sure. The picture on the front of the box has two pink lines. "Hmmm, why would they advertise their product with a negative result? That's dumb," I snort. I unfold the directions and the first thing I see is an illustration with one line in the indicator window. Below that it says, *Not pregnant* and *No esta embarazada.*

"God. If one line means not pregnant, then two lines must mean... *really* not pregnant."

'Cause, you know, I'm sure I'm not pregnant.

"Two lines must mean, like, I broke my uterus or something."

My eyes travel to the left and there's an illustration with two pink lines that says *Pregnant* and *Esta embarazada.*

So I check the stick again. Each line is brighter than the last time I looked.

I am pregnant. After I told Donny, he immediately went to get my strawberry banana french toast.

"I don't even like french toast!" I exclaimed for the tenth time that morning... as I chewed a mouth full of french toast.

The three of us, Kali, Donny and myself, sat on our bed eating away. "Well, I like french toast, and apparently he does too," Donny reasoned, already deciding it's a boy.

"According to the pregnancy calendar, his or her inner ear is forming today. I doubt he or she already knows if they like french toast or not."

"Mommy, are you scared?"

"Umm, I'm kinda afraid of..."

"How much it's going to hurt?"

"Actually, no. I'd kinda forgotten about that part, but thanks for reminding me!"

What you can expect over the next nine months in Blog It Out, Baby:

The Ick Factor: For the past week I've been walking around in a constant state of ickiness. Now I know why. Just like that, you realize that your body will not belong to you for the next two years… at least.

The Sleep Factor: Pregnancy sleep is the best sleep *ever!* When it hits you, there's no fighting it. Don't even try. Just give in and sleep.

The Big Sister Factor: According to Kali, you know what sex the baby is when the doctor "pulls it out" at least that's what she learned on Family Guy. And she's hoping for a little sister so she can put her hair in pigtails when she goes to Pre-K.

The Name Factor:

"Mommy, what are the names you like for a girl?"

"Isabelle."

"And for a boy?"

"Gaius."

"What?"

"GUY-US"

"Spell it."

"G-A-I-U-S."

She's quiet for a second then turns to Donny. "Daddy, do *you* have any boy names?"

Now, if you'll excuse me I have to go pee… again… for the sixth time in the past three hours.

It's Official

December 18, 2007

I'm pregnant.

Right now you're probably thinking, "Yeah, we know. You told us yesterday." But today it's *official* official. You see, I secretly had been having moments of panic yesterday. "What if I'm imagining the whole thing?" You know, the symptoms of pregnancy are very similar to those of getting your period. "What if I'm just *really* late?" What if the symptoms not related to my period (constant queasiness, sleeping a lot, peeing constantly) were all in my head? "What if I'm having a hysterical pregnancy?"

Since I can't get in to see the doctor till after Christmas, I made Donny go get another home pregnancy test last night. I told him to make sure it was different than the first one I used.

"What did you use the first time?"

"First Response with the one or two lines."

"So what should I get this time?"

"Anything but First Response."

Duh.

They have some where the smiley face means pregnant and a frowning face is not pregnant. Which is funny 'cause they're assuming everyone peeing on the stick wants to be pregnant. I bet there are many women staring at that little indicator window making deals with Jesus to see one of those unhappy faces.

Donny brought back and E.P.T. kit. Two for one, in fact. This test has two windows: a small rectangular one that will display a vertical blue line to show the test is working properly, and a larger circular window that will display a plus sign (pregnant) or minus sign (not pregnant.) Of course I didn't know this when I peed on the thing 'cause I didn't bother to read the instructions. I don't do instructions. The only time I read instructions prior to using something is when I'm about to play a board game or the item in question is very expensive and to break it due to incompetence and laziness would cause me great financial pain. For everything else, I'm a wing it kinda girl.

I've started referring to the baby as "Peppercorn" or "Baby baby." Whenever I'm hit with a wave of icky I just take deep breaths and say over and over again, "Oh, baby, baby, baby, baby," until it passes. Peppercorn comes from reading that the baby is currently about the size of one. When I think of it in terms of size, I'm amazed that something so small can be wreaking such havoc. Then when I read what is happening inside of me exactly, I'm amazed that women don't just go into some deep hibernation-like coma for the first few months of their pregnancies. The fact that we still function while a mini brain, heart, liver, kidneys, pancreas, eyes, ears, skin, etc., grows inside of us is amazing.

As I journal the changes, thoughts, and emotions taking place I've noticed an immediate change in my sleeping pattern. I explained it to Donny last night in this way: We were lying in bed when I felt drowsy and my eyes began to droop.

"What time is it?"

"Seven-thirty."

"Oh yeah, it's about that time."

"What?"

"This is usually around the time when the baby is like, 'Mommy, it's time for sleep.' That is until 2 or 3am when the baby is like, 'Mommy, get up and go pee.' I usually stay up for an hour or so. Then around 7am I'm like, 'Ok, baby, it's time to get up and put your sister on the bus.' And the baby is like, 'Oh no it's not.'"

And that's exactly how it is, too. The moment you know it exists, the baby dictates your every action and decision. And that's fine by me.

In related news, my sister shared with me a website that really helped her during her pregnancy: *Baby Fit*. I was pleasantly surprised to learn that it is the sister site to *Spark People*. I've begun tracking my exercise and diet over there. The only difference is that I'm allowed more calories per day to compensate for all the nutrients going to the baby. Right about now I'm saying a big hallelujah to losing 20lbs before getting pregnant.

Morning Sickness & Pregnancy Diet

December 20, 2007

I'm sure you all know that morning sickness doesn't just occur in the morning, but what you may not know is that it can occur *all the damn time*! All day, every day, I feel tired, queasy, and gross. Donny bought me some *Preggy Pop Drops* from Babies 'R' Us yesterday, but I think they're more for mouth nausea than tummy sickness. It's not like I feel like I'm going to throw up, because you'd actually have to eat something for that to happen, but more like my stomach is hosting its very own rock concert.

The worst part is that it's recommended that you eat to make it go away, but eating is the last thing I want to do. Now I see why so many women lose weight in the first few months of their pregnancies. Of course, not eating is not an option so I find myself going through the motions. It's probably no surprise that Donny has completely restocked the fridge and pantry with LOTS of the following:

Apples, pears, bananas, mangos, oranges, calcium fortified orange juice, chicken, pork, broccoli, tomatoes, lettuce, avocado, whole wheat pastas and breads, yogurt, bottled water, eggs, and shitload of other veggies.

He's been grilling all my meat and steaming all the veggies. Not only that, but he's refused to let me lift anything heavy and has been doing the lion's share of the housework in preparation for my friend Emily's visit tomorrow. But above all, he's been putting up with the worst side effect of the early stages of pregnancy: flatulence. *Sweet mother of God*. What's up with that?! Like swelling breasts, heartburn, and constant urination aren't enough?

Here's what's going on with the baby:

The changes to your growing embryo are not quite as drastic this week as they've been in the last few weeks. Growth is now largely focused on their little head, which is starting to develop much more rapidly than the rest of their tiny body. This is because their amazing brain is undergoing some very crucial and rapid development in order to effectively regulate their heart rate, blood circulation, and other vital functions. As for the rest of their miniature body, what were simple limb buds last week are limb flippers this week and the tail is more expressed. Amazingly, within a mere five weeks your little miracle is already developing the rudimentary forms of their liver, pancreas, lungs, stomach and nasal pits while their little heart is already increasing its circulation. Your baby is now a whopping 4-6mm in length.

In other news, Donny and I have allowed ourselves to dream ahead. We usually have these conversations at night and they all start the same way:

"Donny."

"What?"

"We're having a baby!"

"I know."

Silence.

"Nina."

"What?"

"We're having a baby!"

"I know!"

Then we giggle like fools. Then we start making plans for turning the guest bedroom into the nursery and the bonus room into a guest bedroom/rec room. I'd love to install a chair rail in the nursery and paint the top half a light green and the bottom half a khaki color. I think it's a nice gender neutral look. Donny is looking forward to buying a rocking chair to sit by the window. You guys have to see him, he's SO excited.

I prefer to not know the sex of the baby until it's born, but Donny wants to find out as soon as we can. When I told this to my friend David he said, "Why? Tell him it can only be one of two things. It's not like there are five possibilities." But Donny is just *really* excited. We're considering letting Donny find out while I, and Kali, remain in the dark, but I'm sure he'll slip up and tell me somehow.

Because we have a ways to go, I purposely avoid websites with cribs, strollers, and such. Although I'm *dying* to hit up Pottery Barn Kids. You guys know I have zero self control so my ass will probably be window cyber shopping there as soon as this blog is posted.

Finally, we've been discussing whether or not to share every baby name we consider with family and friends. Let me fill you in on a little secret: Expectant parents don't really *want* your opinion on their possible baby names... unless you like them. If you don't, then we expect you to lie and say you do or shut the fuck up. It's like people actually forget that this is someone's child we're talking about and say the rudest shit. So, to preserve this nice little relationship we got going on I may or may not share the names we are seriously considering because I cannot be held responsible for the raging hormones induced cussin' out I give any of you that diss my baby's name. I'm just sayin'.

Baby Like

December 27, 2007

I will not gross you out with tales of *constant* morning sickness. I will not. At least not in this blog. I will; however, tell you all about how my body has been completely taken over by something the size of a raspberry.

I no longer look to my vagina for sexual pleasure. It is simply the place from which I pee... a lot, and the baby delivery chute. My boobs? Milk jugs. And I only eat what the baby likes. Ask my friend Emily. She could be heard asking, "Did the baby like?" after lunch on Saturday.

"The baby liked the rice pilaf. The broccoli smothered in garlic? Not so much. What the baby really likes is his sister's french fries in ketchup."

"Hey!" That from Kali as I reached across the table and snatched a few. Apparently the baby really likes ketchup-covered french fries, which is unfortunate since I don't like ketchup on my fries. Go figure. What else does baby like?

Baby Likes

Joey Bag of Donuts Steak Burrito in a bowl from Moe's Southwest Grill

Ginger Ale

Buttered toast

Buttered toast with jelly

Yoplait Strawberry Banana Yogurt

Multi-Grain Cheerios

Candy Canes

French Fries

Scrambled Egg Whites

Baby No Like

Everything else with a special aversion to orange Juice

The baby used to really like buttered cinnamon raisin bagels... until it decided it didn't... mid-chew. It wasn't pretty, people. The baby has also decided that it doesn't like the aroma of anything.

Baby also dictates how I spend my time. Baby doesn't like riding in a car. We went to my Dad's house Christmas Eve, slept over, and opened all our presents there. He drove us home Christmas night. Sweet mother of God. I immediately hopped out the car, ran into the house, threw up, and went to sleep. The baby doesn't like the winding back roads between here and Grandpa's house. At all. Either that or it doesn't like Grandpa's driving.

Baby likes playing *Rock Band*. Baby will let Mommy belt out songs for at least an hour before he decides, "Alright, enough of this shit, lady. Go lie down." And if I try to squeeze in one more song say, Soundgarden's *Black Hole Sun* or Hole's *Celebrity Skin,* I am hit with a wave of nausea so severe I barely have time to toss Kali the mic before I go running upstairs.

Speaking of Kali, she has taken to saying in a very matter of fact-duh-how dumb can you be voice, "Because you have a baby in your belly!" whenever I say anything like, "I don't feel well." The other night she rubbed my back and cooed, "It will be okay, Mommy." Then, "I can't believe you want to have three kids. You're just going to feel like this again, you know." Good point, kid. Good point.

Anyway, I discovered that the baby really likes music. I feel less icky when I'm just lying in bed, reading a book and listening to Rhapsody via my TiVo. God bless this feature and what I'm going to do in 28 days when the 30-day trial runs out is beyond me. It's like having Tower Records (or Virgin Megastore if you prefer) in my bedroom. If I feel like hearing it, I just search for it and bam, there it is! The baby even allows me to... dance (gasp!) around the bedroom, but only momentarily.

Baby Likes

Marvin Gaye

Stevie Wonder (we're listening to "Do I Do" right now)

The Beatles

Elvis

The Police

Prince

Oasis' *Fuckin' in the Bushes* and *Go Let it Out*

Santana's *Black Magic Woman* and *Oye Como Va*

and very early Madonna

Oh, and I can't front... the baby likes the *Evita* soundtrack. Don't judge me or my baby!

We're about to find out how the baby feels about early Michael Jackson. I'm talking, *Don't Stop Till You Get Enough* Michael. Since Donny has just left for work it's safe to tell the baby how Mommy just knew Michael was going to be his Daddy when she saw that video for the first time.

The Ugly Truth – Part One

January 6, 2008

Every time you do something the experience is unique. Even the things you do all the time. Things you've done millions, thousands, hundreds, and dozens of time. Brushing your teeth, having sex, driving to work every day. Each time, the experience is different than any other time - sometimes slightly, sometimes drastically. We all know this. But for some reason I was totally unprepared for the possibility that this pregnancy would be different than my first.

When I first realized I was pregnant just three weeks ago, yet it feels a lot longer, my emotions went as follows:

1. Shock

2. Fear

3. Happy

Shock: I don't buy it whenever I hear someone say, "We didn't mean to get pregnant." Or, "It was an accident." That's because I grew up with a mother who was fond of telling my brother, sisters, and I, "Don't bring no babies in here." And, "I ain't raising no babies but my own." And you know how, though rare, it is possible for a woman to get pregnant if she has unprotected sex during her period? Well, my mother used that little nugget in her arsenal of fear to ensure that we understood that sex meant possibility of babies. And bringing babies home before we were on our own was a no-no.

And since no form of birth control is 100 percent (except abstinence) I was always convinced that I'd be that .1 percent to get knocked up while on my period, and using a condom, while on the pill, with a guy who had a vasectomy. That could have everything to do with the fact that my mother put the fear of conception into my head or with the fact that I have this over-inflated ego and truly believe that I'm more special, unique, different, etc., than everyone else. Either or.

When Donny and I decided a few years ago that we were going to start trying for another baby I really thought I'd get pregnant like that. (Insert finger snap here.) After two months of trying I was convinced something was wrong. I began charting my ovulation on a spreadsheet I'd devised. Boxes that indicated days when I had my period were shaded in bright red. Days when I was supposed to be ovulating were green. Days when Donny and I had sex were marked with a check mark. I was serious. Each morning, as soon as the alarm went off, I'd reach into the bedside table for my basal thermometer and stick it in my vagina to get my internal temperature. That number determined where each day's box went on the spreadsheet. I'm telling you, I was serious and after about a year, nothing. Then I got laid off, went back to school, blah, blah, blah.

I wasn't shocked to be pregnant because I didn't understand *how* it happened. Like I said, my whole life I just assumed that any time a penis entered my vagina I could get pregnant. It was more like when. For the first week, Donny and I would just shake our heads and go, "Did we even *have* sex in November?" We vaguely remembered having sex maybe twice. But as we know, it only takes once. When Emily expressed her fear of sitting on my bed because she didn't want to catch "baby-making cooties," I told her she was more likely to leave my house and go purchase a flat-screen TV and an Xbox 360 after sitting on my bed. In early November we'd purchased the flat-screen for the bedroom and moved our Xbox there as well. There was more Halo-playing going on than baby making... or so we thought.

Fear: Never mind the fact that I'd already done it. You'd have to be a blazing fool not to feel an overwhelming wave of fear at the thought of pushing out seven to nine pounds of flesh, bones, blood, muscle, and hair from your vagina. Then, being responsible for the overall well-being of (yet) another human being.

Happy: The thought of experiencing all the joys of watching my baby grow, learn, talk, laugh, and just exist, with my husband, was just too good to be true. And not just any husband. Hands down, the best husband ever.

Then, on Christmas Day, everything went to shit.

The Ugly Truth – Part Two

January 7, 2008

You can't be a Mom and be a punkass bitch or a bitchass punk.
Whichever you prefer.

So, what I'm about to share with you today I haven't told ANYONE.
Except Donny and my sister, Christine. And even with Christine I didn't get
too in depth.

We found out I was pregnant on December 16th and from that day till
Christmas Day I was the typical pregnant gal. I was happy, I was excited, I
was wondering if it was going to be a girl or a boy, what we'd name it, what
he'd look like, I was excited about finally being able to convert the guest
bedroom into a nursery, etc., etc., etc.

We spent Christmas Eve at my parent's house. We hauled all of our
presents over there and spent the night. Now, I'm one of those people that
find it hard to sleep on Christmas Eve anyway. I wake up several times during
the night disappointed to see the sun still isn't up and then I finally can't take
it anymore, and around 6 am I'm waking up Kali and Donny to go open
presents. This night was worse. I woke up no less than twelve times each time
feeling sick, uncomfortable, and hot.

Finally, around 5am I was awakened by an ongoing commercial for a *Girls
Gone Wild* video featuring ex-Real World castmates. Um, what the fuck is
wrong with these people? These were like castmates from 10 years ago.
They're in their 30's. They have nothing better to do than to go out and try to
get young white girls to show their tits and make out with each other? What

did they want for their lives *before* they went on a reality show? Get a fucking job, people. And what's up with those girls? Are there really that many white girls in college with Daddy issues? Let's assume they all graduate - they're supposed to be the next leaders of industries? Talk about a national crisis. Somebody needs to do an intervention for young white girls in college.

Anyway, disgusted by both the commercial and my stomach I went downstairs to find my father putting together a race track for my nephew and there was Kali's new bike under the tree in the great room. My sister had taken all of Kali's and my nephew's presents and stacked them around the tree in the foyer. It was a pretty sight. I tried to concentrate on getting into the Christmas spirit while I munched on crackers and ginger ale and chatted with my Dad. But I could feel that something wasn't right.

We had a typical Christmas day and ended it with a nice roast, baked potato, fresh vegetables, buttered rolls dinner. Because it was a holiday we ate in the formal dining room on the good dishes. After dinner I sat around the table with my sister, stepmother, aunt, cousins, Dad and Donny and we discussed baby stuff. One of my cousins is also pregnant (due in March) and she received a baby name book from my sister for Christmas. She already has a little boy, Vincent, and is expecting another and had wanted to name the new baby a V name as well. After we passed the book around the table we realized there are no other good boy V names.

We shared our name choices for both boy and girl. They were met with a lukewarm reception. Everyone loves our middle name for a boy. First name? Not so much. They'll get over it. I'm not sharing it here because on top of everything else I don't want to have to cuss any of you out. In fact, I may do like some other bloggers and just refer to him/her by some nickname or initials.

It was time to go home and my Dad and Donny loaded up my Dad's SUV with all our crap and off we went. That is when shit officially hit the fan. The ride from my Dad's house to ours is about 35 minutes taking back roads. These roads twist and turn like a motherfucker. I spent the whole ride in the backseat trying not to throw up. My Dad has this TV/DVD player installed in the roof and Kali was watching *Madagascar*. At one point she said, "Mommy, look at this part. It's funny." I did and wished I hadn't. It just made me dizzier. I spent the rest of the ride with my forehead pressed against the window because it was blessedly cold.

When we pulled into our driveway I didn't even attempt to help bring the stuff in the house. I hugged my Dad, wished him a Merry Christmas, thanked him for the ride and went upstairs to throw up. Then I stripped out of my clothes and fell asleep. It was around 9pm. From that night forward I threw up everything I ate or drank for the next four days. EVERY. SINGLE. THING.

There was one day in there that I got a migraine. Donny had put his PDA in my face to show me something. I looked up at it for about three seconds and boom... instant migraine. That was not fun. I think that was Thursday, Dec. 27th. The days from Christmas to New Years are kind of a blur. There was a lot of vomiting. A lot of praying for death. A lot of misery. Donny would come home every day and run me a bath, turn out the lights in the master bathroom, light candles and help me into the tub. Then he'd proceed to bathe me. Bathe me because I was too weak to bathe myself. At one point he actually got into the tub with me to do so.

"I look and feel ridiculous."

"You're having my baby."

At just like that I realized I hadn't thought about the baby or being pregnant in days.

Here comes Ugly Truth Number One: Friday, Dec. 28th I hit rock bottom. I told Donny, "This baby hates me." I thought I was being funny and cute. I thought it was a clever way to sum up that the first trimester was kicking my ass. A friend later joked, "It's because he knows that deep down you resent him for making you sick. It's a vicious cycle kinda thing."

At first I laughed. Then I really thought about it. Did I resent this baby? The answer was yeah, I kinda did. This isn't what I wanted. *This* is what I wanted: I want a sibling for Kali. I want a son for Donny. I want a family of four. I want another child in my life. I want to breastfeed again and experience that wonderful feeling you get when you are nursing your baby and they place their tiny hand on your breast, and you can hear them breathing through their nose and swallowing. I want to stand over my baby's crib and watch him sleep on his back and smile, and wonder, "What are you smiling about?!" Watching newborns sleep and dream always amazed me. Their frames of reference are so damn small. They've only been alive like, a month, and they're smiling in their sleep? Their vision is still cloudy those first few weeks. What mental pictures could they have possibly amassed to cause them to smile in their dreams? I want to watch my baby learn to crawl. You know, when they realize they can hold themselves up on all fours and do that rocking thing back and forth with their little diapered butts in the air. Too. Fucking. Cute.

I want a baby. To be pregnant? Not so much. Then I tried to remember if I felt this way while pregnant with Kali. Nope. Why? 1. I didn't know any fucking better and 2. This pregnancy was starting out a lot rougher. When you go from little to no morning sickness in your first pregnancy and massive, constant, please-God-make-it-stop morning sickness in your second, you start to re-evaluate some things. You also start to look at this whole motherhood thing a lot differently. Like I said, you can't be a punkass bitch.

But Friday night, I was this baby's punkass bitch. Donny was sleeping and I was trying to watch *The Nanny Diaries.* I had to pause it numerous times to go vomit. I realized after awhile that I wasn't even throwing up anymore. I had nothing left in me. I went from throwing up food and beverages to stomach acid. It burned and it was coming through my nose. I was having awful thoughts.

"Please God, make it stop."

Then I'd feel guilty. What if I had a miscarriage because God thought I was being ungrateful? Is that what I wanted? No, of course not. But I couldn't take much more of this. I was weak, tired, in pain, miserable, uncomfortable, and sad. So, for the first time in days I referred to my baby.

"Please God, I love this baby. Thank you for this baby. But, you have to help me. I can't do this."

Punk. Ass. Bitch.

Then I stood there over the toilet bowl, bent over, with my hands resting on my knees, trying to catch my breath and praying that the heaving didn't start again. I looked down at my bare legs and thought, "Wow. My legs look great." They did! So I stumbled to the scale and learned I'd lost 6lbs! Six. Fucking. Pounds. In like three days. Then I threw up again.

Then I got in bed and had Breakdown Number One.

"Donny. I can't do this. I can't do this."

I just moaned this over and over again.

"Yes, you can. It will get better. It's just the first three months."

"But I'm only 7 weeks! I can't do this for another five weeks. I can't do this. I feel like I'm dying."

"You're the strongest woman I know."

"No, I'm not. I'm a punkass bitch."

At this point I'm bawling, writhing on the bed in pain, and I'm pretty sure I smelled bad. Saturday morning I had a glass of apple juice and threw it up in minutes. It was time to go to the E.R.

"This baby hates me," I thought as we got into the car. And at the moment, I wasn't too fond of it either.

The Ugly Truth – Part Three
January 8, 2008

I don't think I accurately described what was going on with me before leaving for the hospital that Saturday morning. So, to recap:

- constant, heavy, nausea

- vomiting EVERYTHING I ate or drank for four days

- gas

- heartburn

- lack of sleep

- depression

- lack of emotional connection to unborn child

- aversion to smells that caused more nausea and/or headaches.

Basically, overall misery.

My parents arrived to take Kali for the day, and Donny and I headed to the hospital. I had this thing against emergency rooms until I moved out of New York. Growing up in Brooklyn we'd go to Brookdale Hospital if we needed to go to an emergency room. The wait was always long and one particular experience has stuck with me my whole life. I had to go to the E.R. after that time I busted my knee open on a pipe in a vacant lot. I sat in the waiting area across from an older white man who had on a wife beater and those pants that janitors and garbage men wear. He had a massive amount of gauge wrapped around his head like some bloody turban. The blood was dripping from one side of his head on to his face and chest. He was

265

sandwiched between an elderly lady with a bad cough and a young girl holding a crying infant. I think of that every time I visit an emergency room.

But the emergency rooms in the southern suburbs are worlds apart from the urban New York ones. This particular hospital has a separate pediatric urgent care. We had to take Kali there twice over the years - sprained toe, sprained finger. There's no waiting, no stab victims, no nasty smells, loud noises, etc. It's quite nice. The regular emergency room is the same. It's like sitting in a doctor's office and it's never full.

That Saturday morning, I sat next to Donny while he filled out the form on a clipboard. He leaned over to me, "When was your last period?" I snatched the form from his hands. "Give me that." I furiously scribbled the information. See, I know the key to being seen quickly is to fill out those forms fast. It doesn't matter who got there when or what time you put on the sheet next to "arrival time." What matters is the order in which the lady behind the counter inputs your info into the computer. So, though there were two little old ladies who had arrived before us, I was seen before them because they took too damn long filling out the forms. All is fair in love, war, and the emergency room.

Now, say what you want about doctors and pharmaceutical companies, but when you're throwing up stomach acid and you feel like there's something inside of you sucking the life out of you, all you want is medical intervention... and maybe a little divine intervention as well. All I could think of as I watched the lady behind the counter enter my information into the computer was that behind that counter was the cure, was the answer. They were going to give me something to make me feel better. There was relief coming. Thank God for western medicine. Thank God for doctors and scientists who sat around going...

"What causes nausea?"

"And what can we make to alleviate it?"

"Oh, this works. Now, is it safe for pregnant women?"

"Let's test this shit on some pregnant rats and find out."

"Word."

Thank God for those guys.

We are finally called to the back after about 15-20 minutes. A blonde woman in her late 40's takes my blood pressure, my temperature, and starts asking me questions while entering my answers into a computer. When I tell her about my constant vomiting she says, "Bless your heart." Then she starts telling me about this medicine they gave her when she was pregnant with her first child that knocked her morning sickness right out. Just as I was about to tell her to write that shit down on a piece of paper so I can pass it to the doc in the back and be like, "Hook it up," she said that by the time she got pregnant with her next child, they didn't make the medicine anymore. Fuck.

We head to the back and I'm shown to an examining room and told to just remove my top and bra because it's really cold and put on the usual hospital gown over my jeans. I do so, get up on the table and snuggle under the sheet. Relief isn't far off I tell myself. "If you get cold, let us know. We'll bring you a blanket." After about ten minutes I tell Donny that I need the blanket and he disappears into the hall. He returns a short while later with the warmest blanket ever.

"They made me go get it. It was in a warmer. What kind of hospital makes you go get your own blanket?"

I didn't give a shit. They were my saviors. They had the cure. The doctor comes in. He's this large, elderly, white man. He has a wicked sense of humor and lives in our small town. I like him immediately. He determines that I should get an IV with some fluids and a drug to curb the nausea. Because I have no cramping or bleeding he determines he doesn't need to do a pelvic. Sweet.

Ugly Truth Number Two: When you're pregnant get used to lots of blood being drawn from your body and lots of poking and prodding in your vagina.

We explain to the doctor that we have insurance, but they screwed up our last name and Donny's social security number in their system and it should have been corrected two days ago, but we have no idea if they did it or not and since it is Saturday we can't get anyone there on the phone. He tells me that he'll give me a referral to a good OB/GYN at the woman's center attached to the hospital and a prescription for prenatal vitamins.

"Keep taking the over the counter ones you're taking until they run out. Prenatal vitamins are prenatal vitamins. But when they run out, fill this prescription. If your insurance company pays for them, why not let 'em?"

Then he wrote a prescription for the medicine they were currently pumping into my veins.

"It's called Zofran. It's expensive. Wait till your insurance cards arrive or else you'll pay out of pocket and it's like thirty dollars a pill. It's the good stuff though. One pill dissolves in your mouth and lasts 12 hours."

And then another for medicine that helps with nausea.

"Now this stuff is cheaper and only lasts 6 hours. And it makes you drowsy. You might want to take them until your insurance cards come. And I'm going to go ahead and order an ultrasound for you today. Just to get a look to make sure everything's okay."

A different nurse, a young black girl named Bridget, comes in and begins my IV. I'm so fucking dehydrated and starving that my veins are barely visible. Donny holds my hand as she sticks the needle in and tries to find a plump one. She takes about four vials of blood, hooks up the IV bag, then leaves. Donny continues to sit by my side holding my hand while we watch *Drumline* on TV. After awhile I start to get hungry. I want lemon cake.

"Do you think, if I talk you through it, you can make me a lemon cake when we get home?"

"Yes."

After about ten minutes...

"I want a Sarah Lee pound cake. And a fork."

"OK."

After about twenty minutes...

"I want a cheeseburger from Hardee's."

"OK."

By this time, I'd worked myself into a starving frenzy. I'm so hungry I think I'm going to throw up. I feel weak, hungry, and sick. The nurse keeps coming in asking if the medicine is working.

"I wouldn't know. I'm so hungry I'm dizzy."

They won't feed me though till they know the medicine is working. I try to explain to her that I won't know if it's working if I'm so hungry I die here on the table. She wasn't getting it. When she left the room I told Donny that there was a fortune cookie in my purse from two weeks ago. "Give it to me."

"You're going to get us in trouble."

"Give me the damn cookie."

He gave me the cookie in bits and pieces, so scared we'd get busted. Finally, probably for fear that I'd eat *her*, the nurse brought me a small cup of apple juice (4 sips worth) and three packages of saltine crackers. I wanted to punch her in the head. It was like giving a whale a Tic-Tac. (I in no way mean to imply that I resemble a whale... yet.) I drank the juice and ate two crackers.

A male orderly comes in and announces he's there to take me to my ultrasound. He attaches my IV pole to the bed and makes sure everything is all... orderly, and we're off. It was like a ride at Disney World. I had a bed with one wheel that insisted on veering to the right. Just when I thought he was going to let my ass go crashing into a wall, the orderly would suddenly appear to bump me with his hip and put me back on course. He parks me outside the ultrasound room and congratulates Donny and me on our new baby.

Another white woman in her late 40's comes out and looks at my chart.

"You're just getting an ultrasound, right?"

"Right."

"How many weeks are you?"

"Seven." Seven and one day to be exact.

"Oh, we'll have to do a vaginal ultrasound" she says eyeing my jeans.

Now, all I heard was vaginal so I'm thinking pap smear and poking and swabbing and I'm ready to leave. You'd think I'd be used to it by now seeing as how I've had many in my lifetime especially while pregnant with Kali, but I HATE vaginal exams. Something about the table and the stirrups that seems so... undignified. And it's uncomfortable and personal.

I was prepared though. Before we left I'd taken a bath and made sure my toes were cute, my legs were shaved, and that the vagina was well maintained. I truly believe that vaginal hair conditions are a tricky thing when it comes to vaginal exams. You don't want to be too hairy because that's just inconsiderate. Who the hell wants to be parting palm fronds of hair trying to see into your coochie? But then I feel like being too shaven is kinda... kinky. And rude. So, I always try to find a nice middle ground.

It wasn't until I was on the table with my legs open that I realized she meant that I'd be getting an ultrasound *through* my vagina. I hadn't had one of those before. She explained that she'd be using the cold gel when she inserted the wand with the camera on it because the warming gel wasn't sterile. I was just nervous when I got a look at that wand. It was long as fuck.

"Oh, don't worry," she said seeing the look on my face, "It's just the small part. Like a tampon. The rest is so I can move it around."

Whew.

She covered the tip in the cold gel and pressed it against my vagina. She did that a few times to get me used to the cold before she inserted it. It was like some kinky kind of sex game. It made me feel really uncomfortable with her doing that and Donny standing there watching. Did I mention that Donny has NEVER experienced anything like this? He kept looking at me asking if I was okay and telling me how brave I was. Yeah, right.

Then we look at the screen and I don't see shit.

Great, I think, I'm not even pregnant. I'm going through early menopause. The tests were wrong. I have cancer. I am dying. Then I hear the lady say, "There's the yolk sac." And sure enough there's a small black circle on the screen about the size of a silver dollar. Then she says, "And there's your baby." And sure enough there was our baby. Our baby didn't look like a tadpole at all. It looked like a little tiny person but bigger than I expected. It was in the fetal position and it had a head and little limbs and right where the chest goes was this flashing thing. The heartbeat. It was moving so fast! And then I lost it. I started crying.

"I'm sorry. I'm sorry."

"Shhhh, it's okay" said Donny.

"Oh, honey, bless your heart" said the white lady.

I love southern white women. They will bless your heart all day long.

"It's just... just... I haven't felt pregnant or connected to this baby in a week. I've just felt sick and miserable and there... there... he is. And I just... I just... I feel so bad. Like a bad mother already."

And just like that I had Breakdown Number Two, in front of a stranger who kept blessing my heart while she held a wand stuck in my vagina and my husband who was rubbing my head and hands and telling me I was amazing.

She took measurements of the baby (crown to rump) and my uterus to determine how far along I was. According to my last period I was 7 weeks and 1 day and due on August 15th. According the measurements of the baby and my uterus I was 7 weeks and 5 days and due August 11th. So, as of today I'm either 8 weeks and 3 days into my pregnancy or 9 weeks. She then started checking out everything else down there. She asked if I had both of my ovaries and I told her yes. I noticed she was taking a really long time when she was looking at the right one and asked if anything was wrong. Turns out I have a cyst in my right ovary which she assured me meant nothing. She said women get them all the time and never know it. She said it would most likely dissolve itself. *Great, just great.*

After another hour or so, I was released from the hospital. I felt somewhat better having seen the baby. We stopped at Starbucks and I got… wait for it… a slice of lemon pound cake! I napped at home while Donny ran out to fill the prescriptions. The pills did indeed knock me out and the rest of that day, Sunday, and Monday went by in a blur.

The Ugly Truth – Part Four

January 9, 2008

So, when last we met I was out of the hospital and drugged up for about three days. I wasn't throwing up anymore, but I was sleeping... a lot! Apparently, during that time Donny made a doctor appointment for me, handled everything around the house, went to work, etc.

New Years Eve we were asleep by 9pm. I was awakened a little after midnight by the family across the street setting off severe fireworks. I wanted to strangle each and every one of them. Kali comes into the room, "Can I go across the street? I was looking at the fireworks from the window and Maria waved to me to come outside."

"Absolutely not! Go get in the bed. Happy New Year."

The next few days were better, but still rough. I stopped taking the pills and the vomiting had stopped. Kali went back to school on Thursday, January 3rd so I had to be lucid to get her ready in the mornings. Thursday and Friday were pretty bad. Thursday night Donny told me he'd taken out chicken for dinner and asked how I wanted it prepared. For some reason a recipe he used to make a lot popped into my head and I asked him to make it. I took about five bites and knew it was coming back up. There are some times when I'm eating and my throat will literally close up and not let me finish. I have to spit out whatever I'm chewing and just wait for the vomit.

This particular night I freaked out because the food wasn't in me five minutes before it was coming back up. I can't explain it, but I just lost it. The thought of the food coming back still whole just caused me to freak out. So I'm crying and throwing up and miserable and wailing and it's just a sad sight.

Friday, I was hit with a new affliction. Panic attacks. It would start with waves of heat washing over me. My arms and legs would go weak and limp. My heart would beat really fast and I felt like I couldn't catch a good breath. I started crying uncontrollably. And honest to God, I actually cried out, "I want my Mommy." Donny was trying to calm me down telling me that it wasn't good for the baby. I knew it, but I couldn't stop. I was just miserable. I was tired of being sick and uncomfortable. Donny called my mother and the first few minutes of the conversation was her begging me to calm down before I had a miscarriage and me sobbing relentlessly, "I can't do this. I can't do this." It was horrible. It happened three times that day.

Everyone kept telling me that I just needed to get through the first trimester and that one day I would wake up and not be sick anymore. Because of that, each morning before I even opened my eyes I would lie in bed and do a mental diagnostic of my body. I would try to figure out if today was the day, the day when I would feel normal, when I could finally enjoy this pregnancy. It seemed the day would never come.

I woke up on Saturday (January 5th), and for the first time in weeks didn't feel like I was dying. It was almost too good to be true. I shook Donny awake and asked if he could make breakfast. I couldn't allow myself to get hungry. I can't explain it any better but to tell you that hunger pains now are one hundred times worse than before I was pregnant. If I let myself get hungry now, it's all over. I feel sick, weak, and I get headaches. Even after I eat it's still awhile before I can get back to feeling better. So, the trick around here has been to make sure that I eat every few hours even if it's just crackers and juice or fruit cups.

Saturday and Sunday were very good days. There were small moments of nausea, but nothing like before. Yesterday, I was good. I wrote blogs and spoke with Sophie on the phone and finally felt normal. I had avoided talking to anyone because you feel like all people want to hear is how great everything is. And really, when you have the level of morning sickness that I have, you really just want to tell people to shut up and leave you alone and let you die in peace.

I had a bad spell yesterday evening and had to take another pill which knocked me out, but again it beats being miserable *all day.* Yesterday was also the first day of school for me. Did I mention I'm taking six classes this semester? Yeah. I didn't even have my books until last night. Donny took my student ID and my driver's license and went to the campus bookstore to get them for me yesterday. You know I'm usually the girl that has her books the week before class complete with notebooks for each class and matching folders.

This morning I had a big glass of grape juice before getting Kali ready for school. I was able to see her off to the bus stop before I started to feel weak and dizzy and had to sit on the steps for a few minutes.

So here's the ugly truth in a nutshell. You ready?

Not all pregnancies are roses and sunshine. Some women get morning sickness just in the morning during the first trimester only and then it's smooth sailing. That's how it was when I was pregnant with Kali. Some women get all day sickness so severe it makes them miserable. That's how it is for me right now.

I'm sharing this with you because it's the truth and I wish someone had told me ahead of time how bad it could get. Maybe I wouldn't have felt like such a loser and been so depressed for the past two weeks. You see, I didn't feel pregnant, I felt sick. I wasn't happy and glowing. I was miserable and throwing up constantly. I didn't feel connected to my baby. I actually resented my baby. I even resented Donny sometimes for being able to get all the good stuff out of this experience without having to suffer through any of the bad stuff. I felt immense guilt - guilty for not feeling connected to the baby and guilty for spoiling Donny's experience by being so sick and needy. I felt like he wasn't allowed to express his joy, happiness, or excitement about being a Dad again because it was so the opposite of how I was feeling.

I felt guilty for not spending enough time with Kali so soon after Christmas. She had all these games she wanted to play and I was barely able to participate so the lion's share of it went to Donny who was also doing all of the bill paying, housework, and cooking on top of going to work every day. Go look out a window right now and look towards Georgia. You see that bright light in the distance? That's Donny's halo.

I don't know that if someone had told me feeling like this were possible it would have made the experience any *easier*, and that I wouldn't have had the feelings I had (and sometimes still have) but maybe I wouldn't have felt *as bad* about my feelings. I can't tell you how many times I cried because I couldn't understand why I was feeling the way I was. I want this baby. I love this baby. And if it happens to you, you will too. But there may be moments when you feel like you can't take it anymore. When you feel like being pregnant is the last thing you want. And you know what? That's okay. I would cry for hours because I felt like I was asking God for a miscarriage. Of course I wasn't, but I felt like I was being less than a good woman, a strong woman, a good mother, because I had the nerve to express how miserable I felt, how tired I was, how fucked up bad morning sickness can be.

There is nothing wrong with acknowledging that your pregnancy sucks. That it's difficult. That it's taxing. It doesn't mean you don't want or love your baby. It just means that you don't want to be throwing up everything you consume. It means that you don't love getting headaches and vomiting because the smell of your husband's shampoo now makes you ill. It means that you don't relish the idea of your boobs doubling in size and feeling like they've been gnawed on by trolls. It means you're human. Imagine that.

When I was first thinking about sharing this last week I was going to be all about telling you guys how I'm not ever, ever, ever, doing this again. I even told Donny several times that this has to be a boy because I'm not doing it again. I felt bad seeing the disappointment on his face. I've spoken to women over the past two weeks that agree that you really do forget the worst of it or else no one would have more than one child. Here I am just three days of feeling better and I'm already thinking, "Well, if it's a girl, maybe I'd be willing to try once more..."

What?! *I* don't even know what that's about and I don't have the energy to try and figure it out. You're more than welcome to try. I still have my moments. There are times when I actually forget that I'm pregnant. Sometimes I feel like I'm just laid up with the flu or something. It helps to talk about the baby. Donny will sometimes do that while I fall asleep. We already refer to the baby by the boy name we have picked out. (Positive vibes and all that.) Maybe things will change when I'm finally over this first trimester hump and I can feel the baby moving around. (And that's for another blog because I'm telling you that there are times when I actually feel stuff going on inside of me. I don't care what anyone says.) Maybe I'll feel more connected and better about everything when I know what the sex is for sure. I hope so.

Anyway, I share all of this personal, somewhat embarrassing, stuff because maybe it will help someone else not feel so alone, so guilty, so like a loser. 'Cause if I can get through it, and I will, maybe someone else will know they can too.

The Way You Make Me Feel

January 10, 2008

Is that Michael Jackson song now stuck in your head too? Good.

You will soon discover that my emotions are all over the place. When you see pregnant women on television, crying over any and everything - including toilet paper commercials - that's not really that much of an exaggeration. I'm sick and miserable one day and jubilant and excited the next.

When I was about 19 or 20, I was living in Durham, North Carolina and working as an executive assistant to two high-level managers within IBM. I had a friend, Felicia, who was about my age, maybe a bit older, who had a little girl. One day we got onto the topic of her having more children. She said that she couldn't imagine having another child because she didn't think she could love another child as much as she loved her daughter. The love she felt for her daughter was so immense, she was sure it couldn't be duplicated. I told her I was sure that wasn't true. I had siblings and I guess I didn't want to think that could be possible. Did my mother love one of us more than the others? No, I was sure she was wrong.

Then I had Kali about five years later and I knew exactly what she meant. You know that silly game where someone asks you, "If your mother and your father were both hanging from a cliff and you only had the strength to pull up one and the other would fall to certain death, who would you save?" Now, assuming that the people I'm about to name are in your life and that you have equally healthy and loving relationships with them, who would you save?

Your mother or father? Your sister or brother? Grandma or Grandpa? It's impossible to answer. I think it's because it's all the same kind of love. Now, toss your child into the mix. Your mother or your son? Your daughter or your brother? It's true when they say that the love you feel for your child is unlike any you'll ever feel for anyone else.

Then the moment I hugged Donny after telling him the news, I was filled with more love. More love for him and for Kali. New love for this little tiny thing inside of me the size of a fingernail. And it's weird because he or she has no idea. Donny and I talked about it last night. I told him, "He has no idea how much I adore him already." Seriously. After about a week on Earth this baby is going to try and crawl back inside of me just to get a break from all the attention bestowed upon him from all three of us.

Another thing I've been feeling that I didn't share with anyone until Donny last night, and now here with you, is this urgency to get it all over with. I just want it to be August already. I'm so glad I'm taking six classes this semester because I'm hoping it will make the time go by faster. By the time the semester ends, it will be the end of May and that's a lot closer to August than now. But the main reason, besides the joy I know it will bring to have the baby home, I really want to get this over with is because it's a huge responsibility.

Women, this is the most important thing you'll ever do. It's the scariest thing you'll ever do. On one hand, I'm amazed at how little I seem to be involved. It's kinda like, just fuel the body and it does the rest. The fact that I'm capable of harvesting, for lack of a better word, a set of lungs, a liver, kidneys, fingers and toes, another heart, etc., is AMAZING to me. Since seeing the baby's heartbeat, and hopefully we'll get to see it next week, but insurance companies are notoriously stingy with ultrasounds, Donny has said to me at many random times, "I can't believe there are two hearts beating inside of you right now." And I'm all, "I know." Then I usually go throw up.

One the other hand, you feel like it is so amazing and important you're bound to fuck it up. You should see me walking down the stairs. I'm tempted to start scooting down on my ass one step at a time like a toddler just to avoid falling. Just a few hours ago I was walking up the stairs and I didn't place my foot on the next step firmly enough and I kind of teetered backwards. I don't think I was in any real danger of falling, but it still scared me. With your uterus growing so rapidly your center of gravity is thrown off and that's why pregnant women get so clumsy.

Last night I had another crying fit as I admitted to Donny how scared I am. It's like life is *too* perfect. Perfect daughter, perfect husband, perfect home, perfect grades, perfect eyebrows (don't judge me), and you wonder when that other shoe gonna drop. And you pray to God that it doesn't drop with this baby. You know? Donny couldn't be less afraid and more confident. He says that since we tried so hard for a year to get pregnant with no results, and that this baby was conceived without us really *trying*, that it just proves he's meant to be here. And he's going to be fine.

The other kind of fear I'm feeling comes with not having done this in nine years. I remember April 19th, 1999 so well. It was a Monday and Kali was exactly one week old. Her first week here, I was always surrounded with people – Sophie, my Mom, my Dad, stepmom and sister were visiting. But by that Monday everyone was gone and I was alone with Kali for the first time. Some time that morning I called my mother.

"Hey, um... I need to take a shower."

"So, go take a shower."

"Well, what am I supposed to do with Kali?"

"What is she doing?"

"Sleeping in her little chair."

"Then go take a shower and leave her little butt right where she is."

"Are you sure?"

"What are you going to do? Take her in the bathroom with you?

I snort. "Duh. No."

So, Kali sat in her bouncy chair on the bathroom floor while I took a shower. It was the quickest shower in the history of ass washing. I fear I may do the same thing with this baby. I find myself wondering how I ever slept when Kali was first born. How did I not watch her every moment to make sure she was still breathing? Why are we even decorating a nursery, which now seems miles away from my bedroom, when I know I'm probably going to insist the baby stay in our room? I was at Pottery Barn Kids website yesterday looking at nursery furniture and wondering if I should go ahead and buy the baby a twin bed now... you know, so I can sleep in it in the nursery at night while he sleeps in the crib. Don't judge me!

Finally, I have that fear of "what kind of world am I bringing this child into?" I remember April 20th, 1999 clearly as well. I was home with Kali and called my mother at work once again.

"Ma, these two crazy ass white boys just shot up a school."

Later that day, I watched Kali sleeping in the crib and cried my eyes out. I wanted to put her back inside of me because I thought of all the times her feelings would be hurt, or the times her heart would be broken. I thought I just brought a child into the world, and even the white schools in good areas weren't even safe anymore! Just when I thought I had gotten used to a whole new set of worries for Kali, I'm going to go through all the old ones with this baby.

And physically? Whew. They say that the more times you're pregnant, the sooner you'll feel the signs. This is for two reasons. One, you've done it before so you can recognize the flutters for what they are earlier. Two, your body has that muscle memory thing going on. Even if you had an abortion or miscarriage, you were pregnant and your body remembers. Each time the egg implants I imagine your uterus lets out a weary sigh, "Ok, boys, you know the drill. I'm going to start stretching out a little more every day. You, organs above me, yeah, you. Scoot up. Lungs? Get ready for some company. It's gonna get cramped up there."

And let me tell you, I feel it. I can no longer sleep comfortably on my stomach, back, or left side. Don't ask me why. Well, the stomach is obvious, but when I lay on my left or my back I have shortness of breath. Also, laying on my right side makes gas come out easier when I have it. TMI? Perhaps, but it's true. And unfortunately that position puts my butt right in Donny's direction so we're thinking about switching sides on the bed... again.

And finally, physically, let's talk about the boobs. I can no longer bend forward to pick things up. My boobs feel like they are being pricked with a thousand tiny needles when I do. They have already gotten bigger. When I lean forward it's like all the blood and whatever they're filling with (colostrom?) just rushes to my poor nipples. And speaking of nipples. They are constantly hard. Ok, maybe not constantly, but they spend a great deal of the day at attention and I don't know why.

And guess what, guys? We still got 7 months to go!!

A Great Doctor Visit

January 18, 2008

Let me just tell you that I hadn't left this house since December 29th. As I got ready to go to the doctor this morning (you know, bubble bath, shaving, coochie maintenance) I thought, "What the hell am I going to wear?" My jeans won't close! Correction: They'll close, but it's not comfortable.

Donny came home to take me to the doctor. "Awww, you're so cute. We need to get you some spandex."

"Fuck you. I don't do spandex."

"Oooh, you know what we should get? Those little jogging suits with the hoodies. And you get the ones that say stuff across the butt."

"Yeah, so as my ass spreads the words will be all stretched the fuck out."

"Yeah, and people will have to walk from left to right just to read it."

"Fuck you, Donny. Fuck you."

The woman's clinic where my doctor is located is connected to, and affiliated with, the hospital where we went to the emergency room last month. We decided to stop there and pick up the ultrasound records from our visit in case the doctor wanted to see them. When we got to doctor's office, while we waited to be seen, Donny starts flipping through a magazine. I start noticing a trend in all the articles and flip it over to read the cover, "Conceive."

"Uh, we already did that."

So, we're finally seen and Donny is sent to wait in the exam room while I get weighed and my blood pressure is taken. I warn the nurse, "I can't button my jeans so they're wide open under this sweater."

"Bless you're heart. You're so cute."

As she weighed me I explained that I had just lost 20lbs before getting pregnant. She said she had lost 50lbs and then got pregnant. Twice. I liked my doctor almost immediately after he walked into the room. He was this older white man who has a slight limp. We first talked about the vomiting. He said that it sounds like I have the hyper-thing. The thing (that I can't pronounce) means "vomiting" and the hyper means "vomiting a lot." (Sometimes I spell vomiting with two "t" and I have no idea which is correct, but I'm thinking one looks better.) Anyway, he said I can keep taking the stuff I already have:

1) The Zofran tablets that dissolve under my tongue. They last 12 hours, but I only get nine pills per month from my insurance. It's the stuff they give to cancer patients to help with the nausea caused by chemo and radiation.

2) The phenegran, which is cheaper, only lasts 6 hours and knocks my ass out.

He also suggested Sea Bands. Divers wear them on their wrists to ward off sea sickness. There's a little ball that presses against the inside of your wrists and hits a pressure point that eases nausea. They also have Relief Bands that are larger, like a small watch, and the part that covers your inner wrist is larger and hits more areas so is sometimes more effective. It releases an electrical charge. The Sea Bands are like $6, and the Relief Bands are like $50. Some of the bands come with rechargeable batteries.

Then we talked about the cyst in my right ovary. He explained that it is normal, but he went into greater detail than the woman who took my ultrasound at the hospital. He explained that when you conceive, the ovary grows a little cyst that releases the pre-egg into your uterus. As the egg fertilizes the cyst remains and it releases what the baby needs to grow during the first trimester. Once the placenta is fully formed (anywhere from 10-12 weeks) it begins to take over and release the hormones and stuff the baby needs and the cyst dissolves. He said it's rare, but sometimes the cyst grows, becomes painful, twists, and has to be removed before the baby is born, but again, it's really rare.

He said that over the past 25-50 years they've learned a lot about these ovarian pregnancy cysts. Apparently, many years ago women would have them removed early on because cysts = bad, but then they would miscarry and doctors realized that it was because the cyst wasn't around to do its job. He and the nurse agreed that this should have been explained to me before. He also said that intercourse can aggravate and sometimes rupture the cyst, but the rupture part is really rare as well.

"Don't worry. I'm too busy throwing up to think about intercourse."

And damn if his old self didn't laugh and blush. I love this doctor!! Oh, I didn't tell you guys. The radiology department in the hospital gave us my records on a CD-ROM, so when we told the nurse that she wasn't sure they'd be able to view it. "I've never seen the records given that way." When we told the doctor he was like, "Well, let's go to my office and have a look. My laptop is on." As we headed to his office we passed our nurse who said, "Oooh, I want to go too. You guys will be the first. I want to see if this works."

So, we all sat around the doctor's desk, in his very nice office, and watched as he loaded the disc. And there everything was. It was so cool. I have the disc and I'll try to take some screenshots and see if I can post the pics in a blog. Anyway, he gave me a new due date of 8/12, but he said that may change next week as they take new measurements. Yup, I'm keeping my Tuesday appointment and that's when they'll be doing a new ultrasound.

He explained that it's going to look drastically different than it did just three weeks ago. The baby now has a neck and arms, legs, fingers and toes. Finally, I asked the question I'd been dying to all visit.

"Um, this is going to sound totally vain, but when can I relax my hair and touch up these gray roots?"

I thought his old white ass might not know what relaxing was but he just scoffed, tossed his hand in the air and said, "You can do it now. It doesn't get into your blood. I have patients who have had multiple pregnancies and they're beauticians. They're inhaling that stuff all day and processing their hair and their babies are fine."

Finally, he explained that in another week or so the baby will be done developing and then just growing and gaining weight. I'm so close to being past the hard stuff, he assured me.

After we left we stopped at Old Navy. My baby (Donny) insisted on buying me some more tummy-expanding friendly clothes. We stopped for lunch and then came home.

Oh, and the doc gave me these samples of a liquid medication that helps nausea as well. It's a mixture of B6 and some antihistamine. I'm to take a teaspoon in the morning and two at night. It will make me sleepy, but he said it should help. If it does, he said to just call the office and they'll hook me up with more. Sooo-weeet.

The way this office works is that each appointment throughout your pregnancy you see each doctor at least once. This way, when you go into labor, no matter who is on-call, your baby should be delivered by a physician you know, knows you, and one you're comfortable with. I still have five others to meet, but boy, I really liked this guy. Donny and I both agreed as we left that the entire staff was wonderful and we wouldn't mind in the least if that doctor was the one to deliver little Jack or Isabelle.

Note: He totally was.

Hey, I Remember These Nipples!
January 30, 2008

Since finding out we're having a baby I've only taken a handful of showers. Actually, showers pretty much stopped after the first week. When you're sick and dizzy damn near 24/7, soaking in a hot bath is much more appealing. Taking a bath also gives you the opportunity to comfortably perform a body inspection. It's amazing how many noticeable changes your body goes through in just the first few weeks and months of pregnancy.

Hormones ain't no joke. The first few weeks you're peeing more because of them, you're sleeping more because of them, and you're growing more hair because of them. In all kinds of places. While bathing yesterday I realized that my whole body is covered in this light coating of... fur, bringing new meaning to the term, "mama bear." I've always been hairy and just chalked it up that Latina blood flowing through my veins. I was not prepared, however, for the amount of hair I noticed yesterday. On my chest, tummy, legs, arms, shoulders. What the shit? Again, I'm used to seeing hair in some of these places. Hell, we're all mammals! But everything just seemed fuller.

I dipped my left arm under the water and the hairs immediately stood on end, flowing in the water. It looked like some scientific sea life program on PBS. I was half expecting some British guy's voice to provide commentary. "A woman in her second trimester may notice an increase in body hair. Here, a pregnant woman submerges her arm under water. Notice the thickness of the hair as it sways."

And let's not even talk about my facial hair. Pretty soon I'm going to look like Ming The Merciless.

Then there's the *linea nigra* - the dark line that runs down the middle of your stomach from your belly button and disappears under your baby bump. 'Cause you know after awhile you can't see past your belly. Anyway, that line appears because of the pregnancy hormones as well.

During my body check yesterday, I also noticed something I'm not quite sure has anything to do with pregnancy. I have a bunch of scratches all over. Funny thing is, I don't know how they got there. They're all fairly recent too. One on my knee, two on my arms, one on my left breast, and another on my shoulder. Maybe I'm scratching myself while I sleep? Due to pregnancy hormones my nails are also longer and thicker.

Besides the belly, of course, the most noticeable change occurs in the boobs. And not just the size. The nipples change too. The pregnancy hormones cause your areolas to darken and expand. You may also notice that the skin around your immediate nipple area remains dry. Those are pregnancy nipples. It's like they're preparing themselves for their new role as the conduit from which your child will receive his sustenance. (If you plan on exclusively breastfeeding as I do.) They realize they are not just window dressing anymore and an occasional pacifier for your man. They have to become durable for hours of feeding each day. They now have a *job* to do!

Your normal, non-pregnant nipples are like a cute little purse. It's pretty, it's cute, but it can only hold like a single key and a stick of gum. But you don't care because it's cute. Pregnancy nipples are like a big hefty bag, passed down from your Grandmother. It's leathery, worn, and doesn't match shit in your wardrobe. But it has a purpose. It can hold your keys, your iPod, your iPhone, your laptop, the book you're reading, the book you've been meaning to read, an umbrella, an extra pair of comfortable shoes, some tampons, your gym clothes, your makeup, your wallet, and a midget. Pregnancy nipples do it all! But there's still that dry, cracked, leathery business to deal with.

Ladies, just find a good moisturizer (inexpensive since you'll be using a lot) and don't worry about it because the good news is that after delivery, all of these changes will reverse themselves, and due to the same selective amnesia that allows women to forget all the bad stuff about pregnancy and have more than one child, you will forget all about the hair, tough nipples, and morning sickness. This is why I actually looked down at my tits yesterday while bathing and exclaimed, "Hey, I remember these nipples!"

He Kicks, He Scores

March 14, 2008

It's official: It's a boy! And Jack is also officially a kicker!

Wednesday evening, around 6pm or so, Donny and I were on the bed watching the news. I was telling him how I'd only felt small movement throughout the day while he was at work and how I really wanted Jack to start kicking. Really kicking. More for my piece of mind than anything else, really.

I decided to get out the old doppler and listen to his heartbeat. "Pass me the KY," has become a common heard phrase around our house. So, I lube up and put the wand on my tummy, moving it around trying to find Jack's heartbeat. I found it eventually dead center. He let us listen for a few moments and then he swam away. I found him again, we heard it for a bit, then he swam away again. He's feisty and like his mother, doesn't like to be bothered.

I finally got him to sit still in the center again and while Kali, Donny, and I listened, Kali put her hand right above where the wand was.

"I can feel him moving."

"No you can't."

"Yes, I can. It's this weird vibration."

She moves her hand and puts mine there and sure enough I feel something. Then I take Donny's hand and place it in the exact spot. Not five seconds later, Jack kicked!

Donny yelled out, "I felt that!"

"Me too!"

Kali chimes in, "I wanna feel, I wanna feel."

So now I got about four hands all over my belly and Jack's heartbeat is this steady, fast, and strong rhythm playing throughout the bedroom. He didn't do it again, but we were all happy we got to feel something.

Last night, I was lying on my back kinda propped up by five pillows when I felt him moving center and a little to the left. I grabbed Donny's hand and placed it on my belly. Within a few seconds, a kick!

"Was that you?"

"No! That was Jack!"

"Do it again, Jack!"

He didn't. Like his mother, he only does what he wants to do when he wants to do it. Donny was all excited for the rest of the night. He said he wants Jack to do it more and for longer periods of time. He said the kicks are too quick. I explained that it's not ever going to be like a tap-tap-tap-tap-tap like Jack's tapping his foot in time to movement, but that they will be more frequent and more pronounced as he gets bigger and stronger.

"Are you happy now?"

"Very. I finally feel a part of it."

Aww, he felt left out. He said I would get jealous whenever I'd suddenly tell him, "Ooh, I can feel Jack moving." (By the way, as I type this he's wiggling around right now!)

We had a funny moment last night: If we turn in at the same time, we usually fall asleep with Donny spooning me with one of his hands on my belly. Just in case. Well, last night we turned over right after *LOST* went off and I stayed on my side of the bed, propped up using the laptop to chat with Sophie till about 11pm. Then I read for about fifteen minutes before turning out the light and settling in. I had my back to Donny but I heard him stir so I craned my neck around to see if he was awake.

He was scratching his back so I took a chance. "Hey, you awake?"

"Mmm hmm."

"Do you want some covers?"

I had them all, he had none.

"No, it's hot in here." The ceiling fan was on and I thought it was pretty comfortable.

"Ok. You want to touch me?"

Now I realize I could have phrased it differently, but I wasn't thinking. His head kinda popped up and he immediately started scooting closer. I reached back and took his hand, brought it around, and placed it on... my belly. It was then that I realized his hand was steering a little bit south of where I had intended. Sorry, Charlie. Not tonight.

A Funny Bath Story

May 27,' 2008

This morning I was a mess. My feet were really swollen, every time I had to walk anywhere I felt like my pelvis was on fire and my right calf was killing me because of the horrible charlie horse the night before. Donny helped me upstairs and offered to run a hot bath hoping it would make my leg feel better.

I was in the tub for awhile, reading a book I had propped up on the side of the tub when Kali came in the bathroom and knelt beside me.

"Did Daddy clean the tub?" I haven't been able to clean the tub for months now, as my belly is too big and the tub is too low.

"Yeah, why?"

"Well, what's that?"

I look at the water and see these spots of orange film on top of the water. There were also tiny balls, sand-like, but orange in color, floating in the water. Kali and I stare for a second and I think it looks as if they are floating up right from between my legs... and I can't see anything down there 'cause it's just big old baby belly in the way. I call for Donny who is on our bed right outside the master bathroom.

The three of us are stumped, trying to figure out what the hell is in the water.

"Is it coming from me?" I shriek.

"That's what it looks like."

At this point Donny and I are both thinking the same thing. And it wasn't anything good. I didn't think my water had broken, but I was worried nonetheless. I mean, I don't know what amniotic fluid looks like, and it didn't help that just the night before my mother-in-law was saying that when her water broke with Donny, it came out in small trickles throughout the day. For all I know amniotic fluid looks a lot like orangey-red pond scum when released into a tub of bath water.

Donny takes Kali out of the bathroom and I hear him meet my mother at the top of the stairs and tell her to "come here." She follows him into the bathroom and then the three of us are now trying to figure out what's in the water.

I didn't feel any pain and though I was worried, I knew it wouldn't do any good to freak out. The three of us are trying to get some of the little orange balls (which are also now accumulating along the sides of the tub forming a ring) with our fingertips. When we did, the balls would dissolve. So, I'm naked in the tub with my Mom and husband each inspecting my bath water. Quite a scene, huh? We're touching and sniffing and I remember saying twice, "It has a kind of metal smell, doesn't it?" (Note: Before I got up from the bed to walk to the bathroom I thought I smelled metal too.)

We had just decided that I'd get out and we'd call the doctor just to be safe when finally, my mother sniffs her finger and she says, "You know what it smells like? Vitamins."

And then instantly Donny and I knew what it was. Right before he helped me off the loveseat so we could go upstairs and he could run my bath, I had taken a prenatal vitamin from the end table and stuck it in the pages of my book. My mother had handed it to me a few minutes before, but I didn't take it because I hadn't eaten recently and I don't like taking them on an empty stomach (doing so makes me sick.) So, I stuck it in my book and handed the book to Donny who then helped me off the couch. When Donny told me my bath was ready the last thing I did before rising from the bed was close the book I'd been reading. After I'd bathed and soaked for a bit, Donny asked if I wanted my book and then brought it to me. He sat it and a towel on the side of the tub and the pill must have fallen in the water when I opened it to read.

My mother flicked water in my face. "You scared the shit out of me."

My stepmother later joked that Jack got his daily vitamin straight from my wazoo today.

Little Flames

June 3, 2008

I can't see the bottom part of my stomach which is probably a good thing because that's where the stretch marks live. Out of sight, out of mind. Until, of course, after Jack is born, I lose weight, and it's bikini season again. But, whatever. I'm not going to cry and stress about it. I walk around with my belly bare and Kali is fascinated. Donny's just in love and happy his baby is in there. He doesn't care what the packaging looks like.

"I can't wait to see our baby boy."

"Just wait till he sees how beautiful his mother is."

He ain't slick. He's angling to knock my ass up again in two years.

Last night I was flat on my back with my t-shirt pulled up so Donny and Kali could see Jack moving around.

"Mommy, your belly is like a big pumpkin. Even with those little stretch marks."

"Uh huh."

"They're cute."

"Uh huh."

"And you know, I think pumpkins have little white lines on the bottom too so your stomach really *is* like a pumpkin."

Today, same deal except it's just me and Donny, after watching Jack poke, kick, and roll.

"I'm sorry. I bet this is really ugly, huh? My big old belly with those stretch marks on the bottom."

"No, I think it's beautiful. They're like little flames."

"I should get them tattooed after he's born. Outlined and colored in with orange and red. How white trash is that?"

And we just laughed and laughed. The whole time my big pumpkin belly jiggled.

Big Girl Panties

July 3, 2008

I caved a few weeks ago and bought big girl panties, or as I like to call them, drawers. I couldn't take it anymore. When I was pregnant with Kali, I held on to my Victoria's Secret Angel collection for dear life. I was still sporting those panties into my third trimester. I managed to do the same thing with this pregnancy, finally giving in and buying a three-pack of drawers from Target a few weeks ago.

I'm not a panty-wearer normally, but I definitely buy them. I have this thing about buying sets. I like my panties and bras to match, even if I won't wear the panties. But should I choose to, I think it looks tacky if you're walking around in mis-matched underwear. When you're pregnant, you *have to* wear underwear. Between the hormones in the first and second trimesters and the cervix softening in the third, pregnant women have a lot of discharge and comfortable panties and panty liners can be your best friends.

Plus, I think it's kinda rude going to the doctor without drawers on. Just saying.

The other day I had just gotten out of the shower when I realized I didn't have any clean drawers. Then I remembered that I had two brand new, unopened, three packs in the suitcase of stuff to take to the hospital. I asked Donny to go into Jack's room and grab a pair. He returns with the panties in his hands, holding them up by both ends and waving them like he's fanning the flames of a fire.

Whoomp. Whoomp.

Just imagine the sound of a pterodactyl flapping its wings.

"Donny, stop!"

"What?"

"That makes me feel bad."

"It's fun. Look. They're as big as Kali's shirts."

And to prove his point he spreads my big drawers on the bed and then grabs one of Kali's tank tops from a basket of clean, unfolded, laundry by our bed and places it on top of the panties. Damn if those panties aren't bigger than a Kali shirt.

Son of a bitch.

Discharge

July 5, 2008

We had a doctor appointment this morning. On the way there Donny is all, "You still having discharge?"

"Yeah."

Silence.

"Wait. Why are you asking me about my discharge? Don't be asking me about stuff like that?"

"Well, I was thinking it's something you need to bring up today. Beverly said last week that you could be dilating and they need to know that."

Beverly's our birthing coach.

"You just let me decide what I'm going to bring up."

"You need to bring up *everything*."

See, when you're pregnant with an active partner, you need to be prepared that they expect to have some kind of say in, well, everything... including the status of your vagina and everything it produces and not just the child itself.

When we get to the doctor they do the whole weigh me and check my blood pressure thing and then it's off to the ladies room for a urine sample. I'm sitting on the toilet holding a cup under my pee stream with my head bent down when I am struck by the loveliest aroma.

Is that coming from my vagina? I mean, I know I'm so pretty that I fart fairy dust, but my vagina has never, to my knowledge, released such a lovely odor. I must have sat there with my head between my legs sniffing for about 45 seconds. It wasn't until I was standing up writing my name on the cup with a Sharpie (don't ask why I never write on the cup BEFORE it's filled with piss) that I realized there was one of those time-release air fresheners on top of the cabinet. Duh!

Anyway, the nurse tells me I can call in Donny and Kali from the waiting room and then she'd show us to an exam room. Then she mentions something about "a swab, a q-tip, my vagina, and my rectum."

Say what?

As she leaves the three of us in the exam room with instructions for me to disrobe from the waist down, Donny notices I'm pouting.

"What?' he asks after she left.

"I think they're going to stick a q-tip in my bum."

Kali asks, "What's a q-tip?"

"The things I use to clean your ears."

"What's a bum?"

"Never you mind."

The nurse returns and places a sterile package on the counter and leaves again.

"Kali, hand that to Mommy."

It's the longest q-tip I've ever seen. I start to feel queasy.

Kali is still really sleepy. She stays up late and we had to wake her up early for the appointment. "Why did I have to come?" she whines.

"What else were we going to do with you?"

"Well, I could have stayed home with Daddy and you could drive yourself."

I look at Donny, "Did you want to stay home too?"

"No, someone needs to be here to make sure you're honest."

"Shut up."

So, the doctor walks in (she's the same one from our very first visit. The pretty, young, black, woman who said that it's possible for me to gain only

20lbs during the pregnancy because that's what her little pixie ass did) and we tell her about the contractions. She decides to check my cervix while she's down there doing the q-tip thing. She explains they'll be taking a swab from both my vagina and my anus.

"Lovely."

She laughs. I didn't find a damn thing funny. That was like an hour ago and my ass still hurts. She checks my cervix and it's not even dilated a full centimeter. She could get a fingertip in there, but it was softening hence all the mucus discharge. Isn't childbirth fun?! She said his head is really low and that would explain all my trouble walking and pelvic pain. He's already dropped into birthing position. Yah!

I tell her that whenever I do a lot in one day that by the evening I'm usually all swollen hands and feet. She said that was due to all the excess pressure on my blood vessels and that when that happens I should spend the next day in bed with my feet propped up and avoid salty foods.

"That means no french fries." That from Kali a.k.a. Big Mouth.

"Does Mommy eat a lot of french fries?" asks Dr. F.

Kali just giggles.

I look at both Kali and Donny and say, "Yeah, you're both staying home next time." Dr. F. laughs and says I'm funny.

We're now at the stage where our visits are once a week. I'm officially 34 weeks and 5 days. Just four weeks and 2 days to go! Woohoo!

We were going to go shopping today for the wood blinds and ceiling fan for the nursery, but my asshole hurts and I don't feel like walking.

Full Circle

July 21, 2008

First trimester: We'd just gotten a new flat screen TV and were playing lots of *Halo 3* with Lacey and Brett. I was sick all the time. Miserable and uncomfortable. I felt no connection to my unborn baby because I didn't feel pregnant, I felt sick. I felt like I was going to die.

Now, 19 days till my due date: We just got a new flat screen TV and we're playing lots of Halo 3 with Lacey and Brett. I'm sick all the time. I'm miserable and uncomfortable. I feel connected to Jack, but I catch myself saying, in tears, "He needs to come out. I can't do this anymore!" Not exactly the same song I was singing say, a month ago when it was all, "I can't wait to meet my baby." I feel like I'm going to die.

I tell you the good, you know that. But I'll also tell you the bad. The ugly. And trust me folks, it's very ugly.

I am MISERABLE. And I don't know that I can last another 19 days. I really don't. If I'm not around it's because I don't feel like being bothered for the most part. I'm cranky and sad and depressed and a mess.

Let's start from head to toe:

I'm so depressed that I can't even be bothered to care that I need to dye the gray out of my hair before Jack meets me and thinks I'm his grandmother. I will say that my hair has never been healthier, but I still feel like a spinster when I look in the mirror.

The acne on my face, neck and upper arms is driving me crazy! Donny reminds me that it's all hormones, the same thing happened when I was pregnant with Kali, and that it will go away, but it sure doesn't feel like it. I hate not recognizing myself in the mirror.

The hair growth is out of control! I'm constantly shaving all kinds of places. My boobs are ginormous, which... is kinda nice. But still. They ache because they too are desperate to get this show on the road. Donny tells Jack, "Boy, you got some good stuff waiting for you!"

My stomach is huge. Not as huge as most other pregnant women I see, but big enough. I can't lie back without feeling like I'm going to choke on the acid reflux or suffocate because of everything pressing against my lungs. When I lie on either side I feel Jack and all the fluid flow to that side putting pressure there and then I have to sit up again. When it's time to stand it takes an effort... and an army. Walking is torture. You guys should have seen me on Friday at the movie theatre. I know people were like, "She needs to go home because that looks painful." And it is!

My knees hurt. My back hurts. My pelvic bone hurts. I need to go into labor.

And mentally? I'm a mess. I have a high tolerance for pain. I did over 24 hours of labor with Kali and no drugs. No sweat. I can handle getting a tattoo and already have my second one planned. But I can't stand being uncomfortable. With most serious pain, you know there's an end. Like labor. I know that it can't last forever. But this *all day* uncomfortable feeling drives me crazy.

Sometimes I just cry. For no particular reason I'll just break down and cry and Donny will just sit with me, rubbing me and telling me that I'm doing great and that we're almost there. Problem is: It doesn't feel like it! It's hard to remember this is leading to a joyous event when you're so miserable. And it pisses me off when people say, "Well, Nina, you want him to be healthy so the closer you get to 40 weeks the better."

I'm his fucking mother! Of course I want him to be healthy and I've never once wished to go into labor at his expense. It's a given that I want him to be perfectly healthy when he's born, but it's also okay for me, the one in pain and going through it, to say, "OK, I've 'bout had enough. This shit is hard." I'm allowed!

The other night Donny and I were playing Halo 3 with Lacey, Brett, and Brett's best friend Gabe. I thought I was going to go into labor from laughing so hard. We hadn't had that much fun in forever. Anyway, in between rounds I went to pee and sat my controller and headset on the couch. When I got back, I went to lower myself onto the couch and let out the usual battle moan before doing anything strenuous. They could hear me through my and Donny's headset. Brett says to Donny, "Please tell me that wasn't the sound of her getting off the couch?"

"No, motherfucker! That's what I sound like getting ON the couch!"

It's so sad.

I blew off my doctor's appointment Thursday. I woke up not feeling well and not wanting to go in there just to pee in a cup and have them tell me, "OK, everything's fine. See you next week." Fuck that. So, I called to push it back to later in the afternoon hoping my spirits would rise by then. Well, Donny called. And they said, "We can see you at 1:30pm, but there may be a wait."

Bitch, there's ALWAYS a wait! Why do they do that? Schedule four women for 10:30am? It pisses me off every time I sign in a few minutes early to see other women who've arrived a little before me all checking off that they're there to see the same doctor. There are like seven damn doctors at that practice! So, we rescheduled for today at 3pm. And I don't feel like going 'cause I'm cranky. And I'm getting a cold. And I'm tired of these big girl panties. And I don't feel like wasting my time on them telling me to go home and wait some more. No shit, assholes. How 'bout you check down there and maybe jump start some action, huh?

And I'm tired of looking at all my baby's nice stuff and feeling like he's never going to get here. And I just really, really, really, need to go into labor before I kill someone. Seriously.

Find a Place of Peace

July 23, 2008

That's what the doctor advised me to do yesterday. Find a place of peace.

I went in yesterday because I woke up and couldn't move. The pain in the right side of my back was so severe I thought we'd have to call an ambulance. Donny called Beverly who suggested that he wet a rag, microwave it, and then place it on my back. We did. That helped enough for me to go upstairs and take up her second suggestion of soaking in a hot tub. That helped enough for me to move without screaming and make my way into the office so they could make sure I wasn't in labor. I knew I wasn't. But again, I was hoping for the best.

I saw Dr. F, the pretty, young, black, petite one. She pretty much told me that the pain in my pelvis and back was due to the fact that my husband implanted his ginormous German seed in me and now I'm going to have a mini-linebacker emerge from my vagina any day now. Swell. She felt around and measured and sure enough she thinks he's about 7lbs and will probably be high 7's or 8lbs at birth.

Then she asked, "Now, as for the mental stuff. What can I do for you?"

And I freaking lost it. I was a crying fool. I told her that I knew the cosmetic stuff was temporary, but it didn't help deal with the other stuff. She assured me I'd be my usual beautiful self soon. Her words, not mine. Then I told her about feeling so miserable and hating it because I should be happy and excited. I worry that the feeling won't go away once he gets here. She

307

assures me it will. She doesn't want to prescribe anything because "it doesn't sound like you're suicidal."

"No, I'm not suicidal. Just miserable."

Then she suggested that I go get my hair and nails done. "Get a pedicure to lift your spirits."

Doctors would stop delivering advice like that while sitting on those stools with wheels - so close to your feet as you're sitting up high - if she knew how close I was to kicking her in the face.

Warm Gushes and Nipple Stimulation

July 29, 2008

Oh, what a day!

After a bad night of pain and discomfort Donny called the doctor's office at 9am to see if I could get my 2:15pm appointment today bumped up. They told us to come in right then and there. I jumped in the shower, and by jumped I mean waddled, and we were off.

After the usual check-in stuff (where I *finally* remembered to write my name on the urine cup BEFORE pissing in it) we were shown to a room to wait for Dr. G. I've written about him before. Of all the doctors at my practice, he's my fave; this old white dude that looks like he used to be on *The Sopranos*. I put my panties in my purse, covered my lower half with the sheet and hiked up my dress to get ready for my least favorite part of the pregnancy exam.

Before we left the house I told Donny, "I love Dr. G., but I'm not sure I want him sticking his fingers up my coochie. I mean, he's this old white man."

"Well, if it makes you feel any better I'll be an old white man one day sticking my fingers up your coochie."

No. Somehow that didn't make me feel better.

When he comes in, I tell him how every day just gets harder and how much pain I'm in. He notes that the previous week I didn't get a vaginal exam and he shakes his head in disapproval. "How did they know you were fine if they didn't check?" I ask him to please induce me before I kill myself. "Well, let's see what's going on first... maybe."

The nurse comes in and asks me to scoot down and put my feet in the stirrups. I think Kali might have been in the room once before while I've had a pelvic (yeah, she was there for the infamous anal swabbing) so she kinda knew what to expect and in anticipation she came to the head of the table to hold my hand. I thought it was the sweetest thing. The nurse holds my other hand and then it felt like Dr. G. went in elbow deep.

Oh. My. Fuck. It hurt.

After a few moments I realize I'm squeezing the shit out of the nurse's hand. "I'm sorry. I'm sorry."

"It's okay. Squeeze as hard as you want. But breathe."

It's then that I realize that I'm all tense and holding my breath. I try to relax "down there" as well take a few deep cleansing breaths.

When he's done, Dr. G. says that my cervix is posterior which means it's really far back and it needs to drop down more. He said that it's completely soft and I'm dilated two centimeters. If he sent me to the hospital today for an induction, I'd probably be there for days and I run the risk of having to have a c-section if it doesn't come down during that time.

He said what I needed was more contractions to help move it along and also get more dilation going. Donny asked about the walking I'd been advised to do. He explained that walking doesn't *start* contractions and that any pregnant woman that went for a walk and then got contractions experienced a coincidence; however, once contractions start, walking does help them get stronger and more frequent. In my situation where walking is painful, walking without having any contractions wouldn't be doing myself any favors.

"Are you going to breastfeed?" he asked inadvertently glancing at my huge ta-tas.

I told him I am and he suggested nipple stimulation. *That* he said will definitely bring on contractions. He said I should go home and pump each breast three minutes at a time for like 12 minutes every 2-3 hours.

"Will anything come out?'

"Probably not."

I wanted to hear a resounding NO. I'm a huge breastfeeding advocate. I love it. I'm looking forward to it. It's one of the most beautiful things I've ever done and I'm completely in awe of my body's ability to nourish the child it created. I even get a little judgmental in my head when I hear a woman say she doesn't want to breastfeed. But even with all that, I still feel kinda... icky... at the possibility of seeing something come out before Jack gets here. Also, it's been nine years.

I asked him what his policy was in regards to recording the birth and he shrugged and said, "I don't care. I know what I'm doing. In fact, I like to explain everything that's happening as it's happening so you know what's going on." Which just proved to me that the only reason a doctor would have a problem with it is if they fuck up and don't want video evidence in the malpractice suit. So now I'm praying that Dr. G. is on call when I go into labor, but I'm also going to see if they'll let me request him.

We make an appointment for next Tuesday, which should be my last one, with the one doctor left I've yet to see. For some reason or another I always end up rescheduling my appointments with him. And if I have my way, I won't be meeting his ass next week either cause Jack will be here by then. When we leave, Donny has to bring the car around because I can barely walk. I'm cramping and aching and I feel like my uterus is going to come out of my belly button.

For some reason, on doctor visit days we go to Chic-Fil-A afterwards. Our CFA restores our hope in humanity. The other fast food places always fuck up, but not CFA. Not only do they always get the order right, they're friendly as shit. Today, the girl actually asked us if we wanted a drink tray. Take that ghetto ass Burger King. Donny and I discuss this as we wait for our food. Another observation I'd made before that Donny echoed today while we waited, "And it seems they only hire young, white, blonde girls."

"I know, right?"

Just then who should stroll from the back but a young black girl? We damn near clapped. Yah for black people! We had the same reaction when we found out during the construction of our home that our next door neighbors were a black, male, gay, couple. As an interracial couple in the south we like to see diversity. It gives us hope for the tolerance level in our area and diminishes the chances that one day we'd find ourselves back-to-back, Mr. and Mrs. Smith-style, having to beat some ass.

After we eat, I call my Dad. While I'm chatting with him I feel this tiny, warm, gushing feeling in my panties. "Daddy, I gotta call you back." Donny helps me to the bathroom and on the way I explain what happened.

"Are you wearing panties?"

"Yes, I'm wearing panties!"

Of course, Kali has to follow. There are no secrets in my house anymore. While Donny runs to get me new panties Kali stands and watches fascinated. "Did you pee on yourself?"

"I hope not," I respond grabbing a couple of baby wipes from the back of the toilet.

Once Donny hands me the new pair of underwear I ask him to run out to the car and get a sanitary napkin from the suitcase we packed for the hospital. I can get one foot in the new panties while still sitting but I need Kali to hold open the leg of the other side. She scrunches up her face like I asked her to smell a fart.

"Girl, I've wiped your dirty little ass more times than I can count."

"Are these panties clean?" she asks tentatively, holding them with the tips of as few fingers needed to get the job done.

"Yes!"

"I mean, but, you've worn them before, right?"

"Yes! And they've been cleaned after each time."

What the hell does she think I am? Donny returns with the pad and Kali asks, "What's that?" I know I've kinda explained a period before as she's had to run and get a tampon for me in the past. I explain again that one day she will be getting a period and that the pads are used to absorb the blood. As I talk, I'm un-wrapping the pad and explaining how it's used.

She seemed to take the information well and only displayed a little surprise when I told her that she could be getting it any year now. She thought it was something you had to get when you went to college. Hahaha! She asked if it hurt and I told her that the first day or so of each month that she gets it, she may feel as if she has to take a big poop and her tummy will hurt. She didn't really like the sound of that.

As I'm pulling up my panties she remarks, "That looks like a diaper." Then proceeds to sing and skip, "Mommy's wearing a diaper. Mommy's wearing a diaper," all the way back to the family room.

Donny and I break out the $300 electric breast pump. I'm ready to get this damn show on the road, but I'm also a little frightened. I've never used an electric pump before. I had a small manual with Kali. We decide it would be more efficient to do both breasts at once. I place the suctions over each boob and Donny flips the switch. I felt like a cow. Seriously. It didn't hurt really, but it wasn't the most pleasant feeling either. At least I'm getting prepared though. At exactly three minutes the suction went from quick pumps to long drawn out pulls that actually hurt.

"Shut it off!"

I guess after three minutes it expects you to have a nice steady flow of milk going or something, but I don't have milk yet. Just a few drops of clear liquid and just seeing that made me nauseas. We decide that's enough for now and agree to try again between 3-4pm, which is right about now as I type this.

Donny goes upstairs to pay some bills and Kali is on the floor next to the sofa playing on my laptop when I find myself drifting off to sleep. I didn't even know I was sleeping until a loud noise in my head woke me up. After about two seconds I realize what the sound was.

"Did I just snort?" I ask Kali.

She's laughing so hard she can barely nod and answer, "Yes."

That's another thing I won't miss about being pregnant. Snoring. I used to snore something awful before I got my tonsils taken out a few years ago, but I've been snore-free since then. Until I got pregnant. Now, I'm sawing wood again.

I've had three contractions since doing the breast pump. Hopefully there will be more as we continue to pump every few hours. Between the contractions and Dr. G.'s forearm, I'm an achy mess. But I'm hopeful.

A completely soft cervix and two centimeters must mean I'll be going in soon, right? RIGHT? (Not to mention the fact that it seems I am, in fact, having small gushes of warm fluid that's not urine.) Cross your fingers!

Thank You

July 31, 2008

I know I'm all cranky and pissy lately. I'm just really, really, miserable.

Donny has to help me stand up every time I need to go to the bathroom, which is like every ten minutes. He sleeps bunched up on the love seat because the little bit of sleep I'm able to get is on the couch. During the night I don't have the heart to wake him for my bathroom trips so I end up rolling, yes literally ROLLING, myself off the couch. When I stand up I immediately have pain in my lower back and pelvis. I walk like an old woman. It's not even walking. It's not even waddling. It's like a rumble.

Things have to be placed in special places around the house to accommodate me. Like the toilet tissue has to remain on the back of the toilet tank because I can no longer lean forward to get some off the dispenser on the wall.

I use six pillows at night and basically sleep sitting up. I have contractions, but nothing that ever causes a pattern to signal true labor. I am so depressed that I cry almost every day, several times a day. My latest came about an hour ago when I heard a little boy crying for his mother on some TV show and she was pretty much ignoring him. Because I'm so unhappy and depressed it feels like I'll never be happy again. I woke Donny up and asked him to help me. Help me by making sure that when Jack gets here I'm a good mother, that I take care of him, and that this misery will go away so I can enjoy him and be a good mother to him. He promised me that I had nothing to worry about and held me as I cried and cried.

I really don't know how much more of this I can take. Physically, I'm done. Mentally, I'm a mess.

So, if I don't respond to comments or snap at you when you're just trying to be helpful, I'm sorry. I don't really mean it. Oh, except for those women who don't have children yet feel the need to make comments on my breastfeeding choices. "You're going to do it for *how* long? He's going to bite your nipples off."

Never in the history of titties has a woman lost a nipple to a teething, nursing child. If you've never been a Mom and breastfed a child, I suggest you have a nice, tall, frothy glass of shut the fuck up.

Ok, now that that's out of my system, where was I? Oh yeah... thank you for all your kind words and comments on my profile page. It's nice to know that so many people are thinking of us and praying for a quick, safe, healthy delivery. I sometimes forget that when I'm sitting here feeling like this baby will never come and I'm in so much pain that I cry, and it feels like no one understands or cares.

So, for all of you who have said that something I've written has gotten you through the day or made you laugh, just know that right about now you are returning the favor. Writing this down has kept me (somewhat) sane.

The Big Day

August 3-4, 2008

4:56am - I'm up an hour early. I can feel Jack moving around. I just rub my belly and tell him, "Soon, baby. Soon." There's a really sad movie on Showtime called *The Dead Girl*.

At 6am I'll do my hair, get dressed, and put on some makeup. Donny and I will make sure we have everything we need. Kali's bag for overnights with my parents has been packed and ready to go for weeks. We have to remember to put her toothbrush, toothpaste, and SmartRinse in there. Her iPod and GameBoy Advance have been charging all weekend. She'll be bringing those along in case she gets bored in the hospital.

We've packed the camcorder, the digital camera, the USB plugs for both, the chargers for both, and the tripod. Donny bought a puzzle book to keep himself busy for the down times (if there are any.) All the garbage has been taken out so we don't come home in a few days to a stinky house. Jack's suitcase has been packed and in the car for weeks now. Of course, now I'm having second thoughts on everything I packed for him.

The nightgown I'm wearing smells like baby. We ran out of laundry detergent and yesterday I was too impatient to wait for Donny to get back with more so I washed a load of clothes in Dreft, the baby detergent. Now I smell like newborn which only makes me want to meet Jack more. Yesterday, we kept saying things like, "Today is the last day we'll have lunch in this house as a family of three." We extended all the programs on the TiVos, and the stuff due to record over the next few days, until next week. As I watched the dates go by I thought, "Jack will be here by then."

Every now and then Donny and I would look at each other yesterday and say, "Tomorrow, we're going to have a son. What are we going to do!?" And then we'd laugh and just shake our heads. I told him, "You know what? I'm really looking forward to a few weeks from now when I'm feeling better, and hopefully starting to look more like myself, how great it's going to be to make love for the first time as his parents."

"It will be...." I started to say, "...special," I concluded.

"...crazy," Donny said at the same time.

"See, I was trying to make it romantic and meaningful and you gotta get nasty with it."

"Not nasty. Just passionate. Show you what you've been missing."

That's the wonderful thing about having a baby. You have all these special "last time we did this" moments, and all of these great, "the first time we do this together" moments to look forward to. We were trying to come up with all these "Jack" themed Halloween costumes. Poor boy. One year he'll be a Jack in the Box and another he can be Jack and the Beanstalk... or perhaps he and Kali can be Jack and Jill.

I'm excited. Not really scared or nervous. Maybe because I've done this before. The upside of being so miserable in the final months is that you really don't stress about the delivery. You don't care if you tear or get one drop of epidural. You just can't wait to push! At least that's how I feel.

We called the labor and delivery unit last night to make sure there wasn't something special I was supposed to be doing or not doing, eating or not eating, etc. They said I could do what I want and that they have me on the books for 7:30am. Woohoo! The doctor said I should be on a pitocin IV by 8am.

We get to bring the laptop and if there's Wi-Fi, I'll update as much as I can. I'm hoping for pitocin then epidural. In fact, if they just want to meet me in the parking lot with the epi, that would be swell. I plan on telling the doctor, "You know, when I had my daughter I had to have two shots of epi before it took so feel free to double up on the stuff from the get go. In fact, why don't you figure out just enough to kill me, and then shave off that amount just a tad."

Ok, I'm going to relax for a bit and try not to stare at the clock. It's 5:16am.

5:51am - Ain't this a bitch? It's nine minutes before the alarm is due to go off, and now I just want to go to sleep.

6:52am - We leave in 8 minutes. I think we have everything we need... and probably stuff we don't. We called at exactly 6:30am and fortunately not one inconsiderate bitch went into emergency labor so my induction time of 7:30 is on!

Holla atcha later.

We're Home!

August 6, 2008

There's so much to tell it will probably take three blogs. But here are the highlights:

Jack Ian was born on Monday, August 4th at 5:19pm. He weighed 8lbs and 6ozs and is 20 1/2 inches long. He has a LOT of jet black hair. For the first day or so I didn't think he looked like either one of us. I kept saying, "He looks like his own self." But, the more I look at him, the more I see Donny.

I am married to the most wonderful man EVER. Period. Hands down. It's a wrap. He was so wonderful throughout the whole pregnancy and was my rock while in labor. I also have an amazing daughter who was there the whole time. And the icing on the cake was having my Dad there to witness it as well.

We have video. I'll be sharing some of my Dad's video as he got the PG version. Our video cam was set up on a tripod and got ALL IN MY BUSINESS. What's on that video is between us, the doctor and nurses, and God.

I pushed him out in six minutes and felt every vagina stretching, bone adjusting moment of it. The epidural only took care of the tummy area which was wonderful during most of the day. But once he dropped and it was time to push, I felt it. And what you've heard is correct: it does feel like you have to drop the mother of all dumps. But it was still a wonderful experience. I'm glad I felt it and wouldn't change a thing.

We've been home for about an hour and a half and I'm exhausted. Jack is sleeping and Kali and Donny ran out to the store. My eyes are drooping as I type this.

Pics, blogs, videos, details, etc. to follow soon. Thanks for all your kind words and well wishes.

P.S. Jack is absolutely beautiful. As Donny said, "He has the most beautiful eyes ever. I could stare into them all day." We are all completely in love.

P.P.S. My vagina hurts.

Day One: Drugs 'R Fun

August 7, 2008

So, as most of you know we went to the hospital at 7:30am on Monday morning so that my labor could be induced. Not only was I the only woman scheduled for an induction that day, there were no other women there period. It was very quiet in the labor and delivery wing and we got lots of attention, which as you can all imagine, was right up my alley.

My nurses, Lynn and Jessica, got me settled and hooked up to an IV of fluids while we waited for the doctor on call to arrive and check me before beginning the pitocin drip. Guess who the doctor on call was? Dr. G! Once he arrived, he informed me that he wouldn't be checking me vaginally until after the pitocin kicked in. So, I have no way of knowing how far along I'd progressed from last Tuesday when I was 2 centimeters dilated.

After ten minutes of being on the pitocin, I got a horrible pain in my back. The nurses had shown Kali and Donny how to read the machines hooked up to Jack's heart rate and the one monitoring my contractions. Donny informed me that the back pan wasn't reading as a contraction. Lynn and Jessica came in and I explained that the current pain was exactly what I'd experienced a few days before and they concluded that Jack was most likely pinching a nerve. (This was the cause of the debilitating back pain that warranted an induction to begin with.)

After a while the contractions began and though they hurt, they were tolerable. I just made sure to do my breathing through each one. In the car, on the way to the hospital, I told myself to stick to three things that day. One, *be a big girl* and two, *remain calm and focused* so that, three, I could *enjoy and remember everything.* I was determined to follow through on all three. When they started to get bad (*Mommy, that one peaked at a six! Did you feel it? Yes, honey, Mommy felt it.*) I asked Lynn and Jessica for the epidural. Within ten minutes, Kali was whisked out the room to hang with the nurses at the nurses' station right outside the room and I was hunched over the edge of the bed clutching a pillow.

The doctor administering the epidural was Dr. F. If they made a movie about Dr. F's life Morgan Freeman would play him. I really liked this guy. He was calm and explained everything as he went along. It was kinda scary because they made me recite my full name, the date, my birth date, who the President is, etc., before we began. The three needles he inserted to numb everything stung, but weren't that bad. Then he placed a long, thin, tube in my back and that was tolerable. The most painful part was when he actually injected me with the first drug. It was hot and I felt extreme pressure, but even that wasn't like yell-out-loud pain. I just told myself to breathe, remain calm, and know that it can't last forever. Donny held my hands and told me I was doing a good job.

Up until then I'd been sitting up in bed and keeping a journal on my laptop - like a timeline - for a blog since there was no Wi-Fi to update live, but after I got the epidural the nurses told me I'd have to lie back and remain still so the tubing wouldn't come out... even though they taped it to my back with three large ass strips of tape. See, epidural *and* a free back wax. Sweet. Lynn and Jessica watched the monitors for about ten to twenty minutes and at one point asked, "Do you feel that?"

"Feel what?"

"You're having a contraction. A big one."

Guess the epidural was working.

Then they inserted a catheter and emptied my bladder for me. Didn't feel a thing. I was happy that I couldn't feel pan, but still a little weirded out by the situation. I couldn't move my legs, and when I touched my thigh it felt like it was someone else's thigh. I was reminded of that joke about boys sitting on their hand to make it fall asleep and then masturbating with it so that it feels like someone else's hand. Somehow, I didn't think anyone else would appreciate my little analogy so I kept it to myself.

I don't remember this, but Donny says it's on video. Apparently, I was messing with the controls trying to raise the back of the bed a bit and instead pressed a button that cause the mattress under my butt to rise.

He said I gave a small jump like someone had just stuck something up my butt and said, "Oops. That's my ass."

For some reason Donny and Kali found this extremely funny and busted out laughing which caused my doped up ass to laugh. Donny says that he told me, "Leave it to you to find the ass button." I have to check the video to see this for myself.

There were times when I knew I was having a contraction because my heart would speed up and it felt like someone was sitting on my chest. I didn't like that feeling *at all*, but I guess it beats feeling the pain of a contraction. Dr. G. returned to finally check me down there and hopefully break my water. It turns out that while he was up there looking for my cervix; my water broke on its own. All up his arm, according to Donny who was ALL IN IT. When they looked at the fluid they told me that Jack had had a bowel movement and that it wasn't anything to be too worried about, which of course made me worry, and that it just meant they would have to have a respiratory specialist there when he came out to make sure he didn't ingest any. At this point I was four centimeters and Dr. G. suggested upping the pitocin, which had been increasing throughout the morning anyway.

Kali and I napped and Donny sat by my side. I remember bits of conversation like me telling him I was so happy we worked through our problems and that our marriage lasted so we could share this together to which Donny replied, "Yeah, I'm just glad you didn't leave me." To which I replied, "I know, right? What was I thinking?"

The nurses checked me again and I was at 7 centimeters. They really wanted me to have him before their shift ended at 4pm. We'd all formed a nice little relationship and they were dying to meet Jack. They checked me again 30 minutes later because the contractions were getting stronger, faster, and lower (I was starting to feel them because, as they explained, the epidural only fully covered the stomach, lower pain pelvic pain and anal pressure was all mine to feel though it would be dulled due to the epidural), and I was at 9 centimeters. Yup, I dilated two centimeters in 30 minutes. I wasn't playing around.

At this point I'm wondering where the hell my Dad was. It's after 4pm and we were expecting him around 1:30pm. He called to say that his car had overheated, but he was close by. Swell. I was feeling every contraction and with each one I felt like I needed to push. My new nurse, Becky, would check me and tell me that though I wasn't quite 10 centimeters, I was still in the 9's and I couldn't push. It was sooo hard not to, but I held on. My Dad finally arrived between 4:15 and 4:30. He entered the room carrying his camcorder, huffing and puffing, and said, "OK, you can push now."

"I wish," I replied.

At 4:30 Becky told me she'd check me again at 4:45 because I was really close. It was the longest 15 minutes of my life. It felt like I had to take the biggest shit and no one would let me. At exactly 4:45pm I made Donny page Becky. She checked me and said I felt fully dilated and that she would page Dr. G. After a few minutes she came to tell me that Dr. G. instructed her to start the pushing w/o him and that he'd be there shortly.

I pushed three times for ten seconds each during each contraction. I went through two contractions (six pushes) with Becky and a young nurse named Jennifer. After the pushing for the first contraction Becky said to Donny, "See the head?" And Donny looked between my legs and smiled and nodded. He told me later that Becky had actually pushed open the lips of my vagina and he had to look UP it to see the head. I nearly threw up when he told me that. While we waited for Dr. G., I was told not to push during contractions and to just let Jack move forward on his own with each one. They said he was already really low because the labor had progressed so nicely and at such a good pace.

When Dr. G. entered he instructed Becky to check me and tell him which way she thought Jack's head was turned. She did. Then he said he would check and if she was wrong, he'd explain why. She was wrong and then he said that during each contraction he would work on turning Jack's head in the proper position so she could see how it was done. That made me feel all queasy because, remember, I could feel EVERYTHING going on down there. And though it didn't hurt due to epidural, it was still majorly uncomfortable.

So, with each contraction, Jennifer and Donny are each holding a leg, I'm pushing, Kali is hiding behind a curtain across the room listening to it all (another reason I was determined not to scream), my Dad is somewhere behind me and to my left videotaping, and Dr. G. is twisting his hand inside my vagina.

Donny was amazing. He kept looking down there and would rub my leg, whisper to me that I was doing great and that he loved me. When the head came out I was nervous that they'd say the cord was around the neck or something, but it wasn't. Then Donny told me later that one of Jack's arms also came out with the head because, like his big sister, he seemed to have been resting his head on it. I was instructed not to push because Dr. G. didn't want me to tear and they wanted to situate the arm. Then it was okay to push and I pushed once and he literally just came sliding out. I heard them all say several times, "He's out. He's out." but I thought they were talking about more of his body. I didn't' realize he was *out* out till Donny leaned over to kiss me and tell me, "He's here."

Donny and I both said that we weren't looking forward to that moment where you're just waiting for them to cry. Usually, they wait until they're on the table and they need to be suctioned and stimulated. Not our Jack. He was screaming his head off as Dr. G. was cleaning him up and working on the cord. I could barely see him but I remember thinking that he looked really tiny. I had a moment of panic that maybe they had my due date wrong and he was two weeks early and it was all my fault for wanting an induction if he wasn't fully ready to come out.

They placed him on my chest for a few moments and then they took him away to examine him. Donny and I were a crying mess. On my Dad's video, he follows Jack. But our camera was on a tripod and Donny was too over the moon to think about it right away, and so on our video I now know what it looks like to have someone stick their whole hand inside of me, I'm talking to the wrist or more, and pull out placenta. At the time, I was only vaguely aware of what Dr. G. was doing because I was staying focused on Jack. Donny was crying and kissing me and wouldn't leave my side. I finally told him to go be with Jack that I'd be okay. He told me later that he could see all this blood gushing out of me and he was worried about me so he didn't want to leave.

I remember Dr. G. saying that he was trying to get the bleeding to stop and thinking, "That doesn't sound good." They gave me a shot in my thigh of something that was supposed to help with the bleeding, but I don't remember the name of it. Kali could be heard asking, "Can I come in now?" but me and the nurses kept telling her to wait. I didn't want her to see me all spread open and bloody. But Jack was right next to the curtain so once he was over there being worked on; she spent most of her time cooing over him. Every now and then I'd glance down and see Dr. G. pulling a long piece of bloody thread on a hooked needle and I'd force myself to look away. I found out later from Becky that I only required one stitch (just like with Kali) but that you have to suture several times... I still don't understand what that means, but all I know is that now, my vagina is angry.

You could have knocked me over with a feather when I heard that he weighed 8lbs and 6ozs. He just didn't look that big. Also, I couldn't help but wonder how big his butt would have been should we have gone five more days. I bet I'd have needed more stitches. Once I was all taken care of and cleaned up, I got to hold Jack. Donny had already held him, and by the time he got to me he was knocked out. I nursed him for awhile, but he never opened more than one eye. I hadn't seen his fingers or toes.

Then the shakes began. My body went into shock and I shook for about an hour and a half. My teeth were chattering and everything. I couldn't even talk. I finally passed out while my Dad, Kali, and Donny hung with Jack. When I awoke, the shaking had thankfully passed. We had dinner and my stepmother arrived to see the baby. Around 8pm Becky said I needed to try and walk to the ladies room with her and she would show me how to care for my vagina for the next few weeks and she also needed to make sure I was urinating properly. I had to do this two more times with two more nurses before I would be allowed to go to the bathroom alone.

When you have a baby you really need to check your pride, vanity, and privacy at the door. You will have people from all walks of life, literally, up your ass. Becky had to help me off the toilet and there was one moment when I stumbled and nearly knocked over the little bucket (you have to pee in a bucket placed in the toilet so they can accurately measure the amount of urine you're producing) when Becky and I just busted out laughing. I mean, really, you have to laugh or else you'll cry and go crazy.

A trip to the bathroom just to pee now takes me about ten minutes. I have to fill the spray bottle with warm water, dispose of sanitary napkin, pee, spray vagina with warm water to clean it, pat dry, get new napkin, line it with witch hazel pads, spray those with epifoam, and pull up my gauze drawers.

You heard me. GAUZE DRAWERS. Panties made of gauze. And let me just say... they are FABULOUS! They gave me a bunch to take home. I may never wear regular panties again. They are so comfy and the best part is that if they get soiled, you just toss them away. I love that someone had the nerve to fashion them after boy shorts too. Like, being sexy is the last thing on your mind when you're wearing gauze drawers.

Once it was determined that I was able to go and walk (somewhat) we were transferred to our private room out of the labor and delivery wing and into the Mother Baby wing. My parents and Kali left and it was just Donny, Jack, and I.

He thanked me for all the hard work it took to bring Jack into this world and I thanked him for taking care of me for nine months so I could do it. Then we cried like babies. Jack finally woke up for real and let me look into his eyes. I lost it. I just cried and told him how much I loved him. Then Donny started crying again and told me that the moment Jack came out he thought, "This is what life is about. This is worth living for." And poor Jack just stared out at me like, "Man up, bitches."

The first night was really easy. We were going to take turns getting up with him, but it turns out I still needed help moving around and being able to lift him and place him in the hospital crib. Donny changed the first diaper without me having to ask. And it was a poopy one. He was like a pro; quick, efficient, but gentle and loving. Later in the night, when it was my turn to change a poopy diaper I was like, "Um, so, what am I supposed to do with all this?"

Donny was patient with me. "Make sure you lift his balls and get under there really good. Get in the creases." Just yesterday he awoke from a nap with a soiled diaper and when I opened it, I was greeted with baby boner. I immediately closed the diaper.

"Um, honey, this one's for you."

Day Two and What's Been Happening Since

August 12, 2008

Warning: For awhile my blogs may be kind of (very) long as I won't have much time to update daily as I used to. I find I start typing a blog and then I have to stop to go get my nipples sucked raw, change a diaper, or clean a poopy diaper.

Let me start by saying that labor and delivery nurses are the shit. Even though I believe that one led me astray last week, and one made me feel like a druggie, and some were a little less on the ball as most, overall, those women rock! I mean, you gotta respect a profession where you're expected to check a woman's menstrual pad, help them go to the bathroom, and check their ass for fissures.

Tuesday, our second day in the hospital, was busy. Somehow I ended up alone with Jack while Donny went to my parent's house to get Kali and of course that's when all the shit hit the fan. I don't really know how it happened. I know I called to order our lunch promptly at 11am when the cafe opened for lunch figuring that it would arrive just as Donny was returning. Then for some reason I decided that then would be a good time to take a shower. I pushed Jack into the bathroom with me (he was in the hospital's portable crib) and by the time I was done... like, literally as I exited the bathroom, lunch arrived... and he woke up.

So, I found myself sitting on the edge of the hospital bed totally famished and shaking because I was so hungry, rocking his crib with my left hand and eating with one shaky right hand. My lower back felt like it was on fire because I had obviously done too much too soon (remember, I had given birth less than 24 hours before) and I really thought I was going to pass out. When I managed to eat enough so that I wouldn't faint I had to pick him up to nurse. Of course, during that time a nurse showed up wanting to check my blood pressure, another to check him, and a lady came by asking if I was ready for Jack to take his hospital portraits. I almost chucked my orange sorbet at her.

I know it doesn't sound like it, but I really do enjoy staying in a hospital. I think it's for the same reason I love hotels. I love being waited on. I love that I don't have to worry about making the bed (and seriously, I could have used a hospital bed during my pregnancy. They rock!) and changing the linen. I love that the meals (and the special labor and delivery menu was awesome) are delivered to me. All of my meals were free, Donny got one free meal and then each breakfast was $3 and lunch and dinner were each $4. I think he paid for two meals tops the whole time we were there. People like Donny and are always hooking him up with free shit.

Anyway, at some point on Tuesday I became concerned. It seemed to always be a real challenge in getting Jack to latch on and when he did, he didn't seem to nurse very long. On Monday, he was real mellow. But on Tuesday he was extra fussy and wouldn't fall asleep when laid down. He would fall asleep in our arms, but start screaming bloody murder the moment we put him down. I speculated to Donny that he might not be getting enough colostrum (sweet, thick substance that comes out before your milk comes in.) Even though he was having plenty of wet and poopy diapers, I noticed he wasn't burping after nursing. I wondered if his fussiness was due to hunger or gas. When a nurse came in a short while later she said she could hear his stomach growling as she listened to his breathing. I told her my concern and she suggested we supplement with formula.

I would always offer him breast first, let him nurse as long as he wanted, and then give him formula if he still seemed hungry after that. She brought us these prepared bottles of formula that were only good for one hour after opening. We noticed a difference immediately. Not only was Jack guzzling the stuff down with hearty burps afterwards, but he was sleeping after eating and sleeping for hours at a time. We decided to continue this process until my milk came in.

At some point on Tuesday a nurse came in to "check me." Before she could begin I asked, "Is it just you?" See, when I had Kali a doctor came in to check me and asked if I minded if residents watched because it was a teaching hospital. I looked at the four or five residents huddled by the door and said, "They seem a little long in the tooth to not know how to check blood pressure and temperature, but whatever." Umm, that's not the checking she meant. Next thing you know, I had six or seven people watching as the doctor pulled down my gauze drawers to check the blood on my sanitary napkin and the worst part was being rolled over on my side and having them all watch as the doctor spread my ass cheeks. That's what I get for being a smartass. This time, the nurse was alone so I only had to suffer the indignity of having ONE person looking up my ass.

I swear the nurses' shifts must be like four hours long because it seemed like every time we turned around, a new one was coming in and introducing herself as my nurse. Most were really nice. One got on my nerves. I was told by Becky, the nurse who helped deliver Jack, that I would automatically get 600mgs of Motrin every six hours and I could get a Lortab every four, but I'd have to ask for the Lortab. So, one night as the new nurse came on she said she'd be getting my Motrin in about 15 minutes and I told her that I was also due for a Lortab.

"Well, that is as needed you know."

"Well, I need it." I snapped.

"Well, it can also make you constipated so if the pain is tolerable, you may want to hold off and see if you can move your bowels."

I didn't have the vocabulary necessary to express how much I didn't care if I never pooped again. I was scared I'd bust a stitch. Dr. G. had ordered them to give me stool softeners every so often, but still.

Note: Jack was born on Monday and I made it to Thursday before pooping. Guess what? It wasn't so bad.

Anyway, I waited till that heifer went off duty before I asked the next nurse for a Lortab. Also, I had my prescription of Lortab (prescribed by Dr. G2 on Saturday when she ordered my induction) in my purse so, fuck them.

Ok, so we went home on Wednesday. Donny went to get Kali after breakfast and by the time he came back I was pretty much packed and ready to go. Jack was an angel the whole ride home. He slept the whole way. All that heavy formula no doubt.

From Wednesday to Thursday night I worried that he wasn't nursing enough. It would take him FOREVER to latch on. He would scream and fight it and when he finally did, he'd only suckle for a few minutes and then be done. We thought he was doing it only because he knew the next step was the formula. I was worried that his lack of nursing was causing my milk not to come in. We talked to Beverly and a lactation consultant. Beverly suggested we pump on a regular schedule so Thursday night Donny and I used the breast pump every 2-3 hours for about 20 minutes each time. By Friday morning my breasts were full and achy and I was getting a little milk when I pumped.

I decided to take Jack off the formula cold turkey. The whole weekend was torture. Getting him to latch on was damn near impossible, but I didn't give up. So many times I wanted to just give him a bottle of formula so we could all get some rest, but I held strong. I talked to my friend Carrie (I seriously have the best MySpace friends/readers) and she had some really good suggestions including the old "bait and switch." This involved me cradling Jack in a nursing position but letting him suck on a pacifier. Just as he was getting into it I'd remove the pacifier and stick my breast in instead. That worked quite a few times. Finally, what really worked was Donny making a small bottle of formula and putting a few drops of it on my nipples before feeding. I know, I know, it's heinous fuckery most foul, but it worked.

Sunday was the first day that he latched on as soon as the breast was presented and nursed for long periods of time. The milk was in and flowing because I could hear him taking deep gulps and there'd be milk around his mouth when he was done. Woohoo!

But while this was going on we had a new problem. I have been extremely swollen since delivery. It's most noticeable on my right foot which is huge. Every day it got worse. I'd have trouble breathing when lying down and walking was painful. On Saturday, Dr. G. called in a prescription for Lasix which is supposed to help drain the excess fluid from my body. When I asked if it would affect my milk he said that since my milk was just coming in he doubted it. I wasn't convinced. We waited an hour after he called it in and then called the pharmacy. The pharmacist said that if I took the drug it would dry up my milk. I lost it.

I cried almost all of Saturday and Sunday. I refused to take the medication. I begged Donny hysterically, "Please don't make me do this. Please don't make me do this." Donny told me that at night he would listen to me struggling to breathe and was scared I was going to die. Yet I refused. Even at night when I couldn't breathe and Dr. G. told me it was most likely due to fluid in or around my lungs. On Sunday evening I let Donny go get the prescription but was tempted to flush the six pills when he wasn't looking. When I finally agreed - after my Dad came over to talk to me and my mother talked to Donny and Sophie put in her two cents - I still managed to stall.

Jack was just getting the hang of breastfeeding and I would break down into tears every time I thought that this time would be my last time nursing him.

"When are you going to take it?" Donny would ask.

And I would just cradle Jack and cry and say, "After this feeding. Just one more. I promise." I called Beverly at home and she said that the drug wouldn't hurt Jack and it wouldn't dry up my milk. I was STILL scared. Finally, I looked up a La Leche League leader in my area and called her at home. This poor woman. Here I am, a stranger, calling her at 9:30pm near tears. She looked up the drug and explained that it was sometimes given to newborns directly in higher doses than I'd been prescribed so I probably shouldn't be concerned with Jack getting it in the breast milk and there was no real evidence that it would dry up my milk and that it only said that it *may* reduce my milk supply. To fight that, she suggested that I just feed and pump like crazy. The more milk you put out, the more you produce.

It's Tuesday afternoon as I type this and I have one pill left. Yesterday, we took Jack to the pediatrician. He passed his hearing test, but he's lost four ounces since birth. Considering he just started latching on properly the day before the doctor said it wasn't anything to be concerned about, but did suggest we bring him by tomorrow (Wednesday) without an appointment for a quick weight check. She also said that the medicine wouldn't affect Jack or my milk. Since we were in the building we stopped in to see Beverly and big mouth Donny told her how bad my breathing was the night before and how he was thisclose to calling 9-1-1. She insisted that we go in the back and see Dr. G.

He told me that though the pills say one a day, not to wait 24 hours between doses. He said they only last 4 hours so I should be taking them every 4 hours to get it over with. He also said he was a little mad when he called to check on me and found that I hadn't filled the prescription right away due to something a lactation consultant said. He assured me that he would never give me something that would hurt Jack and that though he understood my desire to breastfeed, if I die of lung failure that doesn't do Jack any good either. True dat.

The pill is supposed to make you pee a lot, but I swear I'm not peeing anymore than usual, but something is working because my right foot looks close to normal. I have to check in with Dr. G. today because he goes out of town tomorrow. He said I may need to have some sort of cardiac scan to make sure I didn't develop cardiac myopathy. Oh, another side effect of excess fluid in your body? Body aches. I would wake up in the middle of the night or first thing in the morning and feel as if I'd been beaten with a bat from head to toe. Not fun.

So, that's the latest. I have one pill left. I feel and look better, though walking still hurts like a bitch. We're going to get Jack dressed soon (the boy sleeps most of the day and likes to hang at night) and take him out in the stroller. Nothing too far. Just up the block and back.

Kali started 4th grade at her new school yesterday. She loves it. Her favorite thing so far? Her Trapper Keeper. Boy, those things have come a long way since we were in school. It's awesome! Her least favorite thing? Her new school bus schedule. She used to get on the bus around 8am and was home between 3:45-4pm. Now, her bus arrives at 7:15am, but she gets home around 3:15-3:20.

As for Donny, he continues to be an *amazing* father. He's so gentle with Jack, but at the same time it's like he's a newborn pro. He changes diapers without having to be asked. It's funny because while Jack's circumcision was healing we had to keep it covered with gauze covered in Vaseline and were instructed not to use a baby wipe on his penis. So, when changing him we'd first prepare new gauze and have it ready on the side with a new diaper and the wipes, we'd keep his penis covered and wipe everything else, put the new diaper under him, and swap out the gauze last minute. This ensured that we didn't accidentally swipe his raw penis with a baby wipe and that we didn't get peed on... though Jack did get Kali on the foot once and spray our bedspread another time.

Yesterday, the doctor said he's all healed so we don't have to use the gauze anymore. Now, all of sudden Donny is looking for something to cover Jack's wee-wee because he doesn't want to get peed on. I had to laugh and give him a big, "I told you so!" Then I tossed him the Wee Block. Bet his ass is glad I bought it now. Jack's belly button stump also fell off Sunday night so he can take a real bath now though I'm waiting till tomorrow so it will be one full week since his circumcision before I put him in water.

Anyway, back to Donny. Donny does all the hard stuff I don't want to do... or I'm too scared to do. If Jack finds his way to the first floor, Donny carried him there. We only had to do it once at the hospital, but Donny was the one to use that bulb thingie to get the excess fluid from his mouth. And when it comes to his long finger nails, Donny files them because we're both too afraid to use the baby nail clippers. (*Or so I thought!*)

As for Jack, his personality (so far) is a mixture of both Donny and I. He's quiet most of the time, like Donny. But when he gets annoyed he goes from zero to eighty in like five seconds. He gives you little warning before he loses his shit, and when he does you better watch out. Just like his Mommy. He's fascinated by Kali and follows her with his eyes whenever she's in the room. She loves holding him until he poops then she's all, "Ok, someone take him."

And, I think that's about it. Life is good. Sleep is elusive. But life is good.

ABOUT THE AUTHOR

Nina Perez is the author of *The Twin Prophecies: Rebirth*, the first in a YA fantasy series. The second, *The Twin Prophecies: Origins* will be released in the spring of 2012. She enjoys spending time with Donny, Kali, and Jack in their suburban Atlanta home. When she's not writing she's watching massive amounts of *Doctor Who*, and wishing she had her very own TARDIS. If you're an adult, you can follow her on Twitter (@AuthorNinaPerez). If you're a fan of *The Twin Prophecies*, follow her at @TwinProphecies. You can also find her on Facebook or by email: nina@blogitoutb.com